ELEVATIONS

Elevations

A Personal Exploration of the Arkansas River

MAX McCOY

UNIVERSITY PRESS OF KANSAS

Published by the University Press of Kansas (Lawrence, Kansas 66045), which was
organized by the Kansas Board of Regents and is operated and funded by Emporia
State University, Fort Hays State University, Kansas State University, Pittsburg State
University, the University of Kansas, and Wichita State University

Library of Congress Cataloging-in-Publication Data

Names: McCoy, Max, author.
Title: Elevations : a personal exploration of the Arkansas River / Max McCoy.
Description: Lawrence, Kansas : University Press of Kansas, 2018.
Identifiers: LCCN 2017054867
ISBN 9780700626021 (hardback)
ISBN 9780700626038 (ebook)
Subjects: LCSH: Arkansas River Region—History. | Arkansas River Region—
Description and travel. | McCoy, Max—Travel—Arkansas River Region. | Natural
history—Arkansas River Region. | BISAC: HISTORY / United States / State &
Local / West (AK, CA, CO, HI, ID, MT, NV, UT, WY). | HISTORY / United
States / State & Local / Midwest (IA, IL, IN, KS, MI, MN, MO, ND, NE, OH,
SD, WI). | NATURE / Ecosystems & Habitats / Rivers.
Classification: LCC F782.A7 M33 2018 | DDC 976.7/3—dc23.
LC record available at https://lccn.loc.gov/2017054867.

British Library Cataloguing-in-Publication Data is available.

Printed in the United States of America

10 9 8 7 6 5 4 3 2 1

The paper used in this publication is recycled and contains 30 percent postconsumer
waste. It is acid free and meets the minimum requirements of the American National
Standard for Permanence of Paper for Printed Library Materials Z39.48-1992.

For Philip Finch, who lives now in our dreams.

Contents

Author's Note

The following is a work of nonfiction and all events happened as described, although they are presented here in thematic, rather than strictly chronological, order. There are no invented or composite characters used, although in cases where I refer to an individual by a first name only, I use a pseudonym to spare embarrassment. In some cases, I have omitted people and events, but only when it had no substantial impact on the narrative.

All photos by Max McCoy, unless otherwise noted.

ELEVATIONS

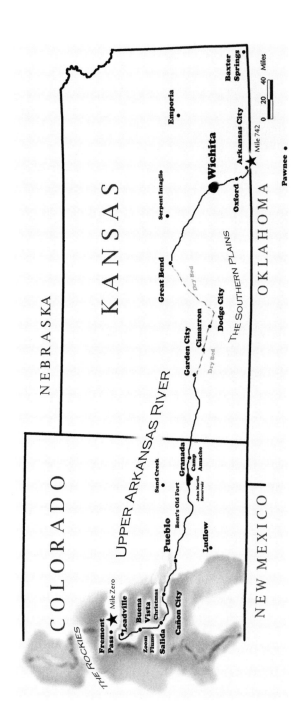

Map of the Arkansas River.

Then come molecules, galaxies, Earth, Denny Creek Granite, life, Leadville Limestone, Rio Grande Rift, humans, present river systems, glaciers, Zoom Flume, and Sunshine Rapid. Finally PVC rafts and tuna sandwiches. It's all there for you now. Don't let opportunity pass.

—*Thomas G. Rampton*, Arkansas River Guide

Standing thigh-deep in the river, my paddle in one hand and the bow toggle of my kayak in the other, I cocked my arm and tossed the double-bladed stick in the direction of the gravel bar. It wasn't a perfect throw, but it was good enough. The paddle skittered to a stop on the bar, with only a part of one blade in the water, in no danger of being swept downstream.

With the 53-degree water gently piling beneath my left hip, I shivered and wished that I had pulled on a wetsuit instead of swim trunks. My chest was warm enough, even though the gray polyester shirts beneath my bulky life jacket were soaked, but my legs felt like they were in a freezer. I stepped toward the bank and the kayak followed, the stem bumping against my legs, the stern drawn downstream by the current.

Then my wedding ring slid from the finger of my left hand.

It hit the hard plastic deck of the kayak and wobbled like a coin, quavering gold in the morning air. I swatted with my right hand, not in a smooth motion but in a heart-in-the-throat kind of jerk, trapping the ring beneath my palm against the swirled yellow and red plastic.

Holy fuck!

Did that just happen?

It's an inauspicious beginning to my first day on the water during a long project that is intended to take me from the headwaters of the Arkansas River near the Continental Divide north of Leadville, Colorado, down the river to the plains. It's more than 700 miles to my destination, the Oklahoma border. My goal is to write a story about the river's journey through Colorado and Kansas, a sort of cultural and natural history of the river, and to weave into that tapestry a deeply personal narrative as well.

I had aimed to tackle the biography of the river, to follow the path from its birth among the highest peaks in Colorado all the rushing way

Headwaters of the Arkansas River near Fremont Pass.

down red canyons to the featureless plains—and beyond. I would pick through the remains of the human hopes and outrageous folly that litter its ancient banks, celebrate the rare sustainable success, and compare evidence of the river past, in the form of written accounts and historic photographs, with the river present. I would consult experts, from river guides to historians to as-yet-undiscovered authorities, who could explain to me why the otherworldly haunts us in the wild. My aim was also to chronicle my personal journey of discovery, noting my reaction to—and interaction with—the water wild.

Desperately, I wanted to avoid writing a travel book. There are many books about things to do and see in Kansas and Colorado, and a few of them are fine books. There is also an avalanche of magazine articles and newspaper features every year, tabloid-sized travel guides of all kinds, and brochures at every welcome center and chamber of commerce along the route. There's plenty of information available, for example, if you'd like to know about the "thriving" arts scene at Salida (as airports sprawl, local arts scenes seem always to thrive in descriptive brochures). You can also find troves in print and on the Web about the Old West experience at Dodge City, or the museums and other civic triumphs along the river in downtown Wichita. Such boosterism is abundant. What I was after were the deeper and sometimes darker stories along the river, the stories that were sometimes harder to find, the stories that rang truer and left readers wiser.

My account would be one of journalism performed naked, rather than clutching at the emperor's cloak of objectivity; I would acknowledge personal biases, share enthusiasms, and embrace advocacy when so moved. Perhaps this new frankness would help me discover what pathology drives me to sometimes leave a wealth of physical and emotional comforts and seek challenges that are physically demanding and often intellectually discomfiting. At least, that was the strategy when my search for the Arkansas began.

So far, I'd plunged my hands into the snow on a high pass from which the river is born, hiked the Arkansas where it was still narrow enough to hop across, and dragged my kayak over barbed wire to find access to bigger water.

But now, things aren't going as planned. My ambitious and high-minded project has been slammed hard against the reality of rocks, water, and talent—physical and otherwise. There is a story here, a story that connects human and wild, past and present, the personal and the transcendent, but standing shivering in the river, I am not convinced that I'm the one to tell it.

Had my wedding ring rolled into the cold, swift water and settled among the jagged rocks below, it would have been gone. Oh, I would have looked for hours, but without being able to mark the exact spot and with no help because I was alone, finding it would have been a long shot. How could I have been so stupid? I had lost some weight, and I knew the ring was loose on my finger, but in the rush to find a place to launch and get on the river, I had forgotten to secure it. How would I have explained the loss to Kim, the woman I had married—and who, more importantly, had married *me*—less than two years before?

Trying not to think about the symbolism inherent in such a catastrophe, I carefully placed the ring in the front pocket of my life jacket and zipped it up.

Then I waded over to the gravel bar, guiding the sluggish kayak across the river, feeling the rocks through the thin rubber soles of my river shoes. I stepped up onto the bar, water streaming from my clothes, and hauled the kayak up, its bottom grumbling and scraping and leaving a V-shaped furrow behind. There was a bathtub full of water in the boat. I leveraged the boat over and let as much water as I could drain from the cockpit—and spilled a Nalgene bottle of drinking water, a plastic baggie of snacks, and a little plastic box with an amber lid that held a collection of spinners and other lures. The waterproof case that held my iPhone and my wallet dangled from the safety cord clipped to an eyelet on the deck. Thankfully, the hatch was still secure over the aft compartment, so at least I didn't have to chase my stowed belongings down the river. Then, I tilted the kayak up onto its nose, letting the boat rest against my shoulder as it drained.

When I had gotten as much water out of the boat as I reckoned was possible, I eased it down and slid the bow a foot or two into the water. Then I began to gather up the small items that had spilled, and when I reached for the fishing tackle I realized my right hand was shaking. In fact, both of my hands were shaking. Tremors rippled through both hands and my fingertips danced. Then I realized I was short of breath and quite cold, and the moment of realization made me fight even harder for air, and made me colder. My vision blurred. I was exhausted and my mind was more than a bit dull. It seemed to me there was a dome of light encircling me, and at the center of the dome was a bright, floating point of light. It was there even when I closed my eyes.

Brilliant, I told myself. *You're going to die here on this gravel bar after having swamped your new boat in Class Zero water, and when people say your name, they're going to laugh.*

But then I tasted blood in the back of my throat, and realized I wasn't having a heart attack. It was a panic attack. I'd had them frequently in the past, mostly years ago, during a previous marriage. The attack was probably made worse by a mild case of altitude sickness. Every trip I made at 10,000 feet or above was accompanied the first couple of days by some sinus bleeding, fatigue, and a bit of depression. Also, I was still recovering from a stomach parasite that I had picked up during my return to Kansas from a writers convention in Las Vegas, an illness that required a trip to the emergency room and IV fluids, and put me in bed for three weeks. I probably hadn't recovered enough for this trip, but the passage of time and the threat of lost opportunity had made me incautious.

I sat down on the deck of the kayak, just behind the seat, holding the little amber plastic fishing tackle case in my lap. Fishing tackle. *What was I thinking?* But I'd had the little box for, what—twenty years? More?— and every time I had fished with my father, usually for trout, I'd had the little box with me. I turned the box over in my hands and the contents shifted and skittered. Inside were even some lures, some small spinners for ultralight rods that I had probably used while fishing with him. There were also little sinkers, like bits of lead shot, and toothpicks and bright bits of felt and a pair of nail clippers to snip line. Of course, *now* I know what I was thinking. My father had died in 1997 and subconsciously I wanted something on this journey that was a direct connection to him. It wasn't about fishing at all.

I slowed my breathing and tried to concentrate on my surroundings. The weird sensation of the dome of light over me began to ease. Trees leaned over the river from high-cut banks and the sky was a deep blue, so deep that I thought it might not be just an optical illusion, that there must be some natural explanation. I felt alone and the immense sky made me feel even more so, as did the far blue peaks of the mountains on the horizon around me. It wasn't more than three or four river miles to the take-out, where my friend Butch would be waiting, and I could manage that. The whole thing had been a stupid idea, anyway. Once I got the kayak on the trailer behind the Jeep, then I could call it quits. Nobody would have to know that I had swamped the kayak in easy water, that I had nearly lost my wedding ring, that I had lost my *nerve*.

But for now, the only way out was down the river.

I fished the ring from the pocket of my life jacket and, with a waterproof Band-Aid from my first aid kit, taped it onto my finger. Then I gathered my gear into the boat, walked it out to where the water was just over my ankles but the stern was on the bar, and sat down in the cockpit. In a moment I was again in the current.

There's no good metaphor for a river. The river is the thing itself, the thing that *other* things are compared to. Time, or more properly change, comes first to mind. "No man ever stepped into the same river twice," said Heraclitus, the weeping Greek philosopher. In Abrahamic tradition, John baptized Jesus in the Jordan River, and the Jordan plays a part in assorted miracles and other stories in the Bible, including a crossing that was the final step in a journey from slavery to freedom. Take a look at American literature, from Mark Twain to Thomas Wolfe, and you'll see that rivers are reliable symbols for journeys, for change, for the nostalgia of our youth and the yearning for the transcendent.

For *everything*, really.

When one does use a metaphor for a river, it is sort of like putting a battery in backward; there's no power. It diminishes that which you are attempting to amplify. I've heard rivers variously described as arteries, pathways, and highways, but those reflect how we have used rivers rather than what rivers are. In their essence, rivers defy description. Even the word *river* is imprecise, at least when you look at the etymology, because it comes from the French for the bank and not the water itself.

It's appropriate that the word *river* comes from the edge where most of our interactions with rivers stops and the wildness begins. Rivers represent the banks of our experience, and the desire to go beyond them. Take even the tamest of rivers, and just a few yards out—say, past the point where you can bend over and touch the bottom while wading— there's a world unknown to anyone without the proper gear. I've seen plenty of river bottoms through a scuba mask, and it is always surprising.

There are plenty of ways to describe how things appear in relation to a river: a ribbon of glittering steel can appear when the sun is low, or mist is a shroud in the early morning, or a boater thrown from her raft becomes a cork bobbing in a rapid. The only time a metaphor works is when a river is damaged or threatened in some way. When the Environmental Protection Agency accidentally released three million gallons of toxic yellow-brown sludge from the Gold King Mine near Silverton, Colorado, into the Animas River in August 2015, it could reasonably be described as having turned the river to shit.

The Arkansas River, the subject of our meditation here, was spared the desecration of the EPA-released (irony noted) heavy metals and other toxic wastewater, because the Animas is a tributary of the San Juan, which is part of the Colorado River System. The Colorado and Arkansas headwaters are only forty or so miles apart, in the high mountains, but are separated by the Continental Divide; while the Colorado flows southwest, through the Grand Canyon and eventually to California and the Pacific Ocean, the Arkansas runs to the southeast—eventually to join in the Arkansas delta with the Mississippi. The Arkansas begins as a brook formed from snowmelt a few miles above Leadville, Colorado, and it was there—near Fremont Pass, where the Continental Divide skews to an east-west orientation, and Highway 91 hosts legions of tourists in their Escalades and Explorers, and squadrons of bikers straddle their Harley-Davidson Road Kings—I began my journey.

Call it Mile Zero.

At least that's what I've named it in one of my dirt- and water-stained notebooks. This location, hard beside (or possibly on) property owned by the Climax mine, is a swamp in summer. It was difficult for me, hiking and attempting to avoid the company's NO TRESPASSING signs, to tell exactly where the Arkansas begins, because the rivulets that combine to form the nascent river are a web running through the soggy land beneath the crooked top of Bartlett Mountain.

The peak of Bartlett Mountain was once 13,555 feet, but the top 150 feet or so have been lopped off during the last seventy years by open-pit molybdenum mining. The Climax mine has produced about three-quarters of the world's supply of moly, an uncommon element used chiefly to produce steel alloys. At the height of production, during World War II, when moly was needed for the production of armaments and radio tubes, the highest human settlement (and US Post Office and railway station) in the United States was located here, at the foot of the mountain near Fremont Pass, at an elevation of 11,320 feet.

The unincorporated town was home to 600 people, notes the Works Progress Administration guide to Colorado, published in 1941. Climax was Colorado's most prosperous mining town, and the company provided dormitories for its single miners that included such comforts as a commissary and a library. "Mining is done by the caving system," the entry for Climax notes, "which has eaten away a large gash in the face of the mountain. Ore bodies are undercut horizontally and broken down with dynamite."

Climax is a ghost town: the post office closed in the early 1960s, and the railway line from Leadville now operates as a tourist attraction. The title of highest community in the United States has been surrendered from the company town of Climax to three nearby contenders, depending on how you define community. Leadville is the highest incorporated *city*, at 10,152 feet; Alma is the highest incorporated *municipality*, at 10,578 feet; and Winter Park became the highest incorporated *town* when it annexed part of a ski resort, although the center of town is only at 9,000 feet. The distinctions are largely statutory, although Leadville has by far the most permanent residents, at 2,580. Living at altitudes above 10,000 feet offers some special challenges, thanks to a winter that lasts for six months. The record low temperature at Leadville is 38 degrees below zero, Fahrenheit. The snow comes by the end of October and typically lasts until May, with an average accumulated snowfall of 10.6 feet. Air pressure, which is 14.7 pounds per square inch (psi) at sea level, is just 10 psi here. Water boils at 193 degrees Fahrenheit and it takes about twice as long to cook anything as it does at sea level.

I've ridden that tourist train that goes north out of Leadville, in an open-air car pulled by a humming diesel, with Kim sitting beside me, for the cost of a pair of twenty-dollar tickets. The depot for the Leadville, Colorado, & Southern Railroad is easy to find because it's on East Seventh, just three blocks east of the town's main drag; if you miss it—as I did, the first time—it's easy to follow the tracks back to where you should be. That was three years ago, during research for another writing project, before embarking on the river journey. Then, it was possible for me to happily climb down from the observation car and stretch my legs with the other passengers when the train reached its northern terminus at a rustic water tank at French Gulch, elevation 10,840 feet, before backing down all eleven miles of tracks to the depot in Leadville. That was before I decided to visit the places beyond the Climax fences where the Arkansas is born—and reborn—every spring.

And even though the river project started in earnest less than two years ago, the idea for it began nearly two *decades* ago. In the 1990s, I was asked to participate for a few years in a summer writing workshop sponsored by Western State College in Gunnison, Colorado, and during the first of those ten-hour drives from Kansas, while following US 50 as it winds ever steeper along the Arkansas River from Cañon City on the approach to Monarch Pass, I was astonished by the sprinkling of snow. I was also fascinated by the river, which seemed as wild as any I had seen, and by the boaters in their yellow or blue commercial rafts and the single paddlers in their neon kayaks. I stopped at the Five Points access, where a wooden observation deck juts out over the water, and from the rail watched as several kayaks slid and bucked and pivoted past the massive red boulders below. I wanted to be in the water with them, for *in* the water they were, not unlike surfboarders, as much water and spray above them as below, their boats sometimes submerged beneath them, but following an invisible line that would lead them to safety at the bottom of the rapids.

It became a routine, every time I made the trip, to stop and watch the boaters. While the rafts of the commercial outfitters looked like fun, I didn't want to be in a boat with six other tourists and a guide steering in the back. No, I wanted to be inside a kayak, to be as deep in the water as I could, to still be in control—but to test that edge between control and surrender.

Growing up in southeast Kansas, I had run miles and miles of Spring River above Baxter Springs in an aluminum boat with an outboard. I had also been with my father on rivers and lakes from Toledo Bend on the Texas-Louisiana line to Lesser Slave Lake in central Alberta, and I knew how to handle a boat before I could legally drive. But those waters, all of them, were calm, save for the occasional chop on a windy day.

Whitewater represented something alien.

My first time in a decked boat came in the mid-1990s, when a friend of mine, Texas writer and treasure hunter W. C. Jameson, invited me on a kayak trip when the Little Red River in Arkansas was at flood stage. He'd bought a pair of touring kayaks, and a rack to carry them on the roof of his black van he called *El Zopilote*, "the vulture." We zipped down the river and never once came close to swimming, even though I juggled the double-bladed paddle to do a little fly-fishing from the cockpit. This was a different kind of boating than I had known before, and the river thrumming past where my thighs and knees were braced against the hull gave me the impression that I was a part of the river, instead of just riding on top of it.

After my research for the Arkansas River project began in earnest, but before my initial hike in the swamp below Bartlett Mountain, I began to think of those places beyond the NO TRESPASSING signs of the Climax company as Minus Mile Zero. The top of the mountain may have been blown to hell long ago, but I wanted to see firsthand what was left. Some of it, I knew from my research, would be artificial; the original stream bed had been buried decades ago by the overburden removed from the mountain in the scramble for molybdenum, and drainage from the mountain was forced into a seven-foot-diameter culvert somewhere above the swampland. That overburden clogging the natural stream bed, as well as acres of other tailings, had been removed under a government-sponsored reclamation project. The brook that flowed through the swamp was a re-creation of what the ancestral headwaters must have looked like. I wanted to see how things looked on the other side of the fence.

Also, I worried that my designation of Mile Zero would prove inaccurate, because it was simply a spot I picked near Fremont Pass where one could identify a rivulet that would become the Arkansas, even if it were narrow enough to easily step across. But there's no topographic or other map that I can refer to that says yes, this is Mile Zero of the Arkansas. There are a handful of boating guides to the Arkansas River, but these generally use the mileposts along Highway 24, above Salida, or Highway 50 below, to provide directions to river access. The best of these boating guides is a self-published book of eighty-eight pages by veteran river runner Thomas G. Rampton, last updated in 2006, that quite sensibly designates mile zero on the river as the Granite Access, below the bridge near milepost 194. This is generally regarded as the uppermost section of the river that is suitable for boating.

You're through Granite in the blink of an eye as you drive Highway 24, a twisting two-lane that serpentines along the river between Leadville and Salida. Here the first gold strikes were made, in 1859. If you're adventurous enough, you can ascend a narrow county road overlooking the west bank of the river and eventually come to Cache Creek, where you can still pan for—and have a reasonable expectation of finding—gold. It's also the point on the river where the Arkansas goes from being a relatively tame river meandering through alpine meadows to a wild one. The hazards include Pine Creek Rapid, which may be the most dangerous stretch of water on the river.

Rampton, in his *Arkansas River Guide,* offers this advice about the river miles below Granite: "A suggestion, if you're going to boat this part of the river but aren't familiar: take a commercial ride with one of the outfitters. And before you launch, make sure you're very good."

Let me state here that I'm not very good.

I won't challenge Rampton's wisdom in designating Granite as his mile zero for boaters. But I decided to keep the spot below the Climax mine, twenty-two miles to the north, as my Mile Zero.

Below would be 120 miles of whitewater, until the river meets the plains.

In 2014, eight whitewater boaters died on the Arkansas River in Colorado, including a fifty-seven-year-old Texas woman who was thrown from an outfitter's raft into the Pine Creek Rapid. The guide had fallen from the boat, according to the sheriff's report, and the raft and its occupants were swept downstream and became trapped in a circulating hydraulic, which spun the boat and threw two of its three remaining occupants into the water. The Texas woman, Mary Johnson, was unable to swim to shore because of the force of the recirculating water in the hole. A safety kayaker—a scout who paddles below the commercial raft to tow clients to safety in the event of such a spill—was unable to reach her before she lost the ability to grab hold, according to a witness.

Pine Creek is a Class V rapid, a violent and challenging stretch of water recommended for expert boat-drivers only. The whitewater classification system goes from Class I, which is moving water with riffles or small waves, suitable for near-complete novices and with little or no risk to swimmers (i.e., those being dumped from the boat) and presenting easy self-rescue, to Class VI, a rapid so treacherous that it is beyond the skills of even expert paddlers and has been rarely, if ever, successfully run.

"Surely this is the most difficult rapid on the entire river," Rampton says of Pine Creek in his *Guide,* "and it is probably the most dangerous water in Colorado after Gore Canyon on the Colorado."

Still, it's important not to overstate the general risk for boaters—while keeping in mind the warnings about places like Pine Creek and, farther down, Frog Rock and Seidel's Suckhole. Deaths among commercial outfitters are rare, and the average whitewater boater has a greater chance of being killed or seriously injured in the drive to the launch point than while in the water, according to American Whitewater, a nonprofit advocate affiliated with more than 100 paddling clubs. The average rapids-running kayaker takes a risk that is somewhat above bicycling but below that of rock climbing and scuba diving. The kayak fatality rate, American Whitewater reports, was approximately 3 in 100,000 participants, according to a 1998 study.

Before we get too comfortable with the idea of relative risk, however, I should note something these numbers don't reflect: that risk increases exponentially at the edges of the spectrum for all three of these highly technical sports. Those most likely to die are novices with little experience who take on too much too soon, or world-class experts who challenge extreme conditions so often that the odds finally catch up.

Two years ago I set out to find the Arkansas River.

What I found was the ghost of a river.

From the headwaters to the plains, we have blasted and choked and diverted and irrigated away the river until those who gave the first accounts of the river would hardly recognize it. Beyond those wildest of places where water and rock collide, only the ghosts of rivers past remain.

The true Arkansas remains in those places where you're most likely to kill yourself, places where if you're foolhardy or just plain unlucky you're at some risk of pinning your kayak against a great red rock or being dragged to the bottom by the unsentimental hydraulics of a legendary suck hole. If you do, of course, it will be your own fault, and don't say that Thomas G. Rampton didn't warn you. As he notes in the introduction to *Arkansas River Guide*, he can only give so much advice, and even though he's seen much of the water as a professional boater, the nature of the river is change. Each water level creates a new river, with its own joys and challenges.

Ultimately, as Rampton notes: "You're operating your boat—not me."

A Certain Grit
Elevation: 10,152' (Leadville)

Leadville . . . is the only land in the world where we have strawberries, mosquitoes and snow all at once. It is the only land where a man puts on his Ulster in the morning and works in shirtsleeves and straw hat at noon. It is the only land where people live two miles above the sea.

—Orth Stein, in a letter to the Lafayette, Indiana, Courier, 1880

Thirteen miles west of the Kansas border, at the welcome center on Interstate 70 in the town of Burlington, there's a three-dimensional relief map of Colorado. The plastic map shows the relative heights of the mountains that tent the middle of the state, from top to bottom, toward the sky.

These are the Rockies, and they begin far beyond the edge of the plastic map, 2,000 miles to the northwest, in upper British Columbia. The range touches six American states, with the longest sections in Montana and Wyoming, and it ends in New Mexico. The state of Colorado claims only 300 miles of the Southern Rocky Mountains, but all of the highest peaks in the entire mountain range are here. The highest of all is Mount Elbert, on the Continental Divide, at 14,440 feet. It is among the fifty-six peaks in the state called the *fourteeners*, mountains with an elevation of at least 14,000 feet. There are higher peaks in the United States—Denali in Alaska is the highest, at 20,310 feet—but Colorado has the most fourteeners of any state.

Looking at the plastic map a certain way—say, after six hours on the interstate and not enough sleep and having guzzled a gallon of black coffee—the mountain ranges look like the back of an old man's gnarled left hand, with the knuckles being the peaks along the Continental Divide, the wrist the western plateaus and canyon lands, the thumb pointing toward Albuquerque. The fingers of the hand reach toward the plains. Between the index finger and the middle finger is a long valley that climbs to the center of the state, toward Mount Elbert.

The river that runs between the fingers is the Arkansas.

Where I grew up in southeastern Kansas, in Baxter Springs, on the edge of the Ozark Plateau and within spitting distance of Missouri, we

Old headframe at Leadville (photo by Karl Gregory).

pronounced the Arkansas River just as you would pronounce the name
of the state. The rest of Kansas, however, takes exception to that, and
residents will take a moment to correct you: "It's the AR-Kansas River."
Well, it is until you reach Colorado, where someplace around Cañon City
you begin to climb into the mountains and the pronunciation switches
back again. But on the plains, I resist a pronunciation that seems foreign
to me. Instead, I have begun to call the river by its nickname, the Ark,
which raises no eyebrows.

As I stand bleary-eyed before the plastic map and drink yet more
coffee from yet another Styrofoam cup, I wonder why I'd never seen
the back-of-a-hand analogy before. I had studied plenty of maps of
Colorado—including poring over several detailed topographic maps—
had zoomed and tilted plenty of interactive maps on the internet, had
twirled plenty of real and virtual globes. Perhaps it was the fluorescent
lighting in the visitor's center somehow interacting with the greens and
blues of the plastic map, adding a kind of hyper-dimensional quality.

Then again, perhaps I was just tired.

Ahead of me was a four-hour drive, not counting stops for gas and
other necessities. My Jeep was loaded with camping gear and warm

clothes and boxes of field guides, maps, and other assorted research books and, attached to a heavy rack mounted on the trailer hitch, a mountain bike. My destination: Fremont Pass and environs, thirteen miles north of Leadville, on the Continental Divide—just a few miles northeast of Mount Elbert, in fact.

Stepping outside the visitor's center and looking to the west, over the façade of the Old Town Museum, a touristy cluster of buildings meant to look like a frontier town, where the biggest attraction today seems to be the ice cream parlor, I can't yet see the mountains, just hazy blue sky. But I've been steadily climbing on my westward journey across the plains, and the elevation at Burlington is 4,170 feet. That's nearly 3,000 feet higher than the elevation at my front steps on Constitution Street, in Emporia in east-central Kansas, which my Garmin GPS tells me is 1,197 feet. By the time you reach Denver, the elevation is famously 5,280.

Western Kansas and eastern Colorado are flat but angle steadily upward like a ramp to the Rockies. According to the books I have in the boxes in the Jeep, this resulted from the erosion of the Rockies over several geologic periods, which deposited silt and sand and gravel across the plains, and also from plate tectonics. About 20 million years ago, the North American plate was shoved over the edge of the Pacific plate, which raised Colorado and much of the American Southwest by about a mile.

"The final sculpting of Colorado's mountains and valleys occurred when global cooling spawned the Pleistocene ice ages," writes Stephen M. Voynick in *Colorado Rockhounding*. "Colorado was not swept by the great northern continental ice sheet, but by regional alpine glaciation over most of its higher elevations. Deep snowfall accumulated and compressed into perpetual snowfields, then into mobile glacial masses that scoured away enormous volumes of rock. When the glaciers finally retreated under moderating temperatures, they released torrents of water that cut deep canyons. . . . At the end of the ice ages, a mere 15,000 years ago, Colorado's topography appeared much as it does today."

The first human eyes—presumably belonging to members of the Clovis culture, named for the distinctive stone tools first found at Clovis, New Mexico, in the 1920s—would have seen the same natural vistas that we see today in Colorado, but with the addition of the occasional woolly mammoth or one of the many now-extinct species of pronghorn antelope. Clovis culture people appeared about 13,000 years ago, lasted for about a thousand years, and then evolved into other Paleo-Indian groups we also identify by their stone tools, including Folsom. It was once thought the Clovis people were the first to inhabit North America, but finds along the coasts are challenging that assumption by thousands of years. Still, Clovis culture may have been the first on the Great Plains.

But I'm not thinking such deep thoughts as I stand in the parking lot outside the welcome center on this day in early June. Those thoughts would come later. What I'm thinking about is the landscape, which is much like Kansas—flat and hot.

It's the beginning of a week that will be remembered for wildfires across Colorado. There will be five days of high winds, dry conditions, and freakish heat; here on the plains, there will be five days that exceed 100 degrees Fahrenheit, including a record high for the year of 110 degrees. In the Black Forest, near Colorado Springs, a 14,000-acre fire will kill two people and destroy 511 homes. At Royal Gorge, on the Arkansas River near Cañon City, another fire will jump the river and destroy forty-three buildings, char the famous Royal Gorge Bridge, and force the evacuation of 905 inmates from the Territorial Prison.

I've been listening to news of the wildfires on my car radio and that's why I'm traveling Interstate 70 rather than following US 50 into Colorado, and following the river through the gate of the mountains at Cañon City. The weather during the summer of 2013 proved consistently uncooperative to my plans to begin my river journey; after the wildfires of June would come the drought of July, and then after that the floods of September. Some parts of Colorado would receive in one week the amount of rain that could normally be expected during an entire year. Ten people died in the flooding, including one involved in a rescue, and damage was pegged by state officials at $2 billion.

The extreme weather of the summer was unexpected and troubling. Fire, drought, flood. The range of the disasters seemed positively biblical, and news accounts did nothing to relieve Kim's anxiety. There had been some tense moments at the dining room table in the days after I'd shared with her my plans for the project, and apart from her alarm at the phrase *whitewater rapids*, there was a concern that my plan was to tackle the project alone. Part of it was a fear for my safety, but there was also her perception that the proposed adventure presented my desire to be alone. Of course not, I protested; well, mostly not. Sometimes, I wanted to be alone, and all of my adult life I have sought challenges that were beyond my normal routine and often beyond any skill set I had, or was ever likely to have.

She wanted to know: *Why?*

I had no answer. Anything I offered would be a neat rationalization, a bit of rhetoric perhaps about personal growth, connecting with nature, undertaking a worthy project. Closer to the truth is this: sometimes I seek out situations that are risky.

I don't know why.

This is my third marriage, and the second for Kim. We tend to walk lightly around one another, seeking a balance between being joined and remaining individuals. I did not seek permission from Kim for the river project, and she would not forbid it. But it hurt her. And what had hurt her the most was that I had made plans for the adventure before sharing with her what I intended to do.

My first bit of research after reaching the high mountains near Leadville, after ten hours of hard travel from Kansas, was something that tourists naturally do: I scooped up a handful of snow.

But I couldn't do it after crossing the pass near Climax, because there was no snow. The year so far had been droughty, and there was no easily accessible snow along the highway. After pitching camp near Leadville, I aimed the Jeep up a dirt road above Turquoise Lake. After many switchbacks and narrow places, and signs warning that the road was for four-wheel-drive vehicles only, there was sudden snow. It lay in patches, and it was melting. Water dampened the narrow road in places, seeking the valley below.

I pressed on, looked for a wide enough spot to pull over and not block the road, and eventually came to an unexpectedly wide turnout near a gated tunnel in the side of the mountain. Although much of the turnout was dry, a tennis court–sized drift lay between the road and the tunnel.

I parked, set the brake, and slowly exited the Jeep. After trying to stretch away the 650 miles of driving, I walked stiffly across the road. I know I walked stiffly because there was a GoPro camera mounted on the windshield of the Jeep; I had wanted to record the twisting and turning mountain lane, with the peaks and the snow above and, after reaching the turnout, decided to just leave it running. When I watch the video now, it seems as if I'm watching a stranger, and yet this motley fellow must be me. There is the untucked orange flannel shirt with the sleeves rolled up to nearly my elbows and the pen in the left shirt pocket, the baggy blue jeans, and the white tennis shoe with one lace dangerously flopping. The green baseball cap is pulled low over my eyes, which sport heavy bags behind the glasses. On my left wrist is a black Luminox dive watch, and on the third finger of my left hand, my wedding ring—still snug, at this point—shines golden. Can this weird character in the video really be me? He doesn't match the mental image of myself at all. This is, of course, the way others see me, and I must make peace with it. In some of my movements—the way I always seem to be looking askance at the world—I recognize my older brother. But my face, increasingly, is my father's face.

I walk over to the drift and scoop up, in my left hand, a great glob of snow. It's wet and shockingly cold, and in the five or six seconds it takes me to walk back with it, it makes my palm ache so that I have to transfer it to my right hand. I'm thinking about the long months the snow must have lain on the mountainside, and how eventually it would contribute to the complicated water system below. As I approach the hood of the Jeep, I hold up the snowball, in both hands, and get closer to the camera. Then I sink my thumbs into it. But before I can break the snowball apart, a great gust of mocking wind comes from seemingly nowhere and snatches it from my hands. The wind billows my shirt and nearly blows the hat from my head, but I turn and catch it by the bill. Wiping my cold and wet hands on the tails of my orange shirt, I walk out of the frame, leaving only the rocky road and the snowdrift, with the gated tunnel in the background, and the mountains and the cloud-laced sky of transcendent blue above.

At the time, I knew I was in the vicinity of Hagerman Pass, which connects the Arkansas headwaters with the upper valley of the Fryingpan River and the Colorado basin, west of the Divide. Later, I would learn from my maps and my GPS coordinates, and from my WPA guide, that I was at the east portal of the Carleton Tunnel, elevation 11,528 feet, and with a bore of nearly two miles through mostly solid granite. In 1887, industrialist John J. Hagerman, who had a controlling interest in the Colorado Midland Railway, decided to extend the tracks from the west side of the Divide and over Frying Pan Pass to Leadville. Putting tracks over the pass was too difficult, so the Colorado Midland made a tunnel near the saddle instead, but the result was unsatisfactory, for the grade was simply too steep.

The lower Carleton Tunnel was begun in 1890, by a private enterprise, as an alternative. It was completed at a cost of $1.25 million, but only after earning a reputation for killing the laborers who worked on it. The Colorado Midland Railway bought the tunnel for a fraction of the cost it took to build. After the railway went bust and the tunnel was abandoned during World War I, it was picked up by Colorado freighting millionaire Albert E. Carlton, who converted it to wagon traffic. The tunnel was eventually acquired by the state highway department in 1924 for automobile use and was renamed the Carleton Tunnel, apparently due to some confusion over how to spell the millionaire's name. In the 1930s the toll to use the tunnel was $1, or $1.50 for a round trip. The tunnel closed for good in 1943 because other routes had made it obsolete.

Today, the name of the tunnel has been changed to reflect the correct spelling of the millionaire's name—*Carlton*—and is used to divert water from the Frying Pan basin to Busk Creek, on the eastern slope. The tunnel is framed in massive timbers, and above the padlocked metal gate is a sign that warns, DANGER—DO NOT ENTER—EXTREME HAZARD—CAVE-INS MAY OCCUR AT ANY TIME. From the left side of the gate, a cement culvert shoots water into a channel that leads to the creek.

To talk about the Arkansas River at Leadville is, necessarily, to talk about mining, and it's difficult to avoid rapine metaphors. From the earliest days just before the Civil War, through the busts and booms that followed, mining has radically changed the land in the upper valley of the Arkansas. In addition to altering the natural topography, the mining legacy left toxic levels of lead, zinc, and other heavy metals in the soil and mine wastes, including contaminated water. A billion gallons of mine sludge is held in a two-mile containment structure called the Leadville Mine Drainage Tunnel, built in the 1940s and now managed by the federal Bureau of Reclamation (BOR). The tunnel—or more properly, an adit, according to the BOR—is located just north of Leadville, and every few years there's a test of a siren system to warn residents if the tunnel fails. In 2008, county officials declared a state of emergency over rising levels of toxic water in the tunnel, and what they saw as an increased potential for a catastrophic release. While the concern continues among some community members about the structural integrity of the tunnel, the BOR claims—on its website, through pamphlets, and via official channels to local news media—there's little chance of a disaster.

The 2015 accident on the Animas River, however, has reminded Leadville residents that a spill is always a possibility. The *Christian Science Monitor* referred to the spill as a possible "Cuyahoga River" moment, a reference to the river in Ohio that infamously caught fire in 1969 and—along with Rachel Carson's *Silent Spring* seven years earlier—helped spur the environmental movement.

But Leadville has already had a Cuyahoga moment.

In 1983, a mine water spill at Leadville turned the Arkansas River blood red. It was alarming enough that the Environmental Protection Agency created the sixteen-square-mile California Gulch Superfund Site and added it to the National Priorities List for cleanup, sparking a grassroots protest that pitted locals against the federal government. Many Leadville residents simply wanted the government to leave them—and their mine dumps—well enough alone. The mining legacy contributed to the character of the people here, with generations of miners and descendants of miners that tend to be conservative and self-reliant.

"Living in Leadville requires a certain grit," wrote Gillian Klucas in her 2004 book *Leadville*, chronicling the fight between the town's old guard and the EPA. "The summers are short, the winters are long and harsh, the air is thin, and the amenities few. Leadvillites reveled in the resilient reputation their rugged existence afforded them. The only glamour to be found in Leadville came from the occasional bride and the coifed tourists, their soft city faces contrasting with the weathered Leadvillites, who tended to look older than their years, the year-round glare of sun and snow plowing deep crevices into their faces, the dry air cracking their calloused hands. It wasn't unheard of to find a man in his eighties wielding a sledgehammer or a ninety-year-old woman repairing fences. They viewed themselves as self-reliant westerners, descendants of that particularly tough and stubborn branch called miners. This remote mountain town had existed for more than a hundred years, and its residents felt they could take care of themselves."

The Leadville Mine Drainage Tunnel notwithstanding, the Superfund cleanup was accomplished over the next couple of decades, with the reclaimed areas being designated mostly for recreational use, including the twelve-mile Mineral Belt hiking and biking trail. In 2014, the EPA declared the cleanup complete.

The Climax mine closed down in 1983, presumably for good, in the wake of a market crash in molybdenum (the mine, however, reopened for limited operations in 2012). The long shutdown of Climax, coupled with the increased emphasis on recreation and tourism, has resulted in a change in the cultural consciousness of Leadville.

Thomas G. Rampton—the author of *Arkansas River Guide,* quoted earlier—has been a resident of the headwaters area since 1979, when he came from California to teach at a private school in Cañon City. He later accepted a job in Buena Vista, where he taught high school chemistry and took students boating after school. Later, he read meters for the local electric company and was responsible for about 400 meters between Buena Vista and Salida.

Now seventy-one, Rampton—who lives in Nathrop, on the river about forty miles south of Leadville—told me during an interview that in the past, residents in the upper valley tended to be miners or ranchers. Now, he says, they are likely to be people like him, who were drawn to the area because of the mountains and rivers.

"The valley here has changed quite a bit," Rampton said. "The people who worked [at Climax] now have gone someplace else. . . . I would say the area is still conservative, but much less reactionary."

The mining legacy still casts a long shadow in the upper valley of the Arkansas, and in Leadville you'll find the ambitiously named National Mining Hall of Fame and Museum. Its promotion materials are proud to point out that it's the "only federally-chartered non-profit national mining museum," and the institution has a decidedly pro-mining vibe. Much of the museum is devoted to Leadville's history, including a scale model of the Robert E. Lee silver mine. There are the usual things you'd expect to find in a mining museum, including the walls of carbide lights and the room with the fluorescent rocks glowing under black light.

The National Mining Hall of Fame has also inherited a separate attraction, on the other side of town from its museum building on West Ninth Street, which tends to be more popular with tourists than with rockhounds or mine fans. For six dollars, every day from late May to the end of September, a mile or so east of town and just off East Seventh Street on Fryer Hill, you can visit the most storied location in Leadville: the Matchless Mine.

It's listed on the National Register of Historic Places, according to the National Park Service, because of its significant contribution "to the social history of Leadville and the state of Colorado, for its contributions made to industry, architecture, and engineering in the field [of] mining, and for its potential to yield more information about the era of the silver boom in Leadville at the turn of the 19th Century. The mine was also made famous by the legend of 'Baby Doe' and Horace Tabor, former owners of the mine, whose scandalous rise from rags to riches ended with their penniless demise."

That unfortunately rhyming "scandalous rise and penniless demise" is a delicate way of putting it. The story of Horace and Baby Doe—and the long-suffering first wife, Augusta—is the foundation story of Leadville, a tale that is equal parts hard work, blind luck, insatiable appetite, blind faith, and tragedy. The story has been told, and retold, in popular books, New York plays, and Hollywood films.

And it all ended here, at the Matchless Mine.

Horace Tabor came to Kansas Territory in 1855 with the first wave of settlers sent by the New England Emigrant Aid Company. This was during Bleeding Kansas, when the fight over whether the territory would enter as a free or a slave state presaged the violence of the Civil War. The company was formed in response to the Kansas-Nebraska Act of 1854, which threatened to upset the delicate balance of free to slave states forged by the Missouri Compromise of 1820, which forbade slavery in former Louisiana Purchase lands above the 36°30′ parallel; the act called for eligible voters in the prospective states to either vote in, or vote out, slavery as a requirement for admission to the union. The company subsidized a portion of the travel costs of about 900 immigrants to establish residency—and voting rights—in the territory, to offset the thousand or so Missouri ruffians who regularly crossed the border to vote in favor of slavery in various territorial elections, legal and otherwise. Blood was spilled on both sides of the political divide in the seven years after the passage of the act. A good argument can be made that the Civil War started on the Missouri-Kansas border years before Confederate artillery fired on Fort Sumter in Charleston Harbor on April 12, 1861.

It was into this Bloody Kansas that Horace Tabor was thrust.

Tabor, listed as a stonecutter from Holland, Vermont, in records held by the Kansas Historical Society, was one of the pilgrims who left Boston on March 13, 1855. Tabor settled in the curiously named community of Zeandale, in northeast Kansas. The name of the town may have been created by mashing up the Greek word for *corn* with the English word for *dale*. Tabor was a farmer, and served in the territorial legislature.

When gold was found at the mouth of Cherry Creek near present-day Denver in 1858, many Kansans—perhaps already weary of the bloodshed on the border—joined what was known, somewhat inaccurately, as the "Pike's Peak Gold Rush." Pike's Peak, named for explorer Zebulon Pike, is sixty miles to the south, as the crow flies. A year later, more gold was discovered higher up in the mountains, and fortune hunters were drawn to claims at California Gulch, Fairplay, and Cache Creek.

Horace and his wife, Augusta, were among the Kansans who decided to decamp for the western regions. All of the gold fields were in Kansas Territory, which extended far beyond the current western border of the state, and included what would become central Colorado and the eastern slope of the Continental Divide. The Tabors arrived in the spring of 1859, and they spent the next few months bouncing between Denver and Idaho Springs and back, then finally settled on California Gulch.

The gulch is located immediately southeast of what is now Leadville. A hundred miles from Denver and across a precarious trail over the Mosquito Range, the narrow gulch was named *California* in hopes that it would prove a bonanza akin to Sutter's Mill on the American River a generation before. While the eastern press made gold mining seem as easy as picking up handfuls of gold nuggets from the riverbed, the truth was that the miners had to remove twelve feet of overburden with hand tools to reach the bedrock, where the placer gold collected. The papers also did not mention the short prospecting season, the brutal winters, or the fierce competition, including claim jumping. Gold seekers came in the thousands—and most of them would go broke and go home. Tabor tried his hand at mining, and some of his claims were profitable, but were no bonanzas; Augusta, meanwhile, turned her attention to keeping shop, because outfitting and feeding the miners proved a much more reliable way of turning a consistent profit.

In 1861, California Gulch and environs were forever separated from

Kansas, as the influx of gold seekers resulted in a population great enough to convene a territorial convention. Colorado Territory was formed, and Oro City—about a mile from current Leadville—was named the seat of Lake County.

After grubstaking various mines, including one that netted him a million dollars when he sold out to his partners, Horace Tabor in 1879 decided he wanted his own mine. He bought the Matchless (named after a popular brand of chewing tobacco) for $117,000. In the next decade, the Matchless would bring Tabor millions—and make him not only one of the richest men in Colorado, but also one of the most influential. At the time he bought the Matchless, he was lieutenant governor of Colorado, and already had his sights set on federal office.

But wealth and influence proved to be not enough for Tabor. By 1880, the fifty-year-old Tabor was seeing a woman who was about half his age: Elizabeth McCourt Doe, twenty-six, twice married and twice divorced. Tabor called her "Baby Doe."

Horace Tabor divorced Augusta twice—first illegally in Durango, and then later in the usual way in Lake County—and married Baby Doe in 1882, while he was serving briefly as a US senator. Her dress alone cost $7,000, at a time when the average monthly wage for a laborer was $20. For a decade after, Baby Doe Tabor lived like royalty on the fortune provided by Tabor and his Matchless Mine. But when the silver market collapsed in the Panic of 1893, Tabor lost everything.

At age sixty-five, Tabor took a job as a laborer in Leadville. Later, he was appointed postmaster of Denver, but held the position for only fifteen months before his death, from appendicitis, in 1899.

And here's where the story veers from fact into legend. On his deathbed, Tabor is alleged to have told Baby Doe to "hold on to the Matchless Mine" because it would be worth millions when the silver market returned.

Baby Doe Tabor moved back to Leadville, where she and her two daughters took up residence in the superintendent's cabin at the Matchless. She had no legal right to the mine, but it didn't seem to matter because the mine was considered worthless, anyway.

In 1929, she was still at the Matchless, reported the *New York Times*.

"Refusing to believe the property has given up its last pay dirt," the *Times* said in an April 21 piece, "she has lived in a deserted shack at the bleak mine entrance, 11,500 feet above sea level, digging and exploring abandoned shafts in the hope of an overlooked vein."

Baby Doe brought with her to the cabin only her wedding dress, volumes of Tabor's love letters, and some photographs, the *Times* reported. She used cardboard to insulate the cabin walls against the cold, and took to wearing a wooden cross around her neck. Even though her daughters grew up and moved on, Baby Doe remained.

She was found dead on the floor of the cabin on March 7, 1935. Apparently, she had frozen to death a few days earlier.

By the time she died, her story was already widely known. A 1932 Warner Brothers film, *Silver Dollar*, told her thinly fictionalized story, and there had been several books. The cabin was opened as a museum in 1954 through the efforts of a group called the Leadville Assembly, whose chief movers were a pair of Denver historians and an antique dealer.

The mine was listed on the National Register of Historic Places by the National Park Service in 2010. On the nomination form, the cabin where Baby Doe died is described as follows: "The one story, ell-shaped, wood frame building is surfaced with unpainted, vertical board siding of various widths and has a corrugated metal gable roof with a metal ridge cap."

It is an ironic monument to the silver queen of the west, and weirdly appropriate to Leadville itself. It conveys, as Gillian Klucas might say, a certain grit.

One of the things about research is that it provides any number of rabbit holes down which to disappear. Research is one of the chief joys in writing a book—joys that I can tell you are precious few, and mostly involve the planning to write something, or the having written something, but never for me the actual damn writing of the thing. I distrust those who claim to enjoy writing, because from my angle they are either liars or graphoholics. If it's not painful, if it doesn't twist your gut with anxiety during the actual composition, then you must not be doing it correctly.

Research is a sure prophylactic to the actual pain of writing, and my inquiries into Leadville's history did not disappoint in this regard. I found many bright and fascinating things connected with Leadville that have no proper place in this story. If given the chance—say, if somebody handed me an all-expenses-paid round-trip time travel ticket to Leadville's frontier past—there would be a number of characters I'd like to meet, but the unhappy love triangle of Horace, Augusta, and Baby Doe would not be among them. First on my list would be Doc Holliday, who after the O.K. Corral came to Leadville to practice his trade as a gambler, was jailed for wounding a man in a gunfight, and probably hastened his own demise from tuberculosis by choosing as his last professional stand a town with brutal winters and high elevation. He died in 1887 in Glenwood Springs, 75 miles northwest of Leadville. He was thirty-six. What I would ask the soft-spoken dentist, over two or six shots of bourbon, is this: *Did you kill Johnny Ringo?* Everyone knows the story of Doc Holliday, or at least they think they do, owing to the many romantic portrayals of him on television and in Hollywood movies. The other Leadville light I'd like to meet, however, is someone you may never have heard of: Orth Stein.

Stein was the son of a wealthy Indiana family, and his father, John, was an attorney and trustee of Purdue University. But young Orth had a talent for journalism, and at the age of fourteen began contributing sketches to the local paper, the Lafayette *Evening Courier*. He also had a taste for the bizarre, and his most popular account was a description of a contraption by which an unbalanced inventor, one James Moon, killed himself in 1876 in an Indiana hotel room. The machine, dubbed a "Kari-kari" by the press, was a kind of automated guillotine that used a candle to burn through a piece of cord, releasing a heavy ax that neatly decapitated the victim, leaving the head in a wooden soap box.

While still a teenager, the bespectacled Stein set out for the West to make a name for himself in journalism, and he soon found himself, in 1880, in Leadville. Among his first pieces was an exposé on the number of quacks practicing medicine in town. Edward Blair's 1980 history of Leadville, *Colorado's Magic City*, describes how Stein posed as a medical student and visited the offices of local physicians, ostensibly to seek work. Few of them had medical training, some bragged about their exorbitant fees, and one even displayed a diploma, high enough on a wall that one needed to stand on a chair to read it, that was just a plasterer's work permit.

Stein also wrote fiction for the *Carbonate Weekly Chronicle*, an honorable journalistic tradition in Victorian America. His most popular tall tales included his description of falling down a ravine into a vast underground cavern north of Leadville, complete with an Alph-like river running through it; the discovery of a skeleton with chains about its neck and bowls of food just out of reach; and a woman prospector who was found frozen to death, carried to the *Chronicle* office, and brought back to life by the warmth of a pot-bellied stove.

My favorite Orth Stein story is about the wreck of a great ship found by two miners. While they are digging a shaft, the bottom suddenly gives way, and the miners find themselves in a cave that contains a junk-like vessel.

"While the whole ship was intact, the wood crumbled like dust beneath the finger's touch," Stein wrote. The ship was about sixty-by-thirty feet, held together with copper nails with octagonal heads, and on the prow was presumably the name of the vessel, in twenty-six characters resembling "Chinese hieroglyphics of the present day."

No human remains or artifacts were found around the ship, with the exception of a large object that appeared similar to a sextant.

"In what strange old seas the vessel sailed, what unknown, ancient waters pressed against its peaked prow, under what prehistoric skies it pitched, what man can tell?" Stein mused.

Stein's work was reprinted in newspapers across the West, and he became a minor celebrity. His path to literary greatness crumbled, however, when in spring 1882 he went to Denver for a much-needed vacation from the *Chronicle*. There, late on the night of April 14 while seeking out friends, he was beaten on the street by an unknown assailant. The motive for the beating was unknown, but Stein's own boss in Leadville theorized that it may have been over a woman, given his employee's nature. The beating, delivered with brass knuckles or another instrument, shattered his glasses and left deep cuts around his eyes. The beating was so severe that newspapers reported Stein was all but blinded, and unable to walk under his own power to his hotel room.

The beating also appears to have done lasting neurological damage, because soon after Stein's personality changed. He had always been flamboyant and expressive, but now he took a turn for the criminal. Changes in personality are not uncommon following head trauma, with the most famous being the case of Eadweard Muybridge, a San Francisco photographer who suffered a head injury in a stagecoach accident on the Butterfield line in Texas—and was then seized with a mania that seems to have contributed to the invention of stop-motion photography and his shooting of his young wife's lover.

In Kansas City, while working for the *Star* under a pseudonym, Stein killed a theater owner named George Fredericks in a row over a chorus girl. He was charged with murder and, after a sensational trial, sentenced to hang. His wealthy family managed to mount a successful bid for a new trial, however, and he was released on bond. He went back to Leadville to work, ran up a number of bad debts, jumped bail, and was later found under an assumed name in Georgia.

In 1897, the Kansas City, Kansas, *Gazette* recapped Stein's career after he made headlines again for drawing a gun on a city prosecutor in Atlanta during a dispute over an exposé about illegal gambling in the city. The *Gazette* noted the time Stein had spent in a local lockup.

"While in jail at Independence Stein was for some time in the same cell with Frank James who was then awaiting trial on the charge of murder for killing conductor Westfall at the Winston train robbery," the *Gazette* said. "After he was released on bond Stein still affected the company of ex-bandits and train robbers and was hand in glove with Dick Liddle and his woman Mattie Collins, the Ford boys who killed Jesse James and other such worthies with which Jackson County was then infested."

Stein never did serve any time for the killing of Fredericks—he was acquitted after a second trial—but he left a long rap sheet behind him, including charges of forgery, according to Robert C. Kriebel's sympathetic biography of the Stein family, published in 1990 by Purdue University Press.

Orth Stein died in New Orleans at the age of thirty-nine. He had retreated to the Crescent City to live among the bohemians there and to write a newspaper column of local sketches. Although contemporary accounts are unclear as to the cause of his demise, influenza—"the gripper"—seems to have been a contributing factor. His death may have also been hastened by a life of dissipation.

"It was as natural for him to write as it was for the mountain stream to leap and bound and sparkle down the mountainside," eulogized an editor at the New Orleans *Herald*. The piece concluded: "When [Stein is buried], the earth will take back to her own a personality and a mind which was so exotically rare and, to those who knew, divinely beautiful."

On my first night in the mountains, in a campground close to Leadville, I pitched camp. There was a Columbia dome tent I'd had for a few years, an air mattress, a Coleman sleeping bag I had bought at a Walmart on the trip out. It was all gear that would, piece by piece, be replaced with lighter and better things as I made my way down the river. I spread a tarp in front of the tent, unfolded a canvas camp chair, and set a blue plastic ice chest next to it. It would be peanut butter sandwiches for dinner, and oatmeal and instant coffee made with water boiled over a Coleman single-burner stove for breakfast in the morning.

After it got dark, I strummed a guitar I'd brought along, then set up a short-wave radio and chatted with another ham radio operator about 700 miles away, in Arizona. Both diversions were impractical, of course, but now that I think of it, my planning had been impractical, and largely based on some emotional fantasy of what I wanted the trip to be. Wouldn't it be nice to write some new songs in the mountains? Or pursue my amateur radio hobby on the side, while exploring the river? I knew the guitar was a bad idea almost right away, because I failed to compose anything new and spent the night worrying what the 30-degree low temperatures would do to the neck. With amateur radio, I would eventually arrive at a more portable and practical solution to operating in the wild, but only because I had a magazine assignment to write about it.

After I finally stowed the guitar and powered down the radio, it was close to midnight. I switched off the battery-powered light that hung from the ceiling and crawled into the sleeping bag, but after five minutes discovered that I hadn't picked a perfectly flat spot to pitch the tent, and that my head was pointed somewhat downhill. So I moved the mattress and the bag until I found a spot where my feet were downhill and I wasn't too close to any of the walls of the tent, which I discovered leaked during a sudden sprinkling of rain. I was so tired that my limbs throbbed and I could taste blood in the back of my throat from my sinuses. The elevation. I closed my eyes and concentrated on being very still and trying not to think about the great amount of crap that I had dragged with me from Kansas.

Then I slept.

At two o'clock in the morning, according to the luminous hands of my watch, I woke. I crawled out of my bag, unzipped the tent, and stumbled outside to conduct some necessary business. The rain had stopped and there wasn't a breath of wind. The sky was mostly clear and the Milky Way arched overhead like a celestial bridge. I stood there, contemplating the couple of thousand stars we can see with the naked eye, and thinking of the billions of others we can't.

That's when I heard the whisper.

For a moment, I wondered who could be out here, conversing ever so gently in low tones. Then I realized the sound I heard was the river, not a quarter of a mile away. The voice was definitely feminine. What was she trying to tell me?

Finding the Line
Elevation: 7,851' (Johnson Village)

When the first light dawned on the earth, and the birds awoke, and the brave river was heard rippling confidently seaward, and the nimble early rising wind rustled the oak leaves about our tent, all people, having reinforced their bodies and their souls with sleep, and cast aside doubt and fear, were invited to unattempted adventures.

—Henry David Thoreau, A Week on the Concord and Merrimack Rivers

My whitewater guide is Brandon Slate, and he owns the Rocky Mountain Outdoor Center (RMOC) below Buena Vista. He came here as a kid from Fremont, Michigan, and he just wanted to kayak in the summer and ski in the winter, and he lived on practically nothing and slept in cars. These are not unusual activities for those who eventually become guides. But Brandon, who is now thirty-three, went to school and learned how to run a business and is now on the city commission and a handful of other boards. Still, he has plenty of memories of the days when he was a river bum, including the one in which he was bitten by a rattlesnake while looking for his favorite paddle, which was hung up in some rocks, and he nearly lost his leg.

Brandon doesn't talk much about himself, but he knows his stuff, and he checks to make sure that my PFD (personal flotation device, but most call it a life jacket) and other gear are up to snuff. He's enthusiastic about what I've come to call my *river project* and he insists I sit on a couch in the common room at RMOC and watch a DVD entitled *Call of the River: A Hundred Years of Whitewater Adventure*. It's a ninety-three-minute documentary produced by Kent Ford, a rather famous paddler, and it describes the evolution of the sport from its beginnings with aluminum canoes in 1949. The most famous *historic* whitewater expedition, of course, is one-armed former Civil War general John Wesley Powell's descent of the Colorado through the Grand Canyon in 1869, in wooden boats.

We ran many of the milder sections I'd read about in Thomas G. Rampton's *Guide*, with Brandon giving me tips. Along some stretches, we floated and we talked, and once we paddled beneath a cliff where a hot spring trickled from above and let it wash over our faces. Under Brandon's instruction, my paddling skill improved, but I still swam a lot. Obviously,

Brandon Slate guiding me on a stretch below Buena Vista (photo by Karl Gregory).

I had forgotten most of what I had once known about paddling. Brandon coached me in picking the best line through a rapid, how to catch an eddy, how to quickly ferry across when needed. He taught me how to stretch before paddling, how to hold the paddle, and how to dip my blades quietly and efficiently in the water. At night in camp, after running twenty or more miles of the river each time, it was hard to sleep because when I closed my eyes, I still felt the motion of the river and saw the trapezoid shapes of the rocks.

How to find the line was essential to everything Brandon taught, because it made the difference between successfully running a rapid or dumping your boat and swimming, or worse, which is called carnage. Competent kayakers can often avoid swimming when capsized by executing a roll, which brings them back upright in one smooth motion. I could never roll worth a damn, so my option in those cases was a wet exit while the boat was upside down and a swim that might include carnage or even a beatdown.

Think of the line as an imaginary thread running down the river that, if you follow it, will lead you safely past any hazards. On easy water, the line is not difficult to follow, and will usually be over the deepest water, typically near the outside of curves. On more difficult water, where the hazards increase, the line might include some tricky technical maneuvers, like a crazy S-turn to avoid some rocks and set you up for the next set of rapids. Because a kayak doesn't track straight but responds to each stroke of the paddle, it takes some practice to keep the bow pointing in the direction you want to go. Novices find this counterintuitive and disorienting, as if they are in some mirror world where reactions are reversed, or in some parallax scroll in which the river is moving but they're not.

In keeping the line, you have to anticipate your moves, lest you miss your chance. If you miss your intended line, you have to recalculate and choose a new one from among a number of competing, and less desirable, alternatives. The line is always changing relative to your position. It's not always easy to see the line, either, because a section is particularly difficult, or perhaps the sun is low on the water and the reflection is blinding. There are other lines on the river as well, such as the line between the current and an eddy, and you can feel that tug at the bottom of your boat as you cross it.

The runs with Brandon were made easier because a friend from Kansas, Butch, was driving the Jeep and shuttling us between access points. Shuttling vehicles is always one of the most tedious parts of paddling, but Butch simplified things by monitoring our progress down the river and being at the take-out when needed. As helpful as Butch was, let me say here it is not always easy to be his friend. Back in Kansas, he's a bail bondsman and he's always armed, usually with a 40-caliber Glock stuffed in a pocket. He will strike up a conversation with absolutely anybody, wander away for a drink with most, and has a bad habit of whistling and talking to himself. But he loves the mountains and the river, and he can perfectly back the trailer down any boat ramp.

One day Brandon and I carried and slid our kayaks down a steep embankment to the river beneath a highway bridge at Johnson Village, below Buena Vista, and set out on a relatively easy run of Class II to III water. After a mile or two Brandon pulled in at an eddy where there was a good-sized tree sticking halfway into the water, and he told me he was going to make me practice self-rescue. And we did, for what seemed like three days, but probably was closer to an hour. He had me climb out onto the trunk of the tree, in my helmet and wetsuit and PFD, and with the neoprene cockpit skirt around my waist—as if I had just done a wet exit—and carrying my paddle. Then he had me jump into the swiftest part of the channel, and try to (1) throw my paddle up on a gravel bar and (2) practice swimming hard to make the bar before the current swept me too far downstream. The first half dozen tries, I managed to fling the paddle up on the bar okay, but didn't swim well enough to reach the bar before being swept downstream. Then, the last couple of times, I angled my body to let the water move me toward the bar while I swam, and made it without much problem. Then he made me crawl up on the bar, instead of stand in the river and walk up on the bar. Get your foot trapped in whitewater, he said, and you're likely to drown. He also made me practice floating down the river, with my feet up and pointed downstream, and practice pushing off rocks. By the time we got back in our cockpits and paddled on, I felt like I had been on the losing end of a street fight. I had some interesting new bruises the next morning. But at the end of the run, not far from the take-out, Brandon tested me by letting me choose my own line through the rocks. I did okay until the water swept me toward a huge, Volkswagen-shaped rock. A hydraulic spun me around, and when I realized I was about to hit the rock broadside, I decided I was through swimming and dug in with my paddle and turned my stern to the rock. The kayak *thunked* into the rock. Then I swept and the bow turned downriver, and I made it without another swim. Brandon laughed and said I had found my *survival* skill. I had a pretty good feeling as we loaded up the kayaks on the trailer.

The next day, that confidence would disappear when I high-centered my kayak on a rock in a riffle near the take-out, and had to step out of the cockpit and drag the boat across to the take-out. The bottom was exceptionally rocky, and some places were thigh-deep, and I used the paddle to tripod myself. Then, about twenty yards from shore, I realized I couldn't lift my left leg. It wasn't trapped; it was just that my muscles quivered and failed to respond. Brandon offered to come help me, but I insisted on doing it myself. I rested for a few minutes, and the movement in my leg came back. After I got home, my doctor checked me out and said the muscles in my left leg were smaller than my right. They had *atrophied*. She could tell even before I slipped off my jeans. She didn't know the cause, but it probably had to do with all the hours I've spent at a desk.

We need the tonic of wildness. . . . At the same time that we are earnest to explore and learn all things, we require that all things be mysterious and unexplorable, that land and sea be infinitely wild, unsurveyed and unfathomed by us because unfathomable.

—Henry David Thoreau, Walden

"Oh, shit," the girl in the chartreuse dry suit at the back of the raft begins to chant. We're floating down a mild stretch of the Arkansas River below Big Bend on the last day of May, and it's placid water, but ahead riffles glitter like diamonds in the sunshine. "Oh shit, oh shit!"

The girl in chartreuse is named Leah, and she's a river guide trainee on her first day on the water. She's sitting sidesaddle on the left tube, with the stick in her hand—the stick is the guide's paddle, typically fiberglass, and longer and stouter than the stubby plastic paddles the rest of us have—and as the guide, she's in command of the raft. She's twenty-something and petite, with a spray of auburn hair spilling from beneath her green helmet, and her Keen river shoes match the rest of her outfit. Her sunburnished face is getting ruddier by the second as she contemplates how to control the raft.

The other four of us in the raft are playing the parts of her paying guests. In addition to me, there's a trainee named Lucas Udley, an athlete and a bike messenger in New York, and two experienced river guides, Kate Stepan and Elisha McArthur. Everybody but me is in their twenties or thirties. Nobody is allowed to assist Leah or give her advice. When she gives a command, we are to respond immediately and without question, even if it's the wrong thing to do. Kate has been making things even more challenging for Leah by engaging in risky behaviors that guides are supposed to prevent their guests from doing, like straddling the tube and dragging a foot in the water, or refusing to keep a hand over the T at the top of her paddle handle—which, in unskilled hands, usually ends with somebody being smacked in the face. Elisha has been kinder, and is handing out makeup glitter from a tiny bottle. It's her trademark, she says, and the kids on her trips love it. All of us crew take some and smear it on our faces, like river woad.

A training session at the low-head dam above Salida.

"What do I do?" Leah asks, panicked.

"You tell us," Kate says.

We're almost to the riffles, and Leah has waited so long to decide what to do that our line is all wrong. We are nearly perpendicular to the riffles, which won't be a problem here, but could result in high siding or even flipping in a serious rapid.

Leah says something, but it's not loud enough to understand.

"What?" Kate asks. "Use your river voice!"

"Forward," Leah says, a bit louder. "Everybody paddle."

So we dig in, but it just propels us forward and fails to correct the line.

"Thank you!" Leah says.

"Does that mean stop?" Kate asks.

"Yes. Stop, please."

Leah's working the guide stick, but not having much luck correcting the angle. Once in the riffle, we begin to slowly spin, and Leah realizes she has completely lost control. Kate finally takes pity on her and makes some suggestions: she needs to use her river voice, which is commanding, confident, and loud; she needs to set her angle early and go with it; and, when needed, she needs to have one side or the other paddle, and make sure everybody with a blade in the water is paddling in time. Leah nods, yes of course, she knew all that but just forgot. Thanks.

We float for a few more minutes, and the rest of us are looking downriver, when suddenly there was a big splash behind us. "Swimmer!" Kate yells. Leah has failed to properly brace herself, and has lost her balance and fallen backward into the river. She is bobbing in the water a few yards out, on my side of the raft, and I lean over the tube to reach for her, but Kate is quicker. In a flash she has belly flopped across the raft and is stretched over the tube, extending her paddle with both hands. Leah grasps the T-shaped handle, and Kate pulls back and uses her legs against the tube to pull her back in—one smooth motion that results in Leah being hauled up over the side like a fish. Kate's reaction was impressive, and it resulted in Leah being in the water the least amount of time possible—the more time spent in the water, the greater the chances of something serious happening. It also kept Kate's center of gravity low, which would help her stay in the raft in rough water.

Leah's face is wet, and now even redder than before. Kate and Elisha tell her not to worry about it. Everybody swims, they say, sooner or later, and it's good that she got it out of the way early.

It takes fifty hours on the water to become certified as a river guide in the state of Colorado, and the trip during which Leah was baptized early was part of a ten-day training session, in class and on the water, that was designed to exceed that requirement. Thirteen aspiring guides had signed up for the training, which was hosted at the RMOC and led by Marcel Bieg, a whitewater safety expert and the western states outreach director for the American Canoe Association (ACA). I had met the group that morning to listen to some of the classroom work, and Bieg—a large man with a river pirate's sense of humor—made me introduce myself and choose a nickname, just as the trainees had. My nickname was Mad Max. I was crazy, I said, because I had this conflicted desire about doing a book on the Arkansas River.

Leah, who approached the training in scholarly fashion, applied herself to the worksheet handouts and asked more questions than anybody else that morning. She wanted to know, for example, about how rapids are rated. Bieg said that the International Scale of River Difficulty was created by the ACA as a consistent way to rate sections of water, and he briefly explained the classes, from I (easy) to V (expert). She asked about the frequency of rescues on the Arkansas, and Bieg said there were no more and no fewer rescues than on other rivers. There would be more in-depth discussion of all of that later, he said. Then we went outside, and Bieg led us in an exercise in tossing a throw bag. A throw bag is a nylon pouch about the size of a one-pound coffee can, in which is stuffed fifty feet or more of floating rope. It's a standard piece of safety equipment, and required carry for guides, but like any other piece of gear, it takes some training to use correctly. From the bank, for example, the throw bag can be used to haul in a swimmer in trouble.

When throwing, you aim for tossing the bag upstream and past the target, so there's a greater chance the swimmer can grasp the line. Then, the swimmer is instructed to clutch the line with both hands to their chest and roll over on their back to be pulled in. Bieg practiced on us by throwing the bags unexpectedly over our shoulders. I missed the line when he threw it at me. Then he had us pair off, about six feet apart, and practice tossing the bag underhand between us. Nobody dropped the bag. Then he had us take a step back every few throws to learn how far we could toss it accurately, and by the time we were twelve feet apart, some of the bags hit the ground. I managed to accurately toss it up to about thirty feet, and a few, including Lucas Udley, the athletic bike messenger, were still going at about fifty feet, when Bieg called a halt.

We loaded the rafts on the trailers and stowed many paddles and the pumps and other gear we'd need, and then we pulled on our wetsuits or dry suits and got into a couple of vans. At the launch, after the rafts were in the water and we had put on our helmets and PFDs, Bieg asked for a volunteer to give a safety talk. Leah volunteered, and she gave an impromptu five-minute talk that seemed to me impressive. She was obviously at ease talking to groups, and in a clear and confident voice she went over the basics, which included: helmets and life jackets are required at all times, use plenty of sunscreen, and hold the paddle with one hand on the shaft and the other over the T-shaped handle, to keep it out of somebody else's face. Follow the guide's commands promptly, and if she calls "High-side!" throw your weight on the downstream side of the raft. When a boat collides against a rock or other obstacle, water piles and threatens to swamp the upstream tube. This can quickly flip the boat or, worse, pin it against the rock. Finally, stay in the boat. If you do fall in the water, keep your feet up, knees bent, and don't try to stand.

Bieg listened, complimented her on her delivery, and then suggested she use some humor to put her guests at ease. For example (and I don't remember if this was one of Bieg's or something I picked up elsewhere): *What's the difference between a raft guide and a mutual fund? One eventually matures and makes money.* Bieg also said to stress that the goal was "to be safe and to have fun."

Sometime after Leah's short swim, on another easy section of the river, I was offered the chance to guide. I flopped in the back, took the stick, and placed myself on the left tube, with my right foot wedged under the bulkhead in front. It was an easy section of the river to read, and shouting commands to the crew, I guided the raft through the deep channels on the outside turns. I tried using the stick to turn the raft, but had forgotten the strokes that had been discussed earlier. I made a few jokes, asked if they were having fun, and shouted commands in my best river voice. Then the river straightened out and there were some mild rapids ahead, and to turn to get the proper line I had one side of my crew paddle backward. When I saw a coffee table–sized rock ahead of us, with a bit of water piling over it, I shouted "Bump!" and the crew shipped their paddles while the raft bopped over it. The best part was riding a wave train a little farther downstream, with the boat going "splish-splish-splish."

I enjoyed playing at being a raft guide, perhaps because I like ordering people about. I was also feeling just the least bit smug that I hadn't fallen out of the raft. But when it was over I was glad to leave the river guiding to others, because river guides have to be everything on the river— friend, boat captain, counselor, comedian, medic, a one-person rescue squad—and they do it all cheerfully and with little pay. The women guides especially are to be admired, because they have proved themselves in a seasonal profession dominated by men, and those men have created a kind of river pirate culture that ranges from the insensitive to the downright misogynistic.

A little farther down we stopped for lunch, just above the boat chute around a notorious low-head dam north of Salida. I had been here before, with Brandon, and I'd flipped my boat and had a short swim on the third drop, at the bottom of the chute. The signs around the dam are better now; they are higher and bigger, for one thing, and illuminated at night. The changes were made by the owner of the dam, Colorado Parks and Wildlife (CPW), after a boating fatality here in June 2014. Amanda Taylor, a thirty-one-year-old woman from Utah, drowned when the private raft she was in flipped after going over the dam at night. Five other people in the raft made it to shore, and a sixth clung to the overturned raft and was rescued by a Salida firefighter. Taylor's body was missing for four days, until her brother found it three miles downriver, snagged on a branch. The family held the body from being swept farther downstream until authorities arrived.

The dam was originally built in 1956, according to CPW, to divert water to the Mount Shavano Fish Hatchery, which produces millions of trout and salmon. The water diversion stopped after an outbreak of whirling disease, in which a microscopic parasite causes deformities in salmonid fish, including trout, and creates erratic tail-chasing behavior. It is thought to have developed in Europe, where trout are immune to it but remain carriers, and is believed by the CPW to have been introduced to Colorado in the 1980s through imported trout from a private hatchery. Although the dam is not currently used to divert water, the state agency says it is an important resource and should be kept for future use.

Above the boat chute, there's a flat, graveled lookout that's good for scouting, and a great flat rock that's also good for sitting and having a sack lunch. I had a hard-boiled egg, some squares of cheddar cheese, and a turkey-and-swiss wrap. The day was warming up, and to keep from overheating I unclasped the Velcro on one shoulder of my farmer John wetsuit and rolled the top down. There were only a few wisps of cloud above, and to the northeast a brick smokestack rose against the blue sky. It was a landmark that could be seen for miles along the river, letting you know you were getting close to Salida.

Then, Bieg called us all together on the overlook above the boat chute and dam to give us a safety lecture on hydraulics. He held a small inflatable raft, perhaps a foot long, a toy or perhaps a promotional item.

Low-head dams, he said, are the most dangerous man-made hazard on any river. Even though they don't look that hazardous, they are responsible for many deaths every year. Because the drop may only be a few feet and typically there is little or no spray at the bottom, inexperienced boaters may think they can just paddle over them. But the problem is that there is a reverse hydraulic, a recirculating current that pushes surface water upstream, toward the hazard at the base of the dam, which traps debris—or boats and paddlers—in a powerful recirculating current. Once trapped, it may not be possible to swim out, even while wearing the best safety gear.

To demonstrate, Bieg went to the water's edge, at the top of the boat chute, and launched the little raft. The drop of a few inches into the first pool represented a full-sized dam. It took him a few tries—and a swim down into the chute—to get the raft positioned correctly, but it eventually flipped and was held in place by the recirculating current. When I had been here earlier, with Brandon, he'd told me a story of somebody he knew who was foolish enough to try to shoot the dam. He survived, with only minor injuries, but the force of the hydraulic had ripped away all of his clothes.

The Flume
Elevation: 7,503' (Browns Canyon)

Search and Rescue itself is a nuisance. Let each person who enters the Canyon, whether on foot, by mule, or by boat, clearly understand that some risk is involved, some rather elementary and fundamental risk, and that nothing can guarantee your safety but your own common sense. Nor even that. Nothing should be guaranteed. Nothing can be.

—*Edward Abbey,* Down the River

The canyon Edward Abbey nominally refers to is the Grand Canyon, but he may have intended the sentiment for any of the canyons in the West with high rocks and fast water. Browns Canyon on the Arkansas River below Buena Vista offers some of the most famous whitewater in the world, and during the summer the river is uncommonly crowded with people, sitting on sausage-like tubes of commercial rafts or paddling their own boats, looking for an iconic wilderness experience. In June 2016 I was among the throng, seeking if not an iconic experience, at least an authentic one.

Like the North Rim of the Grand Canyon, Browns Canyon is also a national monument, albeit a recent one; President Obama used the Antiquities Act to designate its 22,000 wild acres a monument in February 2015. The Antiquities Act was passed in 1906 by Theodore Roosevelt to protect lands that held historic or scientific interest, and the first national monument he designated was Devil's Tower in Wyoming. Presidents since have designated more than 150 sites, from Muir Woods in California to Rose Atoll in American Samoa.

At Browns Canyon, the Arkansas River isn't part of the national monument, because of the abandoned railroad tracks that snake along the eastern bank like a DMZ between the sullied and the untrammeled. It doesn't diminish the beauty seen from the river, however, because the canyon walls are made of weathered pink granite formations, often with spectacular pillars and rounded hoodoos. The canyon is also host to a variety of wildlife, including black bears and mountain lions and bighorn sheep. Of those, the sheep are the easiest to spot, and I've seen many of them standing on the pink rocks overlooking the river, in Browns and throughout the headwaters east of the river.

Failing to run Zoom Flume (photos by Arkansas Valley Digital Imaging).

The night before I ran Browns Canyon, I spent an hour in a budget hotel at Salida, trimming the neck gasket on a dry suit that I had mail-ordered a few days before. Dry suits are expensive, but there is no substitute for protection from long immersions in cold water. I had gotten this one on sale, in about my size, for *only* $636. I felt guilty about the purchase. Besides the kayak and the trailer, it was the single most expensive piece of river-running gear I owned. But good equipment isn't cheap, and a dry suit isn't something you can rent, because they must be altered for a proper fit. It's not a piece of gear for the casual kayaker. The one I bought was a Kokatat Meridian, tangerine on top and gray on the bottom, and it was a one-piece affair that you stepped into. Then you pulled a heavy waterproof zipper diagonally across your chest to seal yourself inside. A major selling feature was that it also had a smaller zipper across the crotch, for urinary relief without removing the entire suit. Water is kept out not only by the heavy zippers, but also by neoprene gaskets at the wrists and the neck, but the catch is that the neck gasket must be trimmed to fit. This must be done slowly, and with repeated fittings, so as not to ruin its ability to keep out water. For an hour, I sat with the dry suit in my lap, the neck gasket stretched over the motel's ice bucket, so that I could cleanly remove the gasket material, ring by ring, with a razor blade. After each cut, I pulled the gasket over my head to test it. Without trimming, the gasket felt like a vise around my neck; after half a dozen cuts, I could only wear it for a few minutes before I felt I would pass out. A couple of more cuts, and I could just tolerate it.

The gasket should be tight, according to the instructions, *but not be too constricting*. How constricting was too constricting, I wondered? I was used to scuba wetsuits and hoods, which are hard to get into and feel impossibly tight until you're in the water, and reasoned this must be about the same. I trimmed a bit more and then pulled the gasket over my head, wormed my way into the rest of the suit and zipped it up, to see if I could stand it. I wore it in the room for about ten minutes, walking about and so forth, and when I peeled it off—with difficulty, because you exit the way you entered, through the big diagonal zipper across the chest—my undershirt was damp with sweat and my face in the mirror looked like a tomato. After I packed things for the next day, in the order I would need them for dressing on the river, including some long underwear for the chilly water, I walked out to the Jeep to retrieve a Pelican case from the back to stow my notebook and pen. Problem was, I had pulled the motel room door shut behind me, and it had locked. The key was inside, on the desk where I had sat and trimmed the gasket.

"Sonuvabitch," I muttered, annoyed at having to go to the office and ask the owner to let me back into my room. That's when I discovered another problem—a handwritten note taped to the door said the lodge keeper, whom we'll call Tom, had gone to the Denver airport to pick up a new housekeeper. He wouldn't be back for another three hours. I felt stupid and unlucky at the same time. Well, the wait wouldn't kill me.

It was still light, so I took my Canon DSLR from the back of the Jeep, slung it over my shoulder, and took a walk downtown to the whitewater park, where I stood on a bridge over the water and shot a pair of young kayakers playing in the waves. They were having a good time, cutting around and through the gates, marked by pairs of red-and-white poles suspended over the water. One of them would also approach the upper end of the hole, where there was a cresting wave, and would paddle like mad to get into position to surf for a few minutes. After his boat sat on top of the wave for a few seconds, the bow would gently turn, and he would cut back into the water, and would do a roll to finish. He made his rolls look effortless, as if the kayak were turning on an axis, and he came back up with just the right momentum so that there was no effort lost in overcorrecting. The paddler appeared to be in his late twenties, and I attributed his skill to youth until a third kayaker joined them, a guy who was perhaps sixty or sixty-five, judging from his white hair and the lines in his tan face. The older man paddled his boat through the gates as easily as if he were on a pond instead of whitewater, and when he rolled he did it with confidence and grace. Like all of the good kayakers I had seen on the river, his back was ramrod straight, and his paddle was always in contact with the water.

As I walked back, I thought about my own skill level. I knew I would never approach the level of athleticism I'd just witnessed at the water park, but I determined not to let it stop me from paddling as much of the river as I could. Back at the motel, I discovered the note still in place on the door of the office, even though it would have been about time for Tom to return. I muttered some more curses. With more time to kill, I stowed the camera in the Jeep and retrieved a small book I'd bought a couple of days earlier at a local restaurant, one I favored because it had reliably good club sandwiches.

I settled into a metal chair outside the locked door of my room and settled down to read the forty-eight-page, locally published booklet. It was titled *Smokestack: The Story of the Salida Smelter*, and it was written in 1987 by a local high school teacher by the name of Dick Dixon. To my surprise, it was a remarkably good account of a feature that you can see for miles as you approach Salida from the north, and one that I'd wondered about since I first saw it from the river upstream: that monolithic brick smokestack that rises 365 feet above the valley floor.

The stack took 264 railroad cars of brick to build in 1917. The walls are six feet thick at the base, and the top is seventeen feet in diameter. When it was built, it was the tallest smokestack west of the Mississippi, and around its base was a maze-like eighty acres of furnaces and railroad tracks. In and surrounding this area were the homes of the workers— Smeltertown, a name that has stuck to this day. The site processed thousands of tons of ore containing gold, silver, lead, and copper. It wasn't the first stack on the site, however. Until the huge stack was built, there were stacks of 150 and 85 feet that carried the fumes away from the site. When the company announced plans for the big stack in 1917, they said the height of approximately 350 feet was necessary to establish a "proper draft" for the furnaces. Dixon, however, says everybody in town knew why a taller stack was being built: the fumes from the old ones were making people sick and killing animals. Although no mention of the pollution ever appeared in the local newspapers, Dixon interviewed plenty of Salida residents who recalled the truth.

"Trees died on the slope of the low Mosquito Mountains down wind to the east of the smelter," Dixon writes, "including those on Tenderfoot Mountain (the low hill with the large S). . . . Ranchers who lived down wind found their crops didn't do as well as they had in the past. Animals sickened and died. In a time before modern medicine and laboratory tests, there were rumors that the smoke wasn't doing human health any good either. Smoke from the stacks carried a high concentration of cyanide." The company paid off ranchers and others to keep quiet. As production increased, it was impossible for the company to keep up with the damages. Lawsuits were filed. A public "permit" system was established, and in exchange for $250 dollars, the company bought the right to pollute a neighboring property to any extent, without liability. It was a stopgap measure until the new stack could be built. Construction began in June 1917 and was completed on November 14, at a cost that exceeded $50,000—which would be about a million in today's money. Arthur Thomson, the smelter assistant superintendent overseeing construction, braved the heights to slip a silver dollar into the cement between a couple of bricks. The same day, Salida town clerk Bertie Roney was hoisted to the top in a materials bucket, presumably in a show of civic pride. Once in operation, the stack also seemed to do what it was designed for, to release fumes high enough in the air to be dispersed to levels that did not immediately poison livestock.

But debt and bad luck, including a fire that destroyed a critical warehouse, and falling metals prices at the end of World War I, doomed the company. In 1919, the Ohio-Colorado Smelting and Refining Company leased the operation to another concern, but the last straw came when the principal lender, the Denver National Bank, called the note. A judge ordered the smelter sold at sheriff's auction on October 25, 1920. The site was wrecked, but the stack remained, perhaps because it would have been too dangerous to fell. In the 1970s interest began to grow in preserving the stack as a symbol of local history. After a long legal battle, it became a National Historic Landmark in 1976.

The smelting operation that ran from 1902 to 1920 at the site had dumped wastes along the banks of the Arkansas River, including arsenic and cadmium. In 1997, the Environmental Protection Agency declared the area a Superfund site, and the contaminated soils were hauled away. New water wells were drilled for the modern-day residents of Smeltertown.

Intrigued, and with some daylight left, I drove to Smeltertown to see the big stack for myself. I was surprised to find some well-made interpretive signs and an ample parking area. The Jeep, parked at the octagonal base of the tower, looked like a toy car from where I'd walked to try to get the entire stack in a photograph. Above, the sky was blue and a smattering of clouds drifted by. Looking up from the base, one gets the unpleasant sensation that the tower is falling toward you. Even though the site is open to the public, you can't climb the tower because it and some adjacent buildings are fenced off and adorned with fierce-looking NO TRESPASSING signs warning that the owner, the Salida Museum, would prosecute violators. But on the afternoon of my visit, there wasn't another soul around, and so of course I slipped through a three-foot rent in the chain link. In the building near the base of the tower, I found evidence of illicit partying—beer bottles, spent condoms, assorted trash. There wasn't much else to see, except the vacant doors and windows.

It was near dark when I returned to the motel, after eating another reliable club sandwich, and still no Tom. Perhaps the flight had been delayed, or he'd had car trouble. There were a couple of windows in the front of my motel room, and one was latched securely, but the other had an air conditioner in it and the lower sash was held in place with just a couple of nails. I briefly considered getting the tire iron from the back of the Jeep and prying it open to climb in, but decided I was hardly desperate enough to risk breaking into my own room.

So I retrieved another volume from the traveling research library in the back of my Jeep—*Down the River* by Edward Abbey—and sat down in the metal chair beneath the light above the locked motel room door. It had turned chilly, so I had slipped on my down vest and a red-checked watch cap. I was tolerably comfortable. Abbey begins by talking about reading *Walden* again, for the first time since his school days, during a float down the Green River in Utah. I had just gotten a couple of pages into it—"Here we are slipping away in the early morning of another Election Day"—when I was interrupted by a feminine voice.

"Pardon me?" I asked.

At the corner of the building, twenty yards away, a young woman was staring at me. She wore a blue-checked flannel shirt that was a couple of sizes too big for her, a pair of pajama pants, and flip-flops. One hip was cocked at a provocative angle. A ball cap was pulled low over her eyes, and from beneath it dark brown hair tumbled over her shoulders. She had one arm crossed, supporting the other elbow, and in her left hand was an unlit cigarette.

"Hey," she said.

"Hello."

"Have you seen Tom?"

"He's on an errand," I said and mentioned the note, allowing a bit of irritation in my voice. "He was supposed to be back a few hours ago. Guess he got held up."

"I need to pay him the rent," she said. "First of the month. I'm just around the corner, in one of the long-term units. Been here a couple of months. My name's Marisa."

I nodded.

She closed about half the distance between us.

"What're you reading?"

I told her.

"What's it about?"

"Well, it's literary nonfiction."

"Oh?" she said. "You reading it for work or something?"

"Something like that."

I returned to the book. There was an age difference of at least twenty years, but the tone in her voice said she didn't mind. I am tempted to say that everything about her spelled trouble, but that's too pat—and shifting the blame. What spelled trouble was my reaction to her, because she was attractive and soft-spoken and I was drawn to her in an old and achingly familiar way. In the past, I would have tried to satisfy that ache. But not now.

She came a few steps closer.

"Got a light?" she asked.

"Sorry," I said. "Don't smoke. Haven't in years."

"Yeah," she said. "I shouldn't."

Still, she remained. She half turned away from me and stared into the night sky, as if she were expecting some kind of answer to appear. She wanted something, it seemed, but whether it was money or something else, I could not tell. Then she brushed her hair behind her left ear with her free hand and smiled in a way that must have been old when the pyramids were new.

"Say, you want to come over to my place?" she asked. "Just around the corner. We could have a drink, maybe. I have some rum."

I looked at her and felt my world hanging on what I said next. Kim had never pressured me or asked for promises. *Nothing should be guaranteed. Nothing can be.* But I had promised myself some things, not the least of which was to avoid causing myself and others pain. An image flashed in my mind: me, standing alone on the bank of the river, somewhere in Kansas toward the end of my journey, and tossing my wedding ring into the water. The thought made me ill. Would that be the last scene in a story that began with the golden band bouncing across the deck of my boat?

"Thanks," I said. "But I really should finish this book."

"Okay," she said.

Still, she remained.

"It was a very kind offer," I said. "Thank you, but no."

She drifted away around the corner.

I don't know for sure what she had been offering. Perhaps I'm flattering myself to think it was more than just a little company. But I knew what my intentions would have been had I accepted.

Tom returned an hour later, with a Filipina housekeeper with an enormous amount of luggage. He complained of delayed flights and traffic and having not eaten since breakfast. He gave me a spare key to get into my room, and once inside I turned on the heater and sat at the desk and made some notes.

When the Grinch loses his jaw, it means high water for the season. At least that's the folk wisdom among the paddlers on the upper Arkansas, and it refers to an image that appears each spring as the snow melts on the east side of 14,235-foot Mount Shavano. The shape does look like the profile of the Grinch from Dr. Seuss, and the Mean One is leering at a better-known image on the mountain, the Angel of Shavano. The angel is a stick-like figure with outstretched arms. When the snow melts enough that the Grinch loses the lower part of his face, usually by mid- to late June, it signals the highest water levels for the season. On the morning I set out for Browns Canyon, the Grinch still had his jaw, but barely.

I met guide Reid Jackson at the Rocky Mountain Outdoor Center and he loaded his kayak on top of one of the center's vans, along with two inflatable kayaks called "duckies." I'd never been in an inflatable before, other than a raft, but Brandon had told me they were "pretty forgiving" and I shouldn't have much trouble paddling one. Brandon was busy running the shop—it was, after all, the peak season—but he had referred me to Reid, who knew the river well. There were two inflatables on the van because running Browns with a guide isn't exactly cheap, and the only way I could afford it was to share the expense with a stranger. The stranger in this case was a woman named Jan, about my age or a little younger, who had her own inflatable back home, and said that she had taken up whitewater paddling following a divorce. She was through with men, she said, and she had been whitewater adventuring to boost her self-confidence. I listened quietly to her story while I tugged on my dry suit over some polypropylene long underwear and contemplated the proper assembly of the ankle gaskets/socks/river shoes/zippered pant cuffs. Leave the ankle zippers undone, Reid advised. They don't really do anything, he said, because it's the gasket that keeps out the water, and it's a sign of a veteran paddler to leave them undone. I left the top down until we reached the launch.

Reid's a high school teacher of English in his thirties, and he spends his summers on the river. That's about 100 days a year on the river, give or take, so of course he knows what he's doing. The launch point was across the highway and some ways north, where Brandon had bought some long-anticipated river access. He intends to move the whole operation there, maybe even open a restaurant, but for now the amenities consisted of a Porta Potty and some open ground where he lets the river guides and trainees camp, a sort of hobo jungle for river rats.

The new place is on a relatively tame section of river called the Milk Run, which I'd paddled with Brandon, but above Ruby Mountain. The plan was to do a run of about ten miles, down to Stone Bridge, and along the way we'd experience some of the best-known rapids anywhere on the river: Canyon Doors, Pinball, Zoom Flume, Egg Beater, the Squeeze, Big Drop, Seven Stairs, Widowmaker, the Graveyard, Seidel's Suckhole. We would also pass Hecla Junction, where Butch and I had spent Christmas about five months before.

Standing at the water's edge, Reid briefed me on the ducky.

The ones we had were NRS-brand boats, bright blue, and about nine and a half feet long. There were eleven-inch-diameter tubes on each side, a self-bailing floor, and an inflatable thwart seat that was like a big pillow. Calling them kayaks is a bit of a misnomer, I think, because they aren't a decked boat. They are more like a cross between a canoe and half a raft, and I can see their appeal, because they are inherently stable. The downside for me was that I didn't feel like I was wearing the boat, as with a decked kayak, and there wasn't a good place to brace my feet that felt comfortable or secure. Reid told me to jam my heels between the tube and the floor. Because of their width, the inflatables are slow, and slow to turn. They would undoubtedly be the safest one-person boat on the river, but I wasn't crazy about them.

The river was running at about 1,000 cubic feet per second, Reid said, which meant a decent ride, but probably not anything too challenging.

"If you swim," Reid said, "the boat is going to flip and you're going to come up beneath it, and it's going to be dark under the mesh floor. You'll be blind. You need to get out from under the boat, and then climb back in. And hang on to your paddle."

Then Reid asked both me and Jan to review basic safety procedures. Summary: don't stand up in the river, float with your feet downstream so you can push away from rocks, swim like hell to get to safety. Then he checked our gear and made an adjustment to my helmet. It was a little loose, he said, and he cinched the strap beneath my jaw. My PFD looked good, he said, and my Nalgene bottle was fine carabinered to a D-ring in the bow. Behind my seat, he clipped a dry bag that contained lunch.

I made doubly sure that my wedding ring was secured with two Band-Aids to my finger; it wasn't going anywhere that I wasn't. The brush with Marisa the night before had made me feel guilty about my past, and having unhappily/happily divorced Jan as a paddling partner seemed oddly inevitable. Also, I wasn't feeling terrific. I had a headache and was tired, as if I were coming down with the flu. But maybe I was just overheated. Even though it had dropped to the 40s the night before, the morning was quickly heating up. It would reach 80 by midafternoon. Zippered in the dry suit, I had begun to sweat. The sweat leached some of the sunscreen into my eyes, which stung. I also began to wish I'd trimmed a couple more rings from the neck gasket, because I felt like I was being slowly but surely strangled. I tugged at the collar, trying to find a more comfortable fit, and I asked Reid how much he usually trimmed from his gasket. He said he never had to trim them, that his suits were always a perfect fit. Don't worry, he said, it would loosen up with wear.

Then we set off.

The first half mile or so was easy water, as I remember it, and because I was feeling suddenly confident, Reid allowed me to take the lead and find whatever line I wanted. He mostly agreed with my choices. I was unhappy with the sluggishness of the ducky and how slow it ferried, but Reid said things would get quick soon enough. When we switched around, and Jan led, I saw that she was more comfortable in her boat—and was a better paddler. Her boat didn't seem slow. The problem with my ducky was me, and I tried to work on my form.

It wasn't long before we were in bigger water with much foam and Class III rapids, and then we shot through the upper and lower Doors of Browns Canyon—so named because of the boulders standing like sentinels over the water. I followed Reid's line through, with no problems. I sometimes bumped into rocks, but the ducky sort of just poured itself around them, without much effort on my part, except leaning in a bit and keeping a blade in the water for control.

We made our way through Pinball, which was thrilling because there are plenty of rocks to avoid, and passed Pink Panther, an enormous boulder that looks like the head of the cartoon character, with his snout in the water as if taking a drink. Then the river calmed down for a half mile or so. I don't remember where we ate lunch, but it must have been on one of the gravel bars in this section. Reid had brought some burritos for us, made that morning back at the RMOC, and they were still wrapped in aluminum foil and warm. But because I'm allergic to a weird variety of foods, including and especially onion powder, I thought it best to pass. I ate a Clif Bar and drank some water. As we ate, Reid said that we'd been making better time than expected, so perhaps the river was up. The Grinch must have lost more of his jaw than expected.

Once back on the water, we paddled some more and then, about 11:30 a.m., Reid called out that it was time to scout Zoom Flume. The river was narrowing here, and we had to paddle hard to river left, so that we weren't pulled by the current down to the tongue of water that represented *commitment*. We landed, pulled the boats out of the water up onto the rocks, then scrambled up onto some boulders, nearly to the level of the abandoned railroad track.

Standing there, we had a good view of the Flume, which is a Class III to IV rapid, depending on the water. "The view," says Thomas Rampton in his *Arkansas River Guide*, "is that feared by Columbus and his crew, had his ships really come to the edge of the world. Boats ahead drop out of sight. Spray shoots up. Zoom is long, rough and narrow, but there's a good eddy below-right." It was the only place, Rampton notes, that he had ever flipped a raft, anywhere.

From our elevated position, the Flume looked like a series of narrow interconnected rapids with one huge rock—Pyramid Rock—in the middle of it all. It's the biggest rapid in Browns. We watched as a half dozen commercial rafts and a couple of private boats shot the Flume, riding a tongue of water down into the first hole, disappearing from view, and then bouncing up out of that to drop into another hole with even bigger spray and waves. Despite the roar of the water, we could hear whoops of joy and fear from the boaters. Reid said the water seemed a little higher and faster than when we had set out that morning, but we'd be okay. We'd have to wait until there was a lull in the river traffic, he said, so as not to trip up anybody's else run, and be ready to go for it. But, he added, Jan and I would have to decide for ourselves which line to run, and we had to do it now, because once we were at the top of Zoom there would only be a couple of seconds to decide. Jan said she didn't want to think about it, she'd just rely on her instinct, and she wanted to go first. I said I would bear center left, because I'd seen some of the boats get slammed if they went too far right. Reid told me not to go too far left.

When it was time, Jan went first, and after she went down the tongue of water into the hole I could only catch glimpses when she bobbed at the top of the waves. Eventually, we could see her boat clear the last hole, and she caught the eddy on the right to wait for us.

Then it was my turn.

I paddled out and in a moment the current had seized my boat and pushed me right down into the trough below the first hole. The spray hit me in the face like somebody had thrown a bucket of ice, as expected, but my sunglasses kept the water out of my eyes. The bow was straight, I was paddling fiercely, and the boat was set up in the direction I wanted to go. *Great*, I thought. *I'm going to make it, no problem.* I punched through a couple of big waves, and then in a split second my angle went too far right, and I was slammed from the left by the biggest wave yet. The ducky rolled over on its right tube and I dug my paddle hard into the water looming beneath me, but it was too late.

The ducky flipped and I was in the water.

Okay, no problem, I thought. *I've been in swift water before.*

But it seemed like a long time before I came up, and when I did I was in darkness beneath the overturned boat, with the sunglasses jammed sideways on my face. The water churned so that it felt like I was in the tub of a giant washing machine on agitate. I bobbed in darkness for a moment, then shoved one of the tubes away and slipped out from under the ducky, bobbing alongside, trying to find a handhold on the wet hull of the inflatable boat. The spray was so high around me that I couldn't reckon my position, but I knew there were some wicked big rocks to river right. All of the excess air in my dry suit had been squeezed up into my arms and chest, so I looked like a tangerine version of the Michelin Man (I should have squeezed more air out of it back at the launch, before zipping up). At least my PFD and my helmet had stayed put. But even with the suit and the life jacket, it seemed I had little buoyancy in the foam. I had a glimpse of my surroundings at the top of the next wave— pink rocks and trees and blue sky and lots of white foam—but the river spun me around and dunked me again in the following trough.

Then came my encounter with the rock.

I had ignored one of the basic safety rules that had been drilled into me since my first whitewater lesson, one that I could repeat without hesitation on command, and one that had completely left me when I found myself in big water. I had failed to keep my feet up and pointed downstream. It was a stupid, dangerous thing to forget.

Tons of water drove me into the granite, and it felt like a stone mallet against my lower back and right flank. I wasn't bobbing any longer, but pancaked against the face of this rock, an unyielding glistening pinkish-gray monolith that rose above my head. My jacket protected my upper back, but the impact still knocked the air out of me and then I swallowed some water trying to recover my breath. Gasping, and with my backside numb from the blow, I sensed that I might be good and royally fucked. I say *sensed* because at this point I was incapable of thought, only feeling. It seemed as if the river were pouring through me, that it would break me on the rocks and then send the pieces to the bottom like a broken jug. It was the only time I'd ever experienced a total loss of control in the water, whether kayaking or scuba diving. I'd had a regulator malfunction once and I ran out of air in a flooded mine in southeast Missouri once, thirty meters down and with a solid rock wall overhead, and had to buddy breathe to the surface, but I had never lost my ability to think; there had been no panic, just a realization of what had to be done. The scary thing for me in the Flume was that it wasn't just a loss of cognition but also a loss of volition, a strange kind of unthinking apathy. Then, dimly, a thought began to form in my panicked brain. It wasn't any kind of thought that would do me any good. It wasn't, *Yeah, this sucks, but you've got a helluva dry suit and a good PFD and all you have to do is make it to the nearest eddy along the rocky bank.* No, the thought was a single sentence, and it was this:

I don't know anything.

The uncaring river had shown me how willfully ignorant I was, that everything I thought I knew was bullshit, and that I had learned nothing. That my particular type of intellectual arrogance had likely killed me. That rationalization and romanticism mean fuck all when faced with the overwhelming power of hydraulics.

I don't know anything.

The punishing water poured down, a baptism of reality that washed the guilt of hubris away. But it did nothing to absolve my lingering existential guilt. There was no white light, no comforting presence, no wilderness epiphany. All my sins remained, the pain of regret was indelible, and there would be no reward for either virtue or vice. What there was, immediate and irresistible, were rocks and water. Our lives are spent in choosing among the rocks and the water, or trying to.

I know my wedding ring is still taped to my finger.

Then a nominal consciousness returned, and I maneuvered around some boulders. River right, the bank closest to me, was filled with too many large rocks to try to make an exit there. The river had flushed me below Zoom Flume, and past the eddy that would have been a good place to rest. Instead, I was still in the current. In what must have been an uncommon display of expert paddling, Reid had kept pace with my misadventure, and had captured my inflatable boat and was holding it for me. He asked me if I was okay, and I said I'd hit a rock with my backside and that it hurt, and he said matter-of-factly that it would have been worse to break a kneecap. He urged me to pull myself up into the boat, and he lifted up the back of the boat to make it easier for me, but my arms felt like spaghetti and the effort set my lower back howling. I said I'd rather swim to shore, and Reid said he'd help me. So I held onto the stern of his boat and he towed me, a big tangerine Michelin Man floating in the water behind him. He cut into the next eddy, and I kept my feet up until it was shallow enough to crawl to the bank, where I unstrapped my helmet and pulled it off, and sat down to rest. I avoided looking Jan in the eye, but I told her she had made a nice run. Reid asked me if I was cold, and I said no, I was hot, too hot. My hands were shaking. I drank some water and yanked the chest zipper partly open and felt inside the suit, and my hand came back wet from my fleece shirt. The suit hadn't leaked; it was sweat.

It had all happened so fast—less than thirty seconds from when I had started the run—that I was not immediately aware of what had gone wrong. I couldn't have recounted it in such detail except for two things: Reid described it to me later that day, and some weeks later I got visual evidence. I didn't know it at the time, but Zoom Flume is one of a handful of places on the river where commercial photographers set up during the season, to sell the images as souvenirs to the legions of tourists on the big rafts. I had known my long swim had been witnessed by a lot of boaters, which was embarrassing enough; to have it captured photographically seemed a special kind of humiliation. But it was also enlightening, because the sequence of thirty photographs is an unambiguous record of misadventure.

Still ahead was seven miles of river, with several named rapids—Big Drop, Seven Stairs, Widowmaker—and one more nominal Class IV run: Seidel's Suckhole. I paddled all of it except Seidel's, because I was spooked. In my mind I confused Seidel's with Frog Rock, above Buena Vista. A twenty-three-year-old off-duty commercial guide, Kimberly Appelson, was thrown out of a raft that high-sided at Frog Rock in July 2010, and she drowned when she was swept into an underwater cave beneath. It took several months—and divers and underwater cameras and heavy equipment—to locate and retrieve her body. At low water at the end of October, a cofferdam was built around the hazard to shunt most of the water away, and divers recovered her body from the rocky sieve. The force of the water had driven her body, like a cork, into a slot at the back of the cave. There was a debate at the time over whether the heavy equipment used to retrieve Appelson's body should also be employed to permanently alter the river and remove the hazard at Frog Rock. Authorities decided to leave the river unchanged, in keeping with conservation ethics and to avoid liability for the agencies involved.

Maybe it was because Appelson and my wife shared the same first name, or maybe it was some heavy equipment on river right (unrelated to anything except some irrigation work) that contributed to my wild misidentification. Reid corrected me, and said Frog Rock was well upriver, but I decided to portage Seidel's anyway. When we reached Stone Bridge, where Brandon was waiting for us with a van, Reid checked the river levels on his smartphone. The flow was above 1,500, stronger by half than when we had begun. On the ride back to the RMOC, I retrieved some wet bills from where I had stashed them earlier, when they were dry. As discreetly as possible, I handed Reid his tip, and said it was not nearly enough.

Back at the RMOC, I changed my clothes and then hung around a bit, chatting with Reid. He asked about my plan for Royal Gorge, the next stretch of whitewater on my list, about seventy miles downstream. Rampton describes the gorge as "dark, narrow, and forbidding," with a Class V rapid called the Sledgehammer. I told Reid it was probably time for me to find a commercial outfitter to take me down the Gorge on one of those big rafts, or maybe even to take the train.

After bidding farewell to Brandon, and thanking him for his help and patience with my crazy project, I climbed gingerly into the Jeep and pulled out of the RMOC parking lot for what I knew would be the last time.

I was tired, hungry, and feeling more than a bit foolish. My flank and butt were hurting worse all the time, and they would continue to hurt, and I would piss blood on and off, and my dehydrated lips would crack and I'd have an ugly scab on my mouth for weeks.

At Salida, I had a steak dinner and a glass of wine at a restaurant near my room, and was surprised to find Marisa working there. I did not speak to her, and she pointedly ignored my presence. While I ate, I made notes about everything I could remember about the day—*when the Grinch loses his jaw, it's high water.* I had already texted Kim that I was off the river, but when I talked to her later that day she told me a story that was as odd as anything that had yet happened while I was on the river.

She had received a call on her cell from a number she didn't recognize, so believing it was a telemarketer, she didn't answer. But the caller left a message on her voice mail, so she thought she'd better check. A shaky male voice identifying himself as Rick said he was calling to relay the news that his nephew had drowned in a boating accident, and that he really needed to talk about it. Shaken now herself, she listened to it again. Obviously, it was a wrong number. But she wanted Rick—who lived in Broken Arrow, Oklahoma—to know he hadn't reached the person he was trying to, so she returned his call. Rick apologized, said he was sorry for the bother, and Kim said she was sorry for his loss.

When Kim related the story, my first thought was that it was a hoax. Somebody must have been pulling her chain, knowing that I was on the river. No, she said. She actually talked to the guy. There was no connection to either of us, and he sounded genuinely upset. When I got back home, she played the voice mail for me.

"Have you ever gotten a call before that somebody had drowned?" I asked.

She said of course she hadn't.

Then we pondered the odds of getting such a call on my worst day on the water, when I was having the stuffing knocked out of me. But we couldn't bear to think about those odds for too long.

Inherent Risk
Elevation: ~7,300' (Seidel's Suckhole)

The woman who died Wednesday afternoon when she was thrown off a commercial raft in a Class IV rapid in Brown's Canyon was identified today. Sue Ann Apolinar, 38, of San Antonio, was swept off the raft when the boat capsized on the Arkansas River at the Seidel's Suck Hole, about 13 miles north of Salida, according to the Chaffee County Coroner's Office.

—Denver Post, June 9, 2011

A month after my swim at the Flume, a fifty-one-year-old Colorado woman was thrown into the Arkansas River during high water when her commercial raft high sided on a rock there. The woman, Sandra Johnson of Littleton, was pulled from the water, but CPR failed, the *Denver Post* reported, and she was pronounced dead at the scene. Johnson was the second river fatality on the Arkansas River in Colorado in 2016, according to the American Whitewater accident database; in May, a sixty-year-old Iowa woman, Debra Lynn Brymer, died after falling into the water from a commercial raft below Royal Gorge.

Fatalities have occurred at nearly every point from Granite down to Cañon City, but some places are worse than others. Frog Rock has claimed at least six lives in the past twenty years. There were seven commercial raft deaths on Colorado rivers in 2015, according to an investigative story by Jennifer Brown that ran in the *Denver Post* a couple of weeks after my swim at the Flume, and most of the deaths occurred in Class IV or V water. The story notes that commercial whitewater boating is commonly safe—outfitters take about half a million visitors rafting in the state each year—but that the risks increase in technically difficult rapids during periods of high water. The danger also correlates with age, and with being overweight or in generally poor condition. Aside from having the proper gear, the strongest indicator of whether a person has the stuff to survive is having the ability and mental attitude to get him or herself out of trouble. "The phrase 'the victim made no attempt to self-rescue' appears repeatedly in investigative reports of rafting deaths," Brown noted. The description rang uncomfortably true to my own experience at Zoom Flume.

The approach to Zoom Flume in Browns Canyon (photo by Arkansas Valley Digital Imaging).

While Colorado has some of the most stringent commercial rafting laws in the country—and advisories are issued at high water, which prompts many outfitters to curtail trips down the most hazardous sections—accidents happen. But the question comes down to how well customers understand the "inherent risk" in whitewater rafting stated in the liability waivers outfitters require them to sign. The *Denver Post* story focused on the death of eleven-year-old Drake Durkee, who was on a commercial trip in June 2015 when he and his grandfather were bounced out of a raft at Big Drop in Browns Canyon. The raft struck the whitewater broadside, according to witnesses, instead of following a line established by other boats in the same Adventure Company trip. While the grandfather was rescued, the fifth-grader drowned when his foot was caught beneath an undercut rock. His body was recovered three days later.

"The rafting company Drake Durkee's grandparents chose for what would become the 11-year-old's last outing was on its second summer of probation for violating state regulations and had been warned it could lose its permit unless it improved," the *Denver Post* reported in a September 2016 follow-up story.

The authority to place an outfitter on probation, or to suspend or revoke a license, rests with Colorado Parks and Wildlife. The list of outfitters subject to disciplinary action, however, is not posted online or otherwise easily accessible. It took the newspaper filing an Open Records request and paying $100 in fees to obtain the information.

"Drake's parents have sued the rafting company," the *Post* reported, "claiming guides were negligent in taking their son and his grandfather, who could not swim, on Class III and IV rapids, for miscommunication when he went overboard, for not rescuing him and for delaying the discovery of their son's body by not immediately talking to rescuers."

The owner of Adventure Company told the newspaper the probation was for paperwork, not safety violations, and that his employees were too distraught immediately following the accident to talk to authorities.

Because of the liability waivers, families who take outfitters to court have a difficult burden of proof. In June 2011, thirty-eight-year-old Sue Ann Apolinar of San Antonio was thrown into the water after the raft she was in flipped at Seidel's Suckhole. The guide managed to right the boat and pulled Apolinar back in, but the raft capsized again in the next rapid, Twin Falls. She was again thrown into the river, where she was washed downstream, became entangled in some branches, and drowned.

Apolinar's adult son filed suit in federal court against the rafting company, Arkansas Valley Adventures, claiming negligence and fraud. The son contended the company misrepresented the nature of the trip, and that Sue Ann was told it was appropriate for beginners and involved, at most, only Class III rapids, when Seidel's is actually Class IV. A federal district court judge granted the rafting company summary judgment, ruling that the waiver Apolinar signed released the company from all liability.

In January 2016, the US Court of Appeals for the Tenth Circuit in Denver affirmed that decision. "The rafting company provided—and Ms. Apolinar signed—a document titled in part 'RAFTING WARNING' explaining that rafting can be 'HAZARDOUS AND INVOLVES THE RISK OF PHYSICAL INJURY AND/OR DEATH,'" the appeals ruling said. "The document proceeded to offer a detailed picture of the sorts of problems that could be (and sadly were) encountered." These included "cold water immersion, hidden underwater obstacles, trees or other above water obstacles" and a risk of drowning from "entrapment of feet or other body parts under rocks or other objects." The appeals court also noted that the waiver clearly said the warnings superseded any previous communications or representations.

One of the three appeals judges, however, offered a dissent on one aspect of the ruling. "In my view," wrote Judge Harris Hartz, "a jury must resolve whether Ms. Apolinar was misled about the danger of the rapids. Although the warning provided to her at the outfitter's office listed all the potential risks that she would face, the description of the rapids is what would convey the probability of those risks. It is not enough to list a risk if the customer has been misled about its probability."

I had signed a waiver similar to one in the Apolinar case for the Rocky Mountain Outdoor Center each time I had gone on the river with Brandon or one of his guides. I hadn't given the liability release much thought because I believed I understood the dangers. Of course, there was always a risk of drowning, just as there is always the chance of a fatal accident when you're behind the wheel of your car. You do what you can to minimize those risks—and in my case, it was finding somebody like Brandon to help me avoid ending up dead or injured in the biggest rapids—but in the end, I always knew my safety was my own responsibility. I am grateful to Brandon for the hours of patient and expert instruction he gave me on the river, but it's not his fault if I do something stupid on the water that results in tragedy.

But I worry about the tourists who are just looking for a little entertainment, the lack of publicly accessible disciplinary reports on outfitters, and whether an eleven-year-old can really grasp the brief safety talk at the beginning of a commercial raft trip.

"Last year, 508,728 commercial raft trips on 29 river stretches in Colorado generated $162.6 million in economic impact," said the editorial board of the *Denver Post* in September 2016. "Fatalities are rare: in the past three years, 18 people died on paid river trips, six of them this year—including [Drake Durkee,] who bounced off a raft in Browns Canyon (the whitewater mecca on the Arkansas River between Buena Vista and Salida) and got trapped by a rock."

The editorial concluded, "Some consumers may find a disconnect between rafting companies' slick brochures and online marketing, which sell serious whitewater trips as fun, big waves, and the legal waivers, where small print whispers that such rivers also can be dangerous. . . . Wild rivers aren't water parks, making it essential that consumers can easily access meaningful information about outfitters' safety records and the risks of the rapids they plan to boat."

The Highest Valley
Elevation: 4,692' (Pueblo)

I've found that there's only one thing that I can't work on and that's marijuana. Even acid I could work with.

—The Art of Journalism No. 1, *Hunter S. Thompson*

Hunter S. Thompson was Colorado's most famous drug and alcohol user and he gave the above quote during an interview with the *Paris Review* in 2000, five years before he pressed a .45-caliber handgun to his head and pulled the trigger. The sixty-seven-year-old practitioner of gonzo journalism left a legacy that included *the* eulogy for the American Dream—"with the right kind of eyes you can almost see the high-water mark—that place where the wave finally broke and rolled back"—speaking of 1968, in *Fear and Loathing in Las Vegas*.

Now, echoes of the wave that Thompson saw with the right kind of eyes from a hill in Las Vegas may be finally washing back, at least in Colorado, where recreational marijuana is now legal. If the American Dream is about freedom and self-expression (and of course it is, along with greed and violence and apple pie), then Colorado is the epicenter for a social tsunami that has been fifty years in the re-making, and is symptomatic of a country that has not been so deeply polarized since the year Martin Luther King Jr. and Robert Kennedy were assassinated, North Vietnam launched the Tet Offensive, and Apollo 8 orbited the moon.

At 8 a.m. on Wednesday, January 1, 2014, the state's first stores licensed to sell recreational marijuana legally opened for business in Colorado. Even though Amendment 64 was approved with 55 percent of the vote, it took a year and a half for the state to handle challenges and determine how to regulate sales. The second state to allow recreational weed dispensaries was Washington, which began licensing operations on a much more limited scale, and not until July 2014. I'm not sure how Raoul Duke would have regarded the legal dispensaries in his adopted home state, but I'm guessing he would have been disdainful, much as heavy drinkers say they regard New Year's Eve as amateur night.

If you are, say, a pot tourist from Kansas—where any amount is

Outside a recreational pot store in Salida.

illegal to possess, even if your physician believes you need it to control your nausea from chemotherapy—you'll have to cross the dreary plain in the eastern third of the Centennial State before finding a place to score your weed. Pot sales are determined by city and county local option, and conservative and rural eastern Colorado appears not to favor such progressive policies. The pot dispensaries, both recreational and medicinal, begin along the populated Interstate 25 corridor, which bisects the state from Fort Collins in the north to Trinidad in the south (there is a lone pot store in eastern Colorado, but it's in the far northeastern corner of the state, near Nebraska in the tiny village of Sedgwick). At least half of the state's five million residents live along the I-25 divide, including those in its most populous cities, Denver, Colorado Springs, and Aurora.

Following the Arkansas River upstream from Kansas, along Highway 50, the first place to buy recreational pot is where Highway 50 crosses the interstate: Pueblo. On a day in June, I pulled the Jeep into a strip mall in a Pueblo suburb and parked in front of a storefront that, not so long ago, might have sold flooring or unfinished furniture. But, there was no doubt now what the storefront was selling; above, a banner with a giant green cross rippled in the breeze.

The buzzwords inside were *care, wellness,* and *natural,* although the interior had a kind of pawnshop security atmosphere, owing perhaps to the amount of cash on hand. (Many dispensaries at the time of my visit were cash-and-carry businesses, because they were denied traditional banking services such as taking credit cards, but banking restrictions have since eased and plastic is welcome in many places.)

After waiting in a queue and showing my driver's license, I was summoned to a counter where I was told that, as an out-of-state resident, I could buy up to seven grams, or a quarter ounce, of weed (the limit per purchase for Coloradans is one ounce). There were dozens of choices, from buds meant to be rolled in a Zig-Zag or stuffed in a pipe to edibles that ranged from things resembling gummy bears to chocolate dinner mints. There was also a variety of types and strains, from those meant to address physical concerns such as aches and pains to those meant for recreation. I had smoked quite a lot of weed in high school but had rarely touched marijuana since; I was clueless as I pondered the contemporary pot menu in all its Starbucks-like variety. Based on the helpful advice of the friendly pot barista, I bought a few grams of buds called "Budderface" and some chocolate that was handily scored for eight doses, each containing about ten milligrams of THC, the active ingredient in marijuana. Then I walked out of the store, the buds stowed in a foil bag, and the mints in a green plastic canister with a pop-off lid. It felt odd, having legally purchased marijuana, a bit like finally buying a legal drink on your twenty-first birthday.

The dangers of overconsumption are analogous as well.

In a 2014 opinion piece in the *New York Times*, columnist Maureen Dowd recounted how she had taken a couple of bites from a marijuana chocolate bar in her Denver hotel room, and then "lay curled up in a hallucinatory state for the next eight hours . . . I became convinced that I had died and no one was telling me." Nobody told her—and it hadn't been on the label, she said—that the candy she munched was meant to provide a recommended sixteen doses for novice users.

When I finally did sample my legally purchased pot, in hotel rooms and along the riverside and sometimes sitting in the open tailgate of the Jeep, from Salida to Leadville, I had no Maureen Dowd–like bad trips. I did find that the pot was stronger than in my youth, and produced a high that was much different than the one I remembered. It was more aggressive and less mellow. I didn't like smoking the stuff. The smoke was harsh, the process was dirty, and it stained one's fingers. It was just too much trouble. The edibles were easier to deal with, and didn't require a pipe or rolling papers or the hunt for a lighter or digging matches out from where they were stowed in my fire kit in my pack. The edibles were stealthy, however, taking up to an hour to kick in.

Dutifully, because this was research, I scribbled down my thoughts. What came out, frankly, was rubbish. It was all predictable, derivative, and sentimental fluff:

> *The warmth of sunshine on my back, the tug of a fish on the line, the magic of late afternoon sun slanting through the trees, placing my palm against the small of a woman's back, the smell of ozone wafting from the back of a tube amplifier, these are some of the things that I imagine I will miss. Of course, if anything is sure, it is that I will miss none of these things. Whether there is eternal dark or an eternal reward at the end of life, there will be no nostalgia. These are the things I am missing now, contemplating my own (hopefully) distant demise.*

No *Kubla Khan* poured from my fevered imagination. Samuel Taylor Coleridge was on opium when he wrote one of the most famous poems in the English language, a work that (he claimed) came to him fully formed in a drug-induced dream. Upon waking, he managed to record only fifty-four lines of the two or three hundred that had been revealed in the dream, before he was interrupted by the mysterious "person from Porlock." After the visitor left, Coleridge was unable to remember the rest of the poem.

It is a long-standing tradition that writers often rely on chemical assistance for inspiration, but knowing the sad ends of Hemingway and Fitzgerald and Thompson and a score of other writers at newspapers and wire services whose names would mean nothing to you, writing is something I've tried to do straight. About the heaviest thing I've pounded the keys on is Apple brand pipe tobacco, and I gave that up years ago, although I miss the smell of it and the satisfying sound a Zippo lighter makes. Perhaps I'd have been a better writer if I'd had a glass of Maker's Mark at my elbow while writing, but I doubt it. I think Hemingway and his brothers and sisters in spirits were geniuses in spite of their alcoholism, not because of it.

While the pot did not give me any writing edge, it did one thing surprisingly well: it eased my depression. This is something that no FDA-approved medication has ever been able to do, and I have been prescribed just about every antidepressant in the pharmacy, from tricyclics to SSRIs to MAO inhibitors. None of them worked, and they came with unpleasant side effects, the least of which were constipation and dry mouth. Talk therapy was more effective, but not as effective as something I called "book therapy"—I would withdraw and engage in deep reading until the depression, in a few weeks or a few months, would ease enough to allow me to function again. But at the worst of it, when I was on as many as three or four medications at once, there was a cognitive dulling so severe that I couldn't concentrate long enough to read a book. Shock therapy was recommended at one point, but I resisted because I was afraid of memory loss. There was only one thing that unexpectedly worked, and that was when I was given a general anesthesia for a minor surgery; when I came out in recovery, my depression was lifted, and remained lifted for weeks. But it wasn't a practical remedy, as anesthesiologists were unlikely to put me under just because I said it helped my mood.

I've been dogged by depression—at its worst, a strange and unthinking apathy—all of my life. Part of it was because of my relationship with my mother, but I won't bore you with all the pedestrian details. As a child I remember being so depressed that it seemed as if I were literally standing beside myself. I became a fat kid because I'd heard somebody say once that "everybody loves a fat man," and I desperately wanted to feel that people liked me. Of course, desperately wanting people to like you ensures just the opposite, so I was an easy target for bullies. Then, when I turned fifteen, I dropped the weight and became the kind of kid who *looks* for trouble, a pot-smoking, drag-racing, and sometimes LSD-dropping redneck—and I found plenty of it. But there was something honest in that. There is something wild in me, and there always has been. It is something that I'm sometimes afraid of and that I try to hide, but it's a part of me. Thankfully, that wild and antiauthoritarian streak was channeled in my adult life into journalism, fiction writing, and other subversive and sometimes creative activities.

But when I turned thirty, the depression returned to flatten me.

My resistance to antidepressants began not because of the side effects—I would have gladly put up with most of them for some relief—but because none of the health care professionals who were prescribing them could give me a satisfactory explanation of how they were supposed to work. I researched the medical literature for proof of efficacy and found little support for the claims made by the drug companies. Now, the fact that antidepressants owe much, if not all, of their therapeutic value to the placebo effect is old news, but for me it was an expensive lesson: the cost of drugs and hospital treatment literally drove me and my family bankrupt. I spent several weeks in the 1990s hospitalized beneath the Menninger clock tower along the banks of the Kaw River at Topeka, and what I remember most vividly is staring in unthinking apathy at the spring rain against my hospital room window. That's a sentence that was hard to type. I still feel the shame of it. Not all of the treatment I received was ineffective—I had a psychiatrist and a therapist who had some success with talk therapy, and a family physician who probably saved my life by simply touching my cheek in a caring manner during a suicidal episode—but frankly, most of the rest was bunk.

During the worst of it, at one clinic, I was told I'd never be well enough to work again; at another, I was told that my only hope of recovery was in devoting myself to a twelve-step program, which I tried, but which made no sense because I wasn't an alcoholic or a drug addict. There were times I wished I were, because then at least there would have been a clearer path to recovery: I could quit, or at least try. But with depression, much of the advice I was given seemed aimed at making me quit being myself. The antidepressants were a large part of what separated me from myself, and a few of the drugs so retarded my mental function that I could not write, even though I was under contract for several books, or even manage *reading* a book. Other drugs sent me into a prolonged manic state, and the behavior that goes with it, which had its own emotional consequences. My return to the world began when I stopped all antidepressants cold, continued *bibliotherapy*, and began teaching a writing class at a nearby college. Within a year, I was writing again and had returned to full-time newspaper work.

For those facing their own battles with depression, I can give no advice. I can only speak with authority about my own experience, and there are so many varieties of mental illness that it is impossible to generalize. We're all wired differently. Alcohol is a far more dangerous drug, and I know this not only from the literature but from personal experience: while on pot, I've never driven like a maniac or picked a fight. Drunk, I've stood on the side of a desert hill near Las Vegas with some writer and editor friends and declared, "This view makes me want to fuck somebody up." Thankfully, they stopped me from doing so.

It has become clichéd to say so, but the fact is that nobody has ever fatally overdosed on marijuana. (In 2014, a nineteen-year-old exchange student fell to his death from a balcony in Colorado after eating all of a pot cookie, but he died from the fall, not from marijuana poisoning.) The biggest dangers associated with pot are the penalties one risks when using in states where it's criminalized, or the violence that is an occupational hazard of the illegal drug trade. But violence often accompanies prohibition, whether the scorned substance is weed, alcohol, or coffee.

Cannabis is among humanity's oldest domesticated plants and has been used medicinally and domestically for thousands of years. It probably was first domesticated some 12,000 years ago on the steppes of central Asia, according to a 2014 piece by Barney Warf in the *Geographical Review*. "From prehistoric Xinjiang to the slums of Kingston, Jamaica, from hashish smoked in medieval Cairo to casual pot users on American university campuses," Warf writes, "psychoactive cannabis has a long and fascinating historical geography." Yet there has been little scholarship about the historical and global impact of marijuana. There have been case studies of marijuana use within individual societies, according to Warf, a geography professor at the University of Kansas at Lawrence, but no attempt to weave the story of the plant's spread across time and cultures into a single coherent narrative. Unlike the world-changing drugs tobacco and opium, cannabis has been largely ignored as a topic for deep study.

The name *cannabis* comes from the Greek *kannabis*, which means "canvas." It includes several closely related species, including the two most common subspecies, both of which have *sativa* in their names, one commonly called hemp that is not psychoactive, and one that is. Hemp is an ancient source of rope, fabric, paper, tents, and sails. It's the other type of *sativa* that produces a high, owing to the psychoactive properties of the sticky resin from its female plants. Another subspecies, *Cannabis indica*, named for India, is also psychoactive and generally more potent. Strains of both *sativa* and *indica* are sold in the dispensaries in Colorado, with the former generally regarded as producing cerebral highs and the latter tending to be soporific.

Societies have long exploited drug addiction for their own ends— "Opium was as central to the foreign policy and foreign exchange of the British Empire in the 19th Century as frigates," Warf notes—but the Industrial Revolution brought about a fundamental change: while agrarian economies could sustain certain significant levels of inebriation among workers, a technological society could not. "A drunken field hand was one thing, a drunken railroad brakeman quite another," historian David T. Courtwright nicely sums up in 2004's *Forces of Habit: Drugs and the Making of the Modern World.*

"Many early prejudices against marijuana (in the United States) were thinly veiled racist fears of its smokers," Warf writes, "often promulgated by reactionary newspapers such as those owned by the Hearst chain. Mexicans were frequently blamed for smoking marijuana, property crimes, seducing children, and engaging in murderous sprees."

By the 1920s, marijuana had been discovered by blues and jazz musicians, and it became part of the bohemian subculture in American cities from Chicago to Kansas City to New Orleans. Horn player Louis

Armstrong was probably the most famous of the pot-smoking jazz musicians.

The campaign to rid the nation of weed was led by Harry Anslinger, the commissioner of the Federal Bureau of Narcotics from 1930 to 1962. Anslinger rejected study after study that showed marijuana did not induce violence or lead to harder drugs. Anslinger particularly disliked jazz because many musicians were black, and he claimed marijuana was a tool used by America's enemies to undermine our determination and our morals. The marijuana crisis was a manufactured crisis that played on American fears of violent and rapacious knife-wielding immigrants. Twenty-nine states had outlawed cannabis by 1931.

In 1937, Congress passed the Marijuana Tax Act, which placed cannabis under federal control and criminalized possession nationwide. In 1948, Congress criminalized the growing of hemp. In 1952 came the Boggs Act, which made penalties for marijuana and heroin the same. From the 1950s to the 1970s, marijuana was common in groups and subcultures that ranged from the Beat Generation to rock musicians to campus radicals opposing the Vietnam War.

Then, by 1971, the law-and-order administration of Richard M. Nixon had officially declared the first "War on Drugs." The move, according to Nixon domestic policy advisor and convicted Watergate co-conspirator John Erhlichman, was a calculated attempt not to fight drug addiction, but to use the power of the federal government to target enemies. Interviewed by Dan Baum for *Harper's Magazine* in 1994, after he had served time in a federal prison for conspiracy and other charges, Erhlichman said that while the administration couldn't make it illegal to be against the war or to be black, they could target those groups by beefed-up enforcement of drug laws.

"By getting the public to associate the hippies with marijuana and blacks with heroin, and then criminalizing both heavily, we could disrupt those communities," Erhlichman told Baum. "We could arrest their leaders, raid their homes, break up their meetings, and vilify them night after night on the evening news. Did we know we were lying about drugs? Of course we did."

Other veterans of the Nixon administration, however, refuted Erhlichman's memory of the motive for the war on drugs. Erhlichman, who wrote a scathing portrayal of Nixon in *Witness to Power*, died in 1999.

Regardless of whether the motivation behind the drug campaign was a noble attempt to rid the country of debilitating addiction or an outrageous abuse of power, the war on drugs has consumed billions of taxpayer dollars and set federal policy for nearly fifty years. It has also resulted in the United States imprisoning more of its population than any other country in the world.

From 1900 to the early 1970s, the prison population hovered at around 1 in 1,000 Americans, with only a slight bump at the end of the 1930s. By 1975, however, tougher drug laws began to swell prison populations. The peak came in 2007, when the nation's total correctional population—those in jail, in prison, or on probation—reached 7.33 million, or about 1 in 31 adults. That's a 500 percent jump in less than forty years.

Since 2007, there's been a steady, but slight, decline per year in the total prison population. The decline has been attributed to a combination of more lenient sentencing, tighter state budgets, dropping crime rates, and shifting public opinion about mass incarceration.

According to statistics from the US Department of Justice, in 2014 there were 6.8 million adults under some kind of incarceration or correctional supervision, or about 1 in 36 adult Americans, the lowest rate since 1996. This includes those in local, state, and federal prisons, and also those on probation or parole. Of the total, about 2.2 million were physically in jail. The overall numbers have declined by about 1 percent since 2007, with most of the decline in the probation population, along with a slight drop in the federal prison population. At the same time, however, those under the supervision of state and local jurisdictions increased slightly.

Despite what appears to be a sea change in the nation's approach to crime and punishment, the United States has the largest prison population in the world. It also imprisons a disproportionate number of blacks and Hispanics, the homeless and the mentally ill, and an increasing number of individuals held for immigration violations. Human Rights Watch, an international nongovernmental organization headquartered in New York, also says that a tough-on-crime default stance by politicians has created disproportionately long sentences, which keeps prison populations high.

"The ratcheting up of sentences for drug offenders and increased drug law enforcement has had a particularly dramatic effect on incarceration," Human Rights Watch said in a 2014 report. "Though new court commitments to state prisons for drug offenders decreased 22 percent between 2006 and 2011, drug offenders still represent 50.6 percent of federal prisoners."

In Kansas, tough drug laws are nothing new. The Sunflower State was legally dry well before national Prohibition. Kansas had a longer prohibition on alcohol than any other state, from 1881 to 1948, but that didn't stop many Kansans from drinking illicitly—or crossing a state line to legally wet their whistle. After 1948, generations came of age amid a confusing mix of state laws, from bans on open saloons to limiting the sale of beer to that which had no more than 3.2 percent alcohol by weight. In the 1970s, zealous Kansas Attorney General Vern Miller raided an Amtrak train that was serving liquor while crossing the state, a move that for a time convinced airlines to stop serving drinks while flying over the state. Things are not quite so strict now, but there are still some liquor laws rooted in the state's puritanical past: all bars must close at 2 a.m., law enforcement can legally use minors in attempts to buy liquor in sting operations, and some counties have never repealed the ban on open saloons.

It's not surprising, then, that Kansas law takes a dim view of marijuana use, and on the transportation of pot across the state line. The penalties for bringing pot into Kansas are severe. If you're caught with any amount, it's likely to result in a felony prosecution.

When I returned to Kansas, I left the pot behind.

But I did bring back a copy of the *Pueblo Chieftain* for Thursday, June 23, 2016. On page 2A, there's a story with the headline, "Marijuana Helps Fund College Dreams." It leads with Janet Calzadillas Chavez, a Pueblo East High School graduate who was among twenty-five in the county to receive a $2,000 college scholarship funded by the county's marijuana sales tax. Chavez, who is eighteen, planned to attend Colorado State University at Pueblo. She and the other scholarship recipients were the first in the state to receive scholarships funded by pot sales—and, according to the *Chieftain*, among the first in the world.

Thirteen Prisons
Elevation: 5,332' (Cañon City)

Warfare and massacre today transformed the Colorado state penitentiary into an inferno as rioting convicts murdered guards and burned buildings.

—Associated Press, October 4, 1929

Coming into Cañon City from the north, you've lost the river for several miles, until Highway 50 makes a hard-almost-hairpin turn to the east, onto Royal Gorge Boulevard, and there's the Ark, like an old friend, across the railroad tracks to the right. To the left is a hogback of pink rocks, and at the point just above the road is a one-person stone guard tower, built by convict labor more than a century ago. Welcome to Prison Valley, as the locals call it. This is Fremont County, Colorado, which has a higher proportion of its population behind bars than does any other county in the United States. This is an unambiguous distinction, because the US Census Bureau counts prisoners as permanent residents. Of the county's 47,000 residents, about 20 percent are incarcerated among the thirteen state and federal prisons here. Those who aren't behind bars either work at the prisons or have family or friends that do.

The most famous prison in the basin is the federal ADX Supermax— the Alcatraz of the Rockies—about 10 miles down the river, near Florence. It's the only facility of its kind in the United States, built for the worst of the worst, and home to terrorists such as Unabomber Theodore Kaczynski and Oklahoma City bomber Terry Nichols. Part of Supermax is underground, and prisoners spend twenty-three hours a day in solitary confinement in what a former warden described as "a clean version of hell." The oldest prison in the valley is the Colorado Territorial Correctional Facility—Old Max—established in 1871. Once you round the curve on Highway 50, it's right there on the north side of the road, hard against the ridge, bristling with guard towers and barbed wire. This is where Alfred Packer, the most famous cannibal of the Old West, was incarcerated until his pardon in 1901; Packer was convicted of manslaughter for eating five of his gold-prospecting companions to avoid starvation in the winter of 1874 (a grill at the University of Colorado at Boulder is named for Packer, who often misspelled his own first name as "Alferd").

Gas chamber at the Museum of Colorado Prisons.

Old Max is the oldest operating state prison in Colorado, and was home to death row for a century, until the 1990s. The institutional green gas chamber is now on display at the adjacent territorial prison museum, and a sign sensibly warns visitors, PLEASE DO NOT SIT OR STAND IN GAS CHAMBER. The chamber was in service from 1934 to 1967, and it was used to execute thirty-two men by cyanide poisoning, typically at eight o'clock on a Friday night. The prison is now a medium security facility, but alert blue-shirted men in dark ball caps and with M-16 style rifles in their hands still occupy the guard towers.

I had a brief encounter with these serious men once, when I pulled to the side of the road, about a block east of the prison, retrieved my camera bag from the back of the Jeep, mounted a telephoto lens, and started to make some photos of the guard towers. Knowing some of the history of the prison, I thought it would be a good idea to have some photos. After I had been shooting for less than two minutes, a couple of cop cars sped down the street and uniformed men told me to stop. I protested that I was on a public street more than a block from the prison, and that I was well within my rights to take photos. Delete the images, they said, or they would arrest me and confiscate my camera—photography was forbidden, they said. I knew I was within my rights, but I had a schedule to keep. And, as the historian Howard Zinn pointed out, free speech and other constitutional rights are what the cop on the beat says they are at the moment. I protested, and deleted most of the images, but kept a couple of shots. Had I been on assignment for a news organization, however, I would have refused to delete any—and would have spent that afternoon in jail. But it wouldn't have been my first time locked up for shooting photos in a public place.

There's an edge to Prison Valley, a kind of hard-nosed approach to life that comes from having an economy based on an inherently dangerous profession. Even those on the outside live on the inside, as the saying goes. It's similar to the cultures I've found in the prison towns of Lansing, Kansas, or McAlester, Oklahoma. During our trips through Colorado my friend Butch, the bail bondsman, seemed completely at home, and once insisted on stopping at a correctional supply store in town to buy a couple of Chinese Tasers, just $28 each. But there's also a softer side to Cañon City, including the parks and museums and the Royal Gorge Route Railroad, which leaves from the old Santa Fe depot at the edge of town, near the river. I took a pleasant trip on the train, in a car that served alcohol, up the gorge and beneath the bridge to Parkdale and back, but I'll waste no space on that here, because you can read accounts of that tourist experience elsewhere.

At Cañon City, I discovered the most humane side of Prison Valley in a corner of Greenwood Cemetery. Most of the cemetery, which has a spectacular view of the Rockies, is what you would expect for a frontier town, including the well-marked graves of civic leaders and sections for Union and Confederate veterans. But in the far corner of the cemetery is a place called Woodpecker Hill, and it's a place for the forgotten.

That's where Tom Monaco led me and Kim and a group of morbidly interested visitors on a tour of the place where prisoners, including those who had been executed, were buried. Monaco is a thin, genial, fifty-something veteran with silver hair and beard who takes pride in his work of locating and caring for the graves on the hill. He is also a bit of an eccentric who dowses with metal rods to find unmarked graves and, as the designated caretaker for the Confederate section of the cemetery, sometimes dresses in a gray Civil War uniform to talk about the history of the cemetery. On the afternoon of our visit, he showed us how he uses the rods to locate graves, showing how they cross when they pass over human remains. The gender of the dead can also be determined, he said. If the rods swing to the right, it means the body is that of a male; to the left, a female. He let us try, and I seemed no good at it—perhaps because of my skepticism—but Monaco proclaimed Kim a natural.

"There are 600 inmates buried here," he said, "but there are markers for only about 350." Finding the missing has occupied him for years. The graves of the inmates went unmarked for decades, and then the same machines the prison used to stamp the narrow, 1920s-era license plates were used to make metal grave markers. Some of the now-rusted markers have names; others say only "CSP INMATE." But one inmate grave that has not only a name, but a stone monument, is that of Joe Arridy.

Arridy was twenty-three years old when he was executed in the institutional green chamber on Friday, January 6, 1939. He'd been sentenced to death for the rape and ax murder of a fifteen-year-old Pueblo girl. But Arridy, who was an escapee from a home for the "feeble-minded" when arrested for the murder, had an IQ of 46. He and an accomplice, Frank Aguilar, were charged. Although Arridy confessed, and placed

Aguilar at the scene of the crime, it was clear to many that he had no idea what he was confessing to, and he was likely prosecuted in order to get to Aguilar. In prison, Arridy's prized possession was a wind-up toy train, and he was described as "the happiest man on death row." After his execution, according to many accounts, the warden wept.

Following a statewide campaign driven in part by advocates for the rights of the mentally disabled, Governor Bill Ritter was convinced of his probable innocence and pardoned Arridy in 2011—seventy-two years after his gassing. A few years before, a local group had replaced the rusted license plate grave marker, which misspelled his name, with a stone monument. Now engraved on the monument is HERE LIES AN INNOCENT MAN, and visitors sometimes leave toy train cars at the base of the marker.

Local folklore has it that Arridy's grave glows at night, as befitting the grave of an innocent child. When we visited, from late afternoon to dusk on a Friday night, I saw no light coming from his monument. But in my photos, I later discovered an image of Monaco, rods in hand, with a spectacular lens flare that seems to float over *and illuminate* the grave of an infant who died in 1882. Even though I understand the physics of the lens flare—I was shooting into the sun, the flare is roughly the shape of the diaphragm in the lens, and the reflection from the UV filter on the front of the lens must have caused the point of light on the marker—it is still *weird*.

Even as some of the inmate dead of Greenwood Cemetery sleep with the innocents, there are many more whose graves must "be in turmoil" with guilt, as Monaco puts it. One of those guilty dead on Woodpecker Hill is Danny Daniels, and his grave is still among the lost, dark and unmarked. Daniels died at the prison just across the road, but he didn't go to glory at the end of a rope. Instead, his death was the end to the bloodiest chapter in the prison's history: a riot that left thirteen people dead and the prison so damaged by fire that the surviving inmates had to sleep in tents. It all ended, of course, on a Friday.

Albert A. "Danny" Daniels is probably the most notorious Roaring Twenties gangster you've never heard of. He operated in my backyard—southwest Missouri and northeast Oklahoma—and although I grew up with family stories about Wilbur Underhill Jr. and other gangsters, I had never heard of him. In his prison mug shots Daniels appears mild, in part because of his round *Where's Waldo?* glasses. But he had begun his criminal career at the age of twenty by holding up a Tulsa cigar store. His weapons of choice were a pair of Luger automatic pistols, which he wasn't afraid of using. For a time, his work vehicle was a Cadillac sedan (stolen from a Springfield, Missouri, newspaper publisher) onto which a truck bed and winch had been grafted. It will soon become clear why he needed the winch.

Daniels was a member of a confederation of gangs that included Ray Terrill and Herman Barker, and its specialty was backing a stolen truck up to a bank, winching the safe into the bed, and taking it away to crack at their leisure. Many banks of the time, unable to afford the construction of a vault, instead used stout "cannonball" safes that weighed several hundred pounds and were circular or barrel-shaped, to resist explosive charges. The gang's hideout was Radium Springs near Salina, Oklahoma, a health resort managed by Barker but owned by a corrupt former judge from Miami, according to *The Complete Public Enemy Almanac* by William J. Helmer and Rick Mattix. The resort was fortified and had an electric beacon to warn gang members of visiting law enforcement. After the safes were cracked, they were dumped from a nearby bridge into Grand River.

"Daniels, in giving battle to the officers who captured him, lived up to the reputation given him by secret service operatives as a gunman and dangerous character," the *Miami Daily News* reported following a shootout at Nowata in 1927. Police in Nowata had been alerted that two men in a car had been shooting at people who crossed their paths, and they confronted Daniels and an accomplice at the city limits. The gangsters fled. "Leaning from behind the steering wheel, Daniels emptied two pistols at the pursuers," the paper said. "As he turned a corner the car skidded into a ditch."

Daniels was shot through the right calf during the battle, but no officers were hit. Daniels was then a member of the Matt Kimes gang, who was being hunted at the time following a bank robbery and kidnapping. Charged with attempted murder in the Nowata case and assorted other crimes, both state and federal, Daniels made $1,000 bond and decided to skip Oklahoma. He left for Wyoming, but along the way decided to stop in Colorado for some quick cash.

In Colorado Springs, Daniels and two accomplices attempted the after-hours robbery of Buckwald Jewelry. They were planning to crack the safe where it sat, because they had covered it with an army tent to hide the intense light from an acetylene torch with a steel-cutting nozzle. It wasn't his preferred method, but Daniels had wrecked his Cadillac-cum-tow-truck at Cardin, Oklahoma, a few weeks before. A beat cop making his rounds discovered the trio on the roof of the jewelry store, and after exchanging some shots, two of them made their escape in a Studebaker sedan. But Daniels was left behind and soon found himself holed up in a coal shed behind the jewelry store and facing off against the entire Colorado Springs police force.

"If you think you guys are so tough, why in hell don't you come after me?" Daniels taunted, according to a wire service account in the *Miami News-Record*. "You won't get me, I'll tell you that, I'm going to lay right here."

The police lobbed tear gas and raked the shed with machine-gun fire. Daniels responded by emptying several clips from his Lugers, then escaped to the kitchen of an adjacent restaurant and flattened himself on the floor to escape the spray of bullets. During a lull in the shooting, he wounded a policeman in the arm who saw him in the kitchen and, believing him dead, ventured too close. He had wounded another officer earlier.

Daniels was convicted of two counts of attempted murder and sentenced to twelve to fourteen years, consecutive, on each count. At Cañon City, where the guards were instructed to refer to inmates only by their numbers, he became 14277. He was one of about 800 inmates inside the walls, where talking to other prisoners at meals and even when in cells was forbidden. The day began at 6 a.m. and ended promptly at 10 p.m., and Daniels's work assignment was the prison laundry.

The best account of what happened in the prison after lunch on Thursday, October 3, 1927, is *Slaughter in Cell House 3*, a slim volume by Wayne K. Patterson and Betty L. Alt. I will rely on it, and contemporary newspaper accounts.

Daniels and another inmate, Jimmy Pardue, who was serving a long sentence for armed robbery, had made what they believed were foolproof escape plans. By bribing guards, they had arranged for two revolvers and other necessary items. Pardue's assignment was carrying coal from the coal pile in the yard to the boiler room, and it was in the coal pile where the smuggled revolvers were hidden. Both Daniels and Pardue missed lunch on the pretext of being on work assignments, but they were armed, and wore civilian clothes beneath their prison dress.

By procedure, there was only one armed guard inside the walls of the prison, and that was the man in the "crow's nest" gun cage that overlooked the dining hall. There were other guards present inside the walls, but none of them were allowed to have weapons, for fear a prisoner would make a try for the guns. Discipline at the prison was tight, owing to a law-and-order platform pushed by the Ku Klux Klan, which was influential in state politics and had its Colorado headquarters at Cañon City. A series of prison riots had swept the nation in the preceding months, and tensions both inside and outside the walls were high.

The man in the crow's nest was sixty-two-year-old Elmer Erwin, and after the prisoners had left the dining hall, he took the bolt from his rifle, placed it on a shelf, and put the ammunition in his pocket. Then he locked the trap door and climbed down the ladder into the empty dining hall, where he was confronted by two armed convicts—Daniels and Pardue. They demanded the keys to the crow's nest. Erwin told them they were crazy, and tried to snatch one of the revolvers.

Pardue shot him twice.

"Damn," Daniels said. "Too bad you had to shoot. That will wake up every tower on the walls."

Not only was Erwin critically wounded, but now there was no clear escape plan. They had counted on a bribed guard to let them pass through the West Gate, or if needed, they would capture a handful of guards and use them as a human shield to get through the gate. Waiting at the gate in a car with the motor running was a childhood friend of Daniels, Jerry Jarrett. He had arranged many of the bribes needed, and was the intended getaway driver, who would take Daniels back to Oklahoma, where his thirty-eight-year-old wife, Elizabeth, was scheduled to be released the next week from the Washington County Jail at Bartlesville, after serving a four-month sentence for violating federal liquor laws.

Now, all that had changed.

But perhaps Pardue, who may have been one of the hardest cases in the prison, didn't care. His real name was Walter Holub, and he was a career criminal in his twenties from St. Louis known as "The Runt" because he stood just five feet, four inches tall, and weighed 125 pounds. The *St. Louis Star,* which sent a reporter to interview his mother during the riot, said he had tattoos that included a grinning skull and crossbones wearing a red pirate cap and "with a pipe jutting from the ghastly mouth. A wriggling snake encircled his forearm beneath the death's head. On his right arm was tattooed the figure of a nude woman." Holub's mother, a poor midwife, blamed his life of crime on a blow to the head suffered when he was six years old, which she said made him seek out "bad companions." After accumulating a rap sheet that went from shoplifting to armed robbery, Holub was sent to the Missouri State Penitentiary at Jefferson City, where he made a spectacular escape from the prison. While on a work crew, he smashed a hole in a sewer pipe and wriggled his way down into it. He crawled a quarter of a mile through the pipe, to emerge in a river. Incredulous authorities at first thought he had died in the sewer, overcome by sewer gas.

But at Cañon City, Holub—known there as Pardue—was an escape artist who had shot a guard, twice. It is unclear if he conferred with Daniels before his next actions, but desperation and perhaps rage drove him to ever more violent measures.

After retrieving Erwin's rifle and the bolt from the crow's nest, Pardue cut the telephone wires to the dining hall. Then, from various vantage points, including windows in the prison dormitory, he used the rifle in an attempt to pick off guards in the towers. Time was important, because if he could kill the tower guards, then their movement would be unfettered in the yard, and perhaps they could escape before the prison was surrounded. First, he shot Walter Rinker, who fell from the tower over the administration building and landed dead on the roof. Then, he killed Ray Brown, who dropped dying onto the wall. Then he missed a guard in a third tower. While trying to get into position to kill another guard, the one in the tower commanding the West Gate, he was instead shot himself. Guard Myron H. Goodwin's bullet shattered Pardue's pelvis, incapacitating him.

Meanwhile, Daniels had gone to Pardue's cell with some other inmates and had dug out of the wall a quantity of guns and ammunition that had been hidden there. It is unclear how these weapons got to the cell, or even their number or type; whatever they were, the guns were distributed among the stripes. There were now hundreds of inmates unrestrained within the walls, and adding to the confusion, one of the inmates used kerosene to set fire to the prison chapel.

At the chapel, seventy-year-old Professor George E. Colgate, a former state senator and the "principal" of the prison school, was understandably alarmed by the fire. Colgate had arrived at the prison a short time earlier for one of his regular literacy lessons. He had heard the shots, but had for whatever reason not thought to investigate, and stayed with a couple of inmates who had been playing piano in the chapel. The professor left the chapel and went downstairs, where he discovered the wounded Erwin, and was soon confronted by Daniels.

"I heard some footsteps out in the hall, and I put my head around to see what they were, and I met Mr. Daniels," Colgate recounted later. "I knew Mr. Daniels. He had a rifle at that time and he flashed it up in my face, then he laughed and said, 'You're not the man I'm looking for.' I laughed because I couldn't do anything else. I said, 'You're not going to kill me?' He said, 'No, I won't kill you. You stay in this building, and you will not be hurt.'"

With some others, Colgate attended Erwin—who had asked that his wife be told that he had gone out fighting—until he died. Erwin's body was rolled up in a blanket and carried by six convicts to the main gate, which was open. Colgate had forgotten his hat, went back to get it, and then walked alone with his hands up to the open gate, which he passed through.

Daniels now decided that Goodwin, the man in the West Tower, had to be removed if they were to have any chance of escape. With a group of other inmates, they crossed the yard and used hammers to break the locks on the door to the tailor shop, which had a second floor that was higher than Goodwin's tower. From this vantage point, an inmate named A. R. Davis shot Goodwin in the chest. It was a mortal wound, as Goodwin died a week later.

From outside the walls, guards with bullhorns ordered inmates to leave their cell houses and go to the bull pen—a low area next to the administration building used as a recreation area—and wait. About 400 did, but that still left many who did not.

"Over a hundred convicts refused to follow the guard's orders, and many of these added to the chaos by scampering around the yard screaming, banging on the bars, setting small fires in the cell blocks, breaking up any furniture they could find and ransacking the barber shop and confiscating all the razor blades," according to *Slaughter in Cell*

House 3. "Coupled with the smoke and fire, calls from outside the walls on the bullhorn, shouting and cursing from the prisoners, and occasional gunshots from townspeople who had gathered on the hog back above the prison yard, the scene was one of complete pandemonium."

The townspeople had armed themselves with rifles from the local hardware store, all available local law enforcement had been summoned to the prison, and by 3 p.m. a local Colorado National Guard unit had arrived and set up several machine guns and a howitzer.

Meanwhile, the critically wounded Pardue asked Daniels to put him out of his misery, but Daniels refused. Both men had shed their prison work clothing and were now in light shirts, dark pants, and dark caps—which made them appear, at a distance, to be guards.

At 4:15, Daniels sent a steward with a message to Warden F. E. Crawford: "We want three cars in the West Gate by dark with plenty of gas, water in the radiators, oil, good tires with lots of air and guaranteed free passage. We will take the guards and convicts out into these cars. When we get ready, we will turn the guards loose, but should we be molested, we will kill the guards."

No deal, the warden said. They could either give themselves up, or go straight to hell.

Around 7:30, Daniels shot the first of the hostages, Jack Eeles, in the head. Eeles was known to be the prison hangman, and this may have influenced Daniels in his decision to kill him first. Daniels had been at the prison for the most recent hangings when, on March 30, 1928, cousins Jasper Noakes and Arthur Osborn were executed. The pair had been convicted of murdering a man for his rare coin collection near Grand Lake, Colorado.

The bullet did not immediately kill hangman Eeles, and Daniels had the dying man carried to the gate, with the warning another would follow if his demands weren't met. When the answer was no, he shot another guard, Abe Wiggins, and sent his body to the gate.

Sometime before midnight, with Pardue in unbearable pain, and it becoming increasingly clear that none of the conspirators was likely to break jail, Daniels made a decision. At least they could escape the noose, which was a certain fate for killing prison guards. He said goodbye to Pardue, and shot him point-blank in the head.

At around midnight, a local Catholic priest, Father Patrick O'Neil, and a Pueblo miner named James Byrne entered the yard carrying fifty pounds of dynamite and wires, and placed the explosives against Cell House 3, where Daniels and the other insurgents had made their stand. O'Neil had earlier asked to talk to the convicts in an attempt to get them to surrender, but was denied. He said he decided to help set the dynamite charge because there were "some good Catholic boys in there" and he couldn't stand what was happening. The first attempt to set off the charge failed, however, so O'Neil again ran across the yard, his cassock gathered around his knees, corrected the fault, and ran back.

The blast was heard for ten miles, broke windows across the city, and made an impressive crater—but it failed to breach the thick stone wall of the cell house. Then, Marion Keating, a Navy veteran of World War I, braved gunfire to throw some tear gas through the bars into the building. As the gas seeped in, the National Guard hammered the house with machine-gun fire. An armored car was driven into the prison yard, but it became stuck in the blast crater next to the cell house.

Daniels shot dead two more guards, J. W. McClelland and Charles Shepherd. He thought he had killed another guard, Marvin Duncan, but managed only to put a round through the man's cap. Duncan survived by playing dead, but was reportedly driven mad by the experience.

Daniels allowed another guard, O. A. Earl, to live—and made a final request.

"We're at the end of our rope, I want you to go out and tell the folks outside that we are all dead," Daniels told him. "I want you to look at us before you go and be sure we are all dead. Don't go before daylight. They will tear this place down and kill a lot of cons if there ain't nothing done."

Later, Earl heard several shots from the southwest part of the cell house. He went to investigate, and by a lighted match saw the bloody bodies of the convicts. Daniels had shot his three remaining partners— A. H. Davis, Red Reilley, and Albert Morgareidge—and then sat on a chair by the door and turned the gun on himself. As instructed, Earl waited until dawn before leaving the cell house. He went to the armored car, which was still stuck in the mud, and told the occupants he was one of the guards. When he was pulled inside, he said he knew he was safe.

The authorities had been gearing up for a full-scale military assault, according to the Associated Press, and were waiting on a 73-millimeter field piece from Pueblo and a tank from Denver. More than 7,000 rounds of ammunition had already been fired, and Crawford, the warden, had been slightly wounded by some buckshot to the chest. By the time Earl brought the news that it was over, the prison was all but destroyed. Cell Houses 1 and 2 had been burned, the dining hall and the chapel had also been destroyed by fire, and Cell House 3 had been rocked by dynamite but remained standing. Dollar estimates of the damage ran between $300,000 and $400,000.

The dead convicts were buried, two coffins to a grave, or perhaps all in one mass grave, on Woodpecker Hill. Accounts differ as to just how many coffins and how many graves. Monaco, the cemetery dowser, said he found the mass grave in 2015, with the five cons buried shoulder to shoulder. Monaco said he has left the graves unmarked, with the exception of an American flag on Memorial Day, because one of the inmates was a veteran.

This is where it happened. There's the flat
where striking miners pitched their tents, the pit
protected by a chain-link fence as if
even now the dead were under guard.

—Ludlow, *David Mason*

The pit where the women and children died is covered by a stout metal
door with rusty hinges and a heavy strap-iron hasp and loop meant for a
padlock. The door is tented, like a playing card creased down the middle,
and rests on a concrete foundation, creating the effect of a mausoleum
sunk into the ground. The area around the pit door is fenced and gated,
like a cemetery—except the wrought iron fence is painted red, white,
and blue. An imposing granite monument overlooks the pit, and at the
base of the monument are three life-sized figures. A virile miner with his
left thumb hooked pugnaciously in his belt gazes to the Sangre de Cristo
Mountains, across the railway tracks to the west, where lightning plays
against the blue foothills. Beside him, there's a mother holding a child.
The mother's eyes seem closed and her left elbow is resting on the stepped
pedestal, as if her burden is too great to bear. A scroll-topped spire rises
above, clearly marking this as a funerary tribute. The monument is ninety-
eight years old, but looks rather recent, owing to a restoration following
a 2003 hammer attack by vandals that decapitated the adult figures.
Thunder rolls across the valley, and suddenly I'm caught in a summer
shower, the drops mottling the granite and gilding the door to the pit. I'm
alone in the rain, and I can't help but ask myself:

What's under the door?

This is the Ludlow Memorial Site where, on April 20, 1914, Labor and
Capital clashed in a bloody confrontation that capped America's most
notorious labor war, and among its deadliest. The front was forty miles
long, stretching along the mine camps that ranged from near Trinidad,
along the coal seams nestled in the hills, to Walsenburg in the north.
After two women and eleven children suffocated in the pit when the tent
colony above them was razed by fire during an attack by the Colorado

The Ludlow monument miner staring perpetually toward Berwind Canyon.

National Guard and the hired guns of the coal company, the strikers waged a ten-day war of retribution that only ended with the arrival of federal troops.

If you've never heard of Ludlow before, it's because this is part of the hidden history of the United States, a chapter from our common book that doesn't make us feel good about belonging to the local chamber of commerce. Seventy percent of tourists who stray from Interstate 25, a mile to the east, expect to find a monument to the *Indian* wars, researchers found in 2005. Despite the best efforts of Woody Guthrie and Howard Zinn, this event has never soaked into the American consciousness the way that Little Bighorn has. Ludlow, and the organized labor movement it represents, exists in the shadowy collective subconscious, in the same way that knowing we should save for retirement does. While a few of us save voluntarily, some of us are in such dire circumstances that we simply cannot, and most of us won't face the facts until forced.

But for the United Mine Workers of America, Ludlow is Ground Zero. The fourteen-foot granite monument, erected in 1918, was paid for by $12,000 (more than $200,000 today) in subscriptions collected by the UMWA. It weighs thirty-five tons. It is one of the comparatively few monuments to organized labor in the United States, and it is arguably the most important. And, every year on the last Sunday in June, the union faithful gather here to picnic, give speeches, and remember the Ludlow Massacre.

There are also observances at important anniversaries, the most significant of which was the hundredth, in April 2014. As has been noted by sages from Gillian Welch (the collective name for the alt-country duo of Welch and Dave Rawlings) to CNN, April is a historically tragic month in American history. Welch's moody "Ruination Day" ballad links three April 14 events: the assassination of Abraham Lincoln in 1865, the *Titanic* striking the iceberg in 1912, and the Black Sunday dust storm of 1935. Other tragic Aprils include, as cited by CNN, the 1993 Waco siege, the 1995 Oklahoma City Bombing, and the 1999 Columbine shootings (all April 19); and the 2007 Virginia Tech Shootings (April 16). Let's add to the list the opening shots of the Civil War, the 1968 assassination of Marin Luther King Jr., and the 2013 Boston Marathon bombing, all of which occurred on different days in April.

In 1914, nearly a thousand striking miners and their families occupied the tent colony on this treeless tract of prairie, close by the mouths of two canyons, Del Agua and Berwind, that led to the coal mines in the foothills to the west. They had spent the seven months since the strike began in this camp where the tents and the stoves were supplied by the fledgling United Mine Workers of America, which also provided $3 per week in strike pay for every miner, and dollars and change for the women and children. On the opposing side was the richest man alive, John D. Rockefeller Sr., who had the largest share in the Colorado Fuel and Iron Company, which had its voracious blast furnaces seventy-two miles to the north, at Pueblo. CF&I owned or controlled the mines in southern Colorado, which it relied on to produce the coke needed to fire the furnaces. The Rockefellers had gained a controlling interest in the firm in 1903; Rockefeller was seventy-five years old, the son of a bigamist and con artist, a high school dropout and the world's first billionaire. A mysterious malady, perhaps psychological in nature, had resulted in the loss of all of his body hair, giving him a somewhat ghostly appearance. He abstained from alcohol and tobacco, taught Sunday school, and although he was an abolitionist, he had hired others to fight for him in the Civil War. He had made his fortune in the oil-refining business and, when kerosene replaced whale oil as lamp fuel, had supplied the world with cheap kerosene. He crushed his competition, in part, by ruling a secret empire that he directed by sets of secret codes and Machiavellian canards. The automobile came along just as the electric light was killing kerosene, and the nation's increasing thirst for gasoline multiplied his fortunes. As the head of the vast Standard Oil trust, which skirted the law against monopolies by hiding single ownership in layers of shell corporations, Rockefeller was the target of muckraking journalist Ida Tarbell, who outlined Standard Oil's transgressions in a series of nineteen pieces for *McClure's* illustrated monthly in 1902. Tarbell concluded that his ghoulish, hairless visage was a reflection of his sins.

The Progressive Era administration of Teddy Roosevelt went after Rockefeller, eventually resulting in a Supreme Court decision that found Standard Oil guilty of restraint of trade through monopoly, and ordered the multinational conglomerate dissolved. But Rockefeller had the last laugh, because the dissolution made stock in Standard Oil worth more as an individual company than it ever had been as part of the trust, and his wealth tripled. As ruthless as he was in business, he was generous in charity, and gave freely to causes he considered worthy. In 1910, he gave $100 million to establish the Rockefeller Foundation to "promote the well-being of mankind." By the time of the Ludlow strike, he had retired, leaving most of the business decisions to his only male heir, John D. Rockefeller Jr. CF&I was just a part of the family empire, but the stock the family owned in it was enough—40 percent in preferred stock and other considerations, worth several million dollars—to make a director of Rockefeller Junior, who relied on the mine operators and plant managers to oversee the complicated affairs in Colorado. Rockefeller Junior, who lived in New York where the corporate empire was directed from a warren of secrecy at 26 Broadway, was cut from a different cloth than his old man; at thirteen, Junior had suffered a nervous breakdown due to "overwork." Now forty, a graduate of Brown University, married, and a father—his son, Nelson, was five years old—Junior had resigned from the board of Standard Oil to pursue philanthropic pursuits. One of those pursuits was attempting to reform fallen women; for three years, he had paid the salary of a female probation officer in a municipal court in the Upper East Side of Manhattan, whose mission was to save young prostitutes from life on the street.

If he cared about working conditions in the mines before the Ludlow affair, he didn't show it, and allowed his managers to handle disasters such as the explosion that killed fifty-six miners at Starkville, a CF&I mine a few miles from Ludlow. The company blamed a spark from a trolley car for the explosion, but a jury found the firm to be criminally negligent in not damping the coal dust, which is explosive, after repeated warnings by state inspectors. The miners died not from the explosion, however, but from being trapped by the collapse of forty feet of tunnel. When the bodies were finally recovered, at least forty of the miners were believed to have died slowly of the deadly, carbon monoxide–laced "afterdamp" many hours after the explosion, because their bodies were intact and their dinner buckets were empty.

In Colorado, about one in every ten workers was employed by CF&I at some phase in the mining, steel-making, or manufacturing cycle. Steel making is an exacting and complicated process, but it can be divided into three steps: producing the purified and carbon-rich coke, melting the iron ore and skimming off impurities, and combining alloys with the molten ore to produce carbon-hardened steel. The last part of the process required plenty of water, and at Pueblo the water was supplied by the Bessemer Ditch, which brought water from the Arkansas River to the CF&I mills on the south side of town, where more than 10 *million* gallons were required per day for the making of steel. The ditch was named for the Englishman who first patented a practical method of steel production in 1856. At CF&I, the cycle continued after the production of steel, including the fashioning of rails, plate steel, and millions of kegs of nails.

The first part of the process, the production of coke, occurred up-canyon from Ludlow, where the coal was mined and then refined in batteries of ovens. It was cheaper to process the coal into coke where it was mined, rather than paying to have it shipped and processed elsewhere. From Ludlow, and all along the coalfields footing the Sangre de Cristo (Blood of Christ) Mountains, the coke was shipped on railcars directly to the furnaces at Pueblo. It was also more convenient (for the owners) to have the miners and their families live near the mines and coke ovens, so that's where the company houses were built, along with the company stores and the company schools. The company towns were wholly controlled by the operators, and the companies decided what newspapers and magazines would be available, what textbooks would be used in the schools, and the price of goods at the company store, which were often inflated for a literally captive clientele. CF&I's stores, for example, turned an unconscionable 20 percent profit. When the miners went on strike in September 1913—egged on by Irish-born militant Mary Harris "Mother" Jones, who said they were cowards if they didn't—they were thrown out of company housing. They came down from the canyons to the union's tent colonies, the largest of which was near the whistle-stop of Ludlow. The colony was also the site of the union's field headquarters, and the union had chosen the spot because it was just 300 yards north of the depot, a strategic location where strikers could keep an eye on scabs transferring from the north-south mainline, the Colorado and Southern, to an east-west branch line. The branch line would take them to company jobs up Berwind Canyon.

English was not the dominant language in the tent colonies, and American citizens were in the minority. The composition of the tent colonies was a diverse and mostly immigrant population, with Italians being the largest group, according to a report by the National Park Service in preparing the Ludlow site for registration as a national historic site. But there were also Slavs, Greeks, Bulgarians, Hungarians, Germans, Scandinavians, Scots, Irish, French, and Spanish. There were also many Hispanics and some African Americans among the striking miners, groups that had been refused jobs in better-paying hard-rock mining (at Leadville, for example) because of racial stereotyping. Of all of these groups, the Greeks were the most militant, and some were rumored to have had combat experience during the Balkan Wars. The leading union organizer at Ludlow, Louis Tikas, was of Greek heritage, having been born in Crete. Tikas had owned a coffee shop in Denver and became a naturalized citizen before turning to labor activism. Employees of the Baldwin-Felts Detective Agency had shot and wounded him in 1910 after he led sixty-three Greek miners in a walkout in northern Colorado. At Ludlow, he was one of only a handful of Greeks who spoke English, and he became a translator for John R. Lawson, head of UMWA District 15, representing Colorado and Wyoming.

The rumblings of labor unrest that culminated at Ludlow had begun decades earlier. Newspaper printers and public school teachers formed the first American unions in the 1850s, but it was the Great Railroad Strike of 1877—which began in the East and spread to the plains, paralyzing the nation's transportation system—that was the first modern labor strike. The United Mine Workers was organized in 1890, and through a series of skirmishes with mine owners across the country over the next two decades, won important but limited concessions.

In the southern Colorado mines in 1913, the average workday could be ten to sixteen hours per day, six days a week. And the work, from the mining of the coal to the production of coke, was dirty, physically taxing, and extraordinarily dangerous. In the mines, the biggest danger was bad air, and the miners had an elaborate lexicon to describe the kinds of "damp" air that ranged from the unpleasant to that which would kill: stinkdamp was marked by a rotten egg smell that could make you sick, blackdamp would rob you of consciousness, and firedamp was an explosive combination of gas and dust. After an explosion, the lingering afterdamp—with its toxic mix of carbon monoxide and other gases—could slowly suffocate you. And the dust in general could cause black lung disease, an accumulation of dust in the lungs that progressively reduces the ability to breathe. The mines reached far into the hogbacks, and the farther back the drifts reached, the more unstable they were likely to be. Mules were used as draft animals in the mines, and with the hay and oats that were carried in to feed the mules came rodents, mostly mice. The mice survived on the scraps from the miners' dinner pails, and according to historian Thomas G. Andrews, it wasn't canaries, but the mice, that the miners kept an eye on as the first sign of trouble. Not only would they be susceptible to bad air, but they would run when spooked by trembling earth.

Miners were paid per ton of coal they produced, and the necessary work of shoring up unstable roofs and walls was uncompensated, so miners were constantly forced to choose between economic need and personal safety. The beehive furnaces used to refine the coal were dirty, fiery hot, and released toxic gases, including ammonia and benzene. In spite of the extraordinary risks and pressure, the miners were aware that they were toiling in what had once been near an ocean, because they found impressions of clam shells and seaweed, and trees alien to present-day Colorado, in the coal. Indeed, these coalfields formed on the lush tropical shores of an inland sea 55 to 100 million years ago. The Colorado Department of Natural Resources has described the environment during this time as resembling present-day South Carolina, "but with dinosaurs."

The strikers were demanding better pay, safer conditions, an eight-hour workday, compensation for dead work (such as bracing shafts), the right to choose their own housing and patronize any store, and company recognition of the United Mine Workers of America. The mine operators balked and, led by CF&I, declared that they would see every mine shut down before giving in to any of the demands. Both sides dug in for a protracted fight. The mine owners recruited the Baldwin-Felts Detective Agency, which had already clashed with striking miners in West Virginia and wounded Tikas in northern Colorado. In the southern fields, the agency employed a specially fabricated armored car with a spotlight and a tripod-mounted machine gun (or, according to some accounts, two machine guns) in back. The three-quarter-inch steel plate had been fabricated at CF&I in Pueblo, and the miners referred to the car as the "Death Special." From photos, the machine gun peeking over the armor plating at the rear of the car appears to be a Colt model 1895, a gas-operated, belt-fed weapon known as the "potato digger" because a swinging lever below the barrel would scrape the dirt if the gun was too close to the ground. It was probably .30-06 caliber, and could fire 450 rounds per minute.

The gun car was used to shoot up the tent colony at Forbes, a few miles south of Ludlow, in October, killing a striking miner and wounding several others. The miners began laying in stocks of arms and ammunition, some of it in the pit-type cellars they had dug beneath the tents, and instructing the women and children to head to the safety of the arroyos if trouble came. What followed was a series of skirmishes that left a score dead—including strikers, company guards, and bystanders—and frayed nerves on both sides. Those watching from the outside, particularly the Denver press, were afraid the strike would generally shut down production and result in a "coal famine."

Under pressure from the mine operators and local law enforcement, Colorado Governor Elias Ammons finally called up the state's National Guard during the last week in October. As soldiers arrived in the strike zone, the governor promised union leaders the troops would remain impartial and were only sent to protect property. Many of the striking miners apparently believed the promises, and appeared to feel some measure of security by the presence of the troops; the National Guard was greeted by immigrant children in white, waving American flags. The

Colorado guard established their camp a short distance south of the Ludlow colony, on the other side of the railway tracks.

At first, the strikers invited the guardsmen to dances and dinners, and played baseball with them on the tent colony field. When the state auditor, a union sympathizer, deferred paying the Guard's expenses in hopes that it would help the strikers, CF&I picked up the tab. Eventually, CF&I would pay the soldiers directly. Former mine employees, sheriff's deputies, and private detectives would also join the Guard, turning it into an undisciplined and heavily armed union-busting force. They called the strikers "rednecks," a term that meant something very different than it does today; in 1914, it did double duty, referring both to the red bandannas the miners wore and to anarchists, or those who sympathized with them.

In November, the governor called strike leaders and mine owners to a summit in Denver, in an attempt to end the strike. But Capital's intransigence and Labor's grievances proved irreconcilable, as the mine owners already knew, according to historian Andrews; the talks were nothing but a ruse to allow the companies to gain some political advantage. The companies claimed that the miners in the southern fields were content with their lot until outside agitators, in the form of the United Mine Workers, arrived. Governor Ammons cleared the Guard to step up arrests of union leaders, who were tried by military tribunal. The state also made it easier to bring in strikebreakers, disperse crowds, and beat and torture prisoners. Hundreds of union leaders were indicted for conspiracy to restrain trade. An order was given that the infamous Mother Jones, the angelic-looking and foul-mouthed labor agitator in her eighties, was to be deported. Although never officially declared, it was martial law in the strike zone, which was christened the Military District of Colorado. Soon, the mine operators were reporting to CF&I that the striking miners had been replaced by new employees, and that coal production in the southern fields continued unabated. There would be no coal famine.

The Pueblo *Chieftain* reported that those workers who had stayed on the job, or replaced the strikers, had received "almost all" of the strikers' demands, including an eight-hour day, a 10 percent raise, twice-monthly paydays, the right to live where they chose, and to refuse to accept company scrip in pay. They were now the highest-paid miners in America, the article asserted, and the only demand that hadn't been met was union representation. The *Chieftain* accused the miners of importing combat veterans from the Balkans to form a "striker army" and intimidate non-union miners by establishing tent colonies around the mines. The refrain was that the trouble had been caused by those outside agitators.

What the *Chieftain* did not report was that the miners brought in to replace the strikers received almost none of the things the operators claimed. In *Blood Passion: The Ludlow Massacre and Class War in the American West*, journalist Scott Martelle uses the experience of itinerant miner James Adams to represent the experience of "scores, if not hundreds" of others. Adams, twenty-three, found himself out of work in Joplin, Missouri, after the non-union lead mine where he had briefly been employed closed down for the winter in 1913. He was recruited by a firm in downtown Joplin to do work on "dams or irrigation ditches" in Colorado, and promised that he would get twenty acres of farmland, already planted in alfalfa and wheat, for $60 an acre, with no money down—the work he was contracted to do would pay for the land. He and fifty-two others who fell for this "land proposition" were under armed guard from the time they boarded the train in Joplin to the time they reached Trinidad, and from there to the Victor-American mine at Del Agua, up the canyon from the Ludlow tent colony. He was told he had no land, that the job was coal mining and had nothing to do with dams or irrigation, and that he would be expected to work off the cost of his tools. After a few days of work, Adams and some others attempted to escape, but were brought back to coal camp by mounted militia. Later, when the militia and mine guards were on a payday drunk, he did manage to escape. Adams later related his tale to a congressional subcommittee investigating conditions in the coal fields, and noted that his only pay for the entire ordeal was a twenty-five cent piece of scrip he had been advanced to buy tobacco.

The elaborate cover story about working on dams and irrigation ditches in exchange for owning your own farm may have been used not merely as bait for men desperate for pay and respect, but also to obscure the nature of the enterprise: importing miners from elsewhere without telling them a strike was in progress was against Colorado law.

An aside: In the interest of transparency, I must tell you here that I was unusually fascinated by the story of James Adams in Martelle's book. Both of my grandfathers were miners in southwest Missouri, my paternal grandfather was nine years old and living in Joplin at the time Adams boarded the train to Trinidad, and I worked for some years as a staff writer at the *Joplin Globe*, which occupies a block downtown near where Adams was suckered by the "land proposition." I never knew either of my grandfathers because both died before I was born, but a staple of my childhood was the brass carbide lamps left over from their mining past, lamps that were no longer used for toil, but to light our way along gloomy riverbanks when we would fish at night, or run trotlines before dawn.

To add to the striking miners' misery at Ludlow came the harshest winter in Front Range history. In December 1913, a blizzard dumped forty-five to sixty inches of snow from Raton, New Mexico, to Cheyenne, Wyoming. In the strike colonies, patrols were hastily organized to brush snow from the tent roofs to keep them from collapsing. In a bit of irony, the only place coal was in short supply was in the colonies, where the little that was available to the strikers was reserved for cooking.

In early January, Mother Jones returned to Colorado. She was arrested by state troops shortly after stepping off the train at Trinidad and hustled off to a city hospital, where she was placed under house arrest. A thousand women marched in the streets, sang "The Battle Cry of Union," and demanded that Mother Jones be released. Their path was blocked by a contingent of cavalry led by Adjutant General John Chase himself, a Denver eye doctor who commanded the state's National Guard. In advancing on the women, according to author Barron B. Beshoar, the general brushed up against a sixteen-year-old protestor, Sarah Slater. Chase berated her and delivered a kick to her breast. Then the general's horse backed into a buggy and he was thrown off, to the delight—and the laughter—of the crowd. The red-faced general regained his feet and shouted to his men, "Ride down the women!" The troopers advanced and swatted at the protestors with the flats of their sabers, but did not trample them underfoot.

When I first read this account, in Beshoar's book about labor leader John R. Lawson, it seemed so cinematically absurd and menacing that I doubted it had happened in just that way. But there are archival photos that show the cavalry, swords drawn, chasing the women from the street. Photos of Chase from the time show an obese fifty-seven-year-old man with a broad white moustache, wearing a National Guard uniform with a corded, flat-brimmed campaign hat. The partisan press dubbed him

"Czar Chase" and claimed he was the real governor of Colorado. In union propaganda, he was described as the "pliant lickspittle of the operators."

If Chase held the power in the state, then in the coalfields the man to be reckoned with was thirty-seven-year-old Karl "Monte" Linderfelt. A high school dropout, Linderfelt was a US veteran of the Philippines Insurrection and the Boxer Rebellion, and had been a mercenary in the Mexican army. At the outbreak of the 1913–1914 strike, he was a mine guard who became a deputy sheriff, and then a lieutenant in the Colorado National Guard. According to the later testimony of some of the strikers, Linderfelt had pronounced: "I am Jesus Christ, and my men on horses are Jesus Christ—and we must be obeyed." He had lashed out at twenty-seven-year-old Louis Tikas in January 1914, taking out his anger that one of his men had been injured when his horse had tripped—or been tripped—by some fence wire. He battered Tikas, cursed him, held a gun on him. "This is the time I clean you out of this place," Linderfelt said, according to Tikas's testimony shortly after to a state labor board, "and also any God-damn other strikers and dagos living in this country." Linderfelt disputed these assertions, and said it was the strikers and their foul-mouthed women who were inciting violence.

Even though Rockefeller Junior had not been directly involved in the day-to-day operations of the family interests in Colorado, he was increasingly expected to directly answer questions from the press and the federal government about CF&I's handling of the strike. On April 6, he was called before a subcommittee of the House Committee on Mines and Mining. The following exchanges are taken from the official record of the proceedings. The chair is Martin D. Foster, an Illinois Democrat.

> CHAIRMAN: But the killing of these people, the shooting of children, and all that that has been going on there for months has not been of enough importance to you for you to communicate with the other directors, and see if something might not be done to end that sort of thing?
> JUNIOR: We believe that the issue is not a local one in Colorado; it is a national issue, whether workers shall be allowed to work under such conditions as they may choose. And as part owners of the property, our interest in the laboring men in this country is so immense, so deep, so profound that we stand ready to lose

every cent we put in that company rather than see the men we have employed thrown out of work and have imposed upon them conditions which are not of their seeking and which neither they nor we can see are in our interest.

CHAIRMAN: And you are willing to go on and let these killings take place—men losing their lives on either side, the expenditure of large sums of money, and all this disturbance of labor—rather than to go out there and see if you might do something to settle those conditions?

JUNIOR: There is just one thing, Mr. Chairman, so far as I understand it, which can be done, as things are at present, to settle this strike, and that is to unionize the camps; and our interest in labor is so profound and we believe so sincerely that that interest demands that the camps shall be open camps, that we expect to stand by the officers at any cost. It is not an accident that this is our position.

CHAIRMAN: And you will do that if it costs all your property and kills all your employees?

JUNIOR: It is a great principle.

The day after Junior testified before Congress, the Pueblo *Chieftain* sent out a public letter to newspapers across the country, asking that it be reprinted in order to set the record "straight" about what was going on in Colorado. The letter repeated the claim that all of the strikers' demands had been granted to those still employed at the mines, and that the southern coalfields were not the hotbeds of violence that had generally been reported. At the same time, it also said a state of insurrection existed. The letter defended the right of Governor Ammons to "arrest and detain all whom he thinks are menacing law and order," citing the Supreme Court's 1909 *Moyer* decision, which was brought following a mine strike in Colorado's northern fields. Charles Moyer, president of the Western Federation of Miners, had signed a poster, featuring an American flag, denouncing the state's denial of civil liberties, including habeas corpus, to striking miners. Moyer was arrested for defacing the American flag, and then was ordered to be held indefinitely as a military necessity. Although Moyer was released after four months, he sued the governor of Colorado at the time. But a unanimous Supreme Court decision made it legal for the governor or officers of the National Guard acting under "good faith" to imprison American citizens during an insurrection and deny their writs of habeas corpus. The ruling, in essence, made it legal to use military force against organized labor. A century later, in 2004, *Moyer* was cited as a precedent for the treatment of "illegal enemy combatants."

The *Chieftain's* public letter, penned by Managing Editor Fred H. Marvin, asserted that the paper was "not interested in either side of this controversy" but did not like to see the state slandered. "Colorado has a constitution," Marvin declared. "Human rights and property rights are as sacred here as in any other state of the union. . . . The governor of Colorado is as fair, as honest and as capable as any other governor in any state in the union. The militia which has been in the field is no different from [sic] the militia in any other state. In other words we, of Colorado, are just as normal."

Marvin appealed to "correct the impression that a state of anarchy exists in Colorado; that armed bands of men are in and about our coal mines killing each other, that 'Mother Jones,' or anyone else, is being unjustly deprived of liberty; that the strikers in their tent colonies are being driven in the cold by a cruel, heartless militia."

By the time Marvin's letter was printed on April 23 in the *Eau Claire Leader* in Wisconsin—from which I take the text—the tent colony at Ludlow would be in ashes. Historians, anthropologists, and archaeologists are still puzzling out what happened on Monday, April 20, the day after Greek Orthodox Easter.

Most of the militia had been withdrawn, because the state was already $600,000 in debt for the occupation. Also, Ammons wanted the troops withdrawn by the time he left for Washington to plead for national help in mediating an end to the strike. He had intended to withdraw all of the militia, but had been persuaded by the mine operators to leave thirty-eight men, including the remnants of Monte Linderfelt's company, in the strike zone. Nerves remained taut, however, because of rumors of a new cache of arms at the Aguilar camp; the militia was also worried that their diminished numbers were an invitation to violence from the strikers. But the trigger for the inevitable wasn't a rifle shot; it was a letter sent by a woman who claimed her husband was being held against his will in the Ludlow colony. Linderfelt had the letter first, then sent it on to Ludlow, where another lieutenant dispatched a four-man detail from the Ludlow depot to the tent colony to look for the man, Carindo Tuttolimando.

The guardsmen went to the office tent, and Louis Tikas was summoned. Tikas questioned the authority of the soldiers, because he said military rule had ended with the withdrawal of most of the troops. Tikas also said the man they wanted wasn't there. The soldiers were unconvinced, and threatened that if Tuttolimando wasn't handed over by noon, they would conduct a tent-to-tent search. The soldiers returned to the Ludlow depot and reported to their commander, a Major Hamrock, who made a telephone call to the colony to ask that Tikas come up to the train depot. Tikas refused, rejecting the military's right to make demands. The insistence of the guardsman, and the noon deadline, had alarmed the miners, and some armed men began trickling out of the camp, despite Tikas's pleas for them to remain.

Linderfelt was dispatched with the company's "baby"—a tripod-mounted machine gun like the one in the gun car—to join some other soldiers with another gun who had already established a position on Water Tank Hill, which overlooked the Ludlow depot, the tracks, and the tent colony beyond. With an effective range of 2,000 yards, the National Guard's potato diggers on Water Tank Hill commanded the field from the depot to the tent colony, the entrances to the canyons, and beyond. The guardsmen were also well out of the range of the striking miners' rifles.

Soon, Tikas phoned Hamrock back and agreed to a meeting at the depot, where Tuttolimando's wife and daughter were now also present, at military request (if there are names in the record for the wife and daughter, I sadly cannot find them). Tikas recognized the wife, and told her that her husband had left the colony the day before.

Meanwhile, the order of battle was being established. The militia had Water Tank Hill and some of the west side of the Colorado & Southern tracks that ran north from the depot. The strikers occupied the ground between the tent colony and the C&S railway tracks, with some taking cover in the depressions the guardsmen believed were rifle pits, and many others dropping into a strategically important railway cut in a curve on the branch line, the east-west Colorado & Southeastern. The C&SE cut, south of the colony, offered plenty of cover from which to discourage guardsmen from advancing on the colony.

"The details of what happened next are in dispute," recounts Andrews, the historian. "The confusion that characterizes any battle, the irregular makeup of both fighting contingents, the weak chain of command in each, the absence of neutral witnesses, the partisan worldviews of two sides staring past each other, the yawning gulf of hatred and misunderstanding that separated them—these and other complications make it foolish to think that we can know with any certainty what actually occurred on April 20."

Andrews suggests the fighting began with a single gunshot, fired by a person unknown. But our journalist, Scott Martelle, is not quick to adopt so neutral an approach.

"Relatively nonaligned witnesses suggest the battle began in confusion, fueled by distrust and fear," Martelle writes. A train station manager at the Ludlow depot recalls that two large explosions opened the battle, but he does not recall any gunshots coming before. The militia had already agreed to set off explosives in the event of trouble, to warn all soldiers in the canyon. A National Guard internal investigation also found that these warning explosions were the start of the battle. Plenty of gunfire followed, from the Springfields carried by the militia to the assorted small arms of the strikers. Above it all was the hammering of the machine gun on Water Tank Hill.

Tikas came down the road from the depot, waving a white handkerchief. A private from Denver, thirty-year-old Alfred Martin, was shot in the neck when the militia tried unsuccessfully to rout the strikers from their position along the railway cut. Martin was left on the field, as the strikers pushed the militia back to Water Tank Hill, and he bled to death.

News of the battle spread quickly over the telephone and telegraph wires, and Linderfelt's wife, Ora, called the National Guard Armory at Trinidad, which dispatched troops, another machine gun, and thousands of rounds of ammunition. The reinforcements were delayed by an hour while a replacement was found for a union train crew that refused to take the soldiers to Ludlow. These new troops were Company A, freshly recruited, and largely composed of former mine employees. Most of them did not have uniforms yet, nor had officers been selected for the company. In addition to Company A, guards currently employed in the camps and other anti-union personnel came to the aid of the militia. The battle continued for hours and, under fire from two machine guns and increasing numbers of guardsmen and others, most of the striking miners were driven to the north and east. Private Martin's body was recovered, and it appeared he had been shot after death and his body battered. A less-than-impartial report by a military commission found he "had been shot through the mouth. Powder stains (indicated) that the gun was held against his lips. His head had been caved in and his brains had exuded to the ground. His arms had been broken. In such a way does the savage blood lust of this southern European peasantry find expression."

Martin was the only guardsman killed that day.

The women and children in the colony either fled, seeking cover in the arroyos, or they burrowed into the ground, in the cellars beneath the tents. The largest of these underground spaces was beneath the colony's water well, to the north of camp, which had wooden platforms and ladders going eighty feet below ground. It was probably the safest place to be that morning. Others, such as Mary Petrucci and her three children, were huddled in the cellars beneath their tents. The Petrucci tent was designated Tent No. 1, and it was at the very southwest corner of the colony, closest to where the road crossed the railway tracks.

Just before sunset, a Colorado & Southern freight pulled onto a siding at Ludlow to let a passenger train through. In spite of the battle, it was apparently important to maintain a regular schedule. As the freight approached, the conductor noted that the tent colony was on fire; the brakeman saw two burning tents in the colony's southwest corner, and a man in a military uniform setting a torch to a third tent. The crew also saw that many women and children, including those who had been hiding in the water well, used the cover of the freight cars to make their escape to an arroyo, and beyond. More women and children were hidden in the cellars beneath the tents, however, and there were still a few non-combatant men in camp, including Tikas.

Linderfelt's squad, who had led the advance from Water Tank Hill, arrived in the colony about the time the fire started. The soldiers were on a whooping and hollering rampage, and their sounds were soon joined by the wailing of the dozens of frightened women and children. Linderfelt was unnerved, and later said it was the "most unearthly" sound he had ever heard. Then the soldiers, many of whom were recent recruits, began looting. This mob was beyond the control of the officers, and the list of items they carted off includes jewelry, clothes, tools, and bicycles. The soldiers also ripped down the colony's American flags, witnesses said, and threw them on the ground.

The first tent to catch fire seems to have been the Petrucci tent, beneath which Mary and her three children were hiding. Fleeing the flaming tent, she encountered some guardsman who, she said later, shouted and then shot at her. With the children, she darted into Tent No. 58, directly behind her tent, and raced down the earthen steps leading to a larger cellar (the women called it a "cave") the colony used as a maternity ward. There, she found eleven other women and children hiding: Patria Valdez and her four children; Alcarita Pedregon and her two children; and a pregnant young mother named Fedelina Costa, with her two children.

As the tent above Petrucci and her children burned, smoke began to collect in the maternity cellar. Petrucci wanted to flee once more, but the pregnant mother convinced her it was safer down in the hole. The women prayed while the older children attempted to climb out, but they fell back when their hands were burned. It wasn't long before the fire, which was drawing air from the cellar, had depleted enough oxygen in the maternity cave to make the women and children drowsy. Oxygen makes up 21 percent of the air we breathe, and if a fire reduces the available amount to 17 percent, we become disoriented and our judgment is impaired. At 9 percent, we fall unconscious, and death follows at 6 percent.

Above the maternity cave, strikers and others saw guardsman igniting more tents, some with flaming brooms. Tikas was helping some of the remaining women and children to escape, and even Linderfelt was urging flight. But many of the families refused to accept any help from the militia, believing they would be killed, and even fought against being carried to safety. The guardsmen later testified that they had not realized there were women and children hiding in the pits below the tents until they heard their screams. Tikas eventually slipped out of the camp, too, and made his way to hide in a pump house to the north.

Once the colony had been taken, the guardsmen flushed out the few remaining armed strikers in the surrounding area. Other soldiers rounded up some unarmed men at the pump house, including Tikas and others who had fled the burning colony.

Tikas was marched down the tracks to the crossroads at the southwestern corner of the colony and presented to Linderfelt. After an argument about who was responsible for the violence, Linderfelt swung his rifle by the barrel, like a baseball bat, and broke the stock over the Greek's head. The blow sent Tikas to the ground and left a bloody gash on the right side of his head that exposed the white of his skull. Then Linderfelt walked away, leaving Tikas and two other prisoners in the charge of a sergeant—and surrounded by a mostly uniformed mob of fifty armed men.

As he lay on the ground, with the adjacent tent colony in flames, Tikas was shot three times in the back. The other two prisoners were killed as well, one with a shot to the face that blew out his brains. The bodies would be left on the road for three days.

The sergeant later testified that Linderfelt had ordered the executions, but a military commission found conflicting testimony; some said the three were killed in crossfire during the battle, which was unlikely because the battle was over, while others said the prisoners were shot while attempting to escape. But then, all the witnesses were militia. The only unchallenged evidence was the autopsies.

About 5:30 the next morning, Mary Petrucci—who had, somehow, escaped death—climbed out from among the bodies in the black hole that had been the maternity cellar. Still not fully conscious and reeling as though drunk, she was instinctively seeking water. Staggering up to the Ludlow depot, covered in black soot, stinking of smoke, she must have seemed an apparition worthy of Shakespeare.

Just twenty-three, Petrucci was a child of the southern Colorado coal fields. The daughter of a miner and an Italian American Catholic, she had been born in the company camp of Hastings, only three miles away in Del Agua canyon. Her homes had been company homes, and her meager education a company education, except for the instruction she received from the church. She had married Thomas Petrucci, a company employee and naturalized citizen, at the age of sixteen, and their lives had been defined by the hard realities in the coal camps. When Thomas, who operated a coal tipple, went on strike and the family came down out of the canyon to the tent colony, Mary found that she liked it so much she would have preferred to live in the colony year-round. She later said that she found her tent warm, there had been enough coal, and the only sadness was the death of one of her children in March.

The Ludlow postmistress, who knew Petrucci, recognized her beneath the grief and the grime, and asked where her children were. Petrucci said she left them in a hole and expected they were dead. Another woman who had been in the maternity cellar with her, Alcarita Pedregon, had also regained consciousness and escaped the maternity cave sometime before Petrucci did that morning, but the record is unclear on where she went that morning. The postmistress woke Linderfelt, who was asleep in the depot, and he directed some men to accompany her to the camp to investigate, but the men refused, saying it wasn't safe. The postmistress, waving a white handkerchief, went down alone and searched, but Petrucci was confused and told her to look in the wrong spot. A few hours later, the correct location was found—and the bodies of the two women and eleven children. The dead were pregnant Fedelina Costa, twenty-seven, and her two children, Onofrio and Lucy, ages six and four; Patria Valdez, thirty-seven, and her four children, Rudolph, Eulala, Mary, and Elvira, ages nine to infancy; the Pedregon children, Rodgerio and Cloriva, ages six and four; and the three Petrucci children, Joe, Lucy, and Frank, ages four to infancy.

Fedelina's husband, Charles Costa, was also killed during the battle.

The morning the dead were found, there were a few tents left standing, but the guard finished burning those, too. Over the next two days, the women and children who had escaped to the arroyos began trickling into towns, after having spent cold nights with few provisions. One woman gave birth, alone on the prairie, and stumbled with her naked infant into a coal camp. Passengers on the Colorado & Southern were shocked by the bodies of Tikas and the others left at the crossroads. If the violence had shaken some sense into the guardsmen, some showed no sign; a few knelt to shake Tikas's dead hand and mockingly wish him well in the afterlife.

It wasn't until two days after the battle that the bodies of the women and children were removed from the death pit. Beneath a Red Cross flag, a local contingent of clergy and nurses, bolstered by a state labor official and a UMWA leader, went to the site to retrieve the bodies. Fire survivor Pearl Jolly helped the group locate the pit, and as the National Guard soldiers watched and Trinidad photographer Lewis R. Dold documented the event, the bodies were taken out of the ground and placed in wagons.

By the time the corpses were removed, news of the thirteen dead women and children had made headlines across the country. The *Topeka Daily Capital* described it as the "Colorado Civil War." A subhead in the

New York Times declared, "Women and Children Roasted in Pits of Tent Colony as Flames Destroy It." In southern Colorado, the union issued a nationwide "Call to Arms" asking for miners to come to the defense of the strikers in southern Colorado.

A ten-day war ensued.

The militia held Ludlow, but the union made the coalfields from Trinidad to Walsenburg bleed. By Wednesday night, a force of several hundred armed strikers had killed guards and burned mines. By Friday, the fighting had spilled northward to Cañon City, where there was more killing and another mine destroyed. The strikers established a military camp near Trinidad, and made plans to dynamite the county courthouse. State officials pleaded for federal intervention and on April 28, a week after the bodies of the women and children were discovered, Woodrow Wilson relented and sent in the US Army—with the demand that both the strikers and the militia lay down their arms. By the time the troops arrived, the front extended more than 200 miles, from Trinidad to north of Denver. The ten-day war ended April 30, when a company of soldiers from Fort Leavenworth in Kansas arrived in southern Colorado by train. The strike had finally come to an end, and the strikers had lost.

The coal war had claimed at least seventy-five lives, making it the bloodiest labor conflict in American history; the deaths of the thirteen women and children made it the most notorious. With a journalist's passion for quantification, Scott Martelle tallied the death toll in *Blood Passion*, using autopsy reports and funeral registers. Martelle points out that while the strikers are typically portrayed as victims, they were more effective at combat; the miners lost nineteen men, while they killed thirty-seven soldiers, guards, and strikebreakers. This tally, of course, does not count the women and children who died in the pit, one man who died after being jailed in harsh conditions, or five bystanders who were fatally shot during the insurrection.

Although the union lost the strike, it won the public relations war. In addition to the newspaper headlines, there were congressional investigations that produced thousands of pages of testimony, and some of the women who had survived the tent colony fire went on speaking tours. The Rockefeller family, already linked in the public mind with greed, was now a symbol of the collateral damage caused by uncaring, unbridled capitalism.

The Rockefellers hired former newspaper reporter Ivy Ledbetter Lee to deal with the public relations nightmare that had bottomed out at Ludlow. Lee could rightly be called the father of modern public relations, because he created two staples that are with us today: the press release and the photo opportunity. He would use variations of both in his campaign against the union, a campaign that would prove instrumental in rehabilitating the Rockefeller family image with the American public.

Lee was thirty-six, a graduate of Columbia and Princeton, and a man who—according to his hometown newspaper, the *St. Louis Star*—never once in his life failed to send "a post card, letter, gift or telegram" to his parents. He was six feet tall, bookish and courteous, but he could fly into a fist-pounding rage over the "stupidity" of humankind. He had worked for Adolph Och's *New York Times*, Joseph Pulitzer's *New York World*, and William Randolph Hearst's *New York Journal*, but he didn't fit the mold of the typical newspaperman. He was too polite, for one, and too ambitious, for another. In 1903, he left straight journalism for good and established his own brand of press agentry. He understood that convenience was the key to getting your client's message in the news columns, and to that end he provided reporters with reams of clean copy ready to be set into type.

In 1906, when advising eastern coal operators on how to respond to a strike, Lee had established a "Declaration of Principles" for his public relations firm. "This is not a secret press bureau," the declaration said. "All our work is done in the open. We aim to supply news. . . . Our matter is accurate. Further details on any subject treated will be supplied promptly, and any editor will be assisted most carefully in verifying directly any statement of fact." He gained the trust of journalists by allowing access to newsmakers and, in the case of one client, the Pennsylvania Railroad, even to accident scenes.

But Lee's declaration might as well have been written in sand (or torn up and the pieces messengered to him, as in *Citizen Kane*). Before the strike was over, he would not only be operating a secret press bureau but also helping to spread the most malicious of lies. Among the publications that Lee produced, but which did not bear his name, was a series of "bulletins" under the collective title, *The Struggle for Industrial Freedom in Colorado*. These were issued to newspaper editors and other opinion leaders over the course of several months after the massacre in 1914 and attributed publication to the "Committee of Coal Mine Managers," composed of J. F. Welborn, president of Colorado Fuel and Iron; John C. Osgood, chairman of the Victor-American Fuel Company; and D. W. Brown, president of the Rocky Mountain Fuel Company. "The struggle in Colorado has ceased to be, if it ever was, one between capital and labor," one bulletin intoned. "The fundamental question is: Shall we preserve law and order?" Another bulletin carried a letter signed by twenty-five Colorado newspaper editors calling for an end to the strike, with the claim that the coal companies already paid more in wages and other benefits for workers who remained on the job than what was being demanded by the union. The bulletin failed to point out that CF&I either owned or controlled all twenty-five state newspapers.

But the most notorious of all the bulletins was one that flatly declared that there had been no "massacre" of women and children, suggested the strikers themselves were responsible for the conflagration, and offered a justification for the murder of Tikas.

"The bulletins were sometimes loaded [on] one side, leaving the door open for criticism," writes Lee biographer Ray Eldon Hiebert, journalism chair at American University in Washington, DC, with considerable understatement in 1966. "Bulletin Number 8, for instance, contained a quotation from Mrs. Helen Grenfell, vice-president of the Law and Order League, to the effect that the Ludlow disaster was precipitated by the strikers, that the fire had been started accidentally by 'an overturned stove or an explosion' and that the two women and eleven children were suffocated, not shot."

What the bulletin did not mention was that Mrs. Grenfell was the wife of a Denver railway executive and that her league was organized as a response to a pro-labor group called the Women's Peace Association.

Grenfell's letter claimed that the Greek contingent had shot first at the National Guard, that "elaborate" rifle pits had been constructed in the colony in preparation for the attack, and that the soldiers, when alerted by the screams of the victims, risked their own lives while under fire to rescue women and children from the flaming tent colony. The murder of Tikas was referred to as the "unsoldierlike offense of striking the prisoner . . . by an officer of the State troops." But, Grenfell said, such acts of violence may be understood when placed in the context of the viciousness of the strikers, and she used imagery that was sure to strike a nerve with Coloradans. Quoting Bulletin No. 8 directly: "The discovery that all wounded or dying men, whether soldiers or civilians, who fell into the hands of the strikers had been tortured and unspeakably mutilated may explain, if it does not excuse, the wrong doing charged."

While archaeological evidence has revealed that there were, probably, caches of ammunition in at least some of the tent cellars, there has been no conclusive evidence of rifle pits, only trash pits, according to National Park Service documents. The allegation of wholesale mutilation of bodies by the striking miners is unsupported, and was apparently based on the condition of Private Martin's body.

By 1915, at the urging of Lee, Rockefeller Junior was visiting the coal operations in Colorado, and staged photographs of him in a miner's cap and togs with company officials were reprinted in newspapers across the country. About the same time, Junior instituted policies at CF&I that gave the miners almost everything the strikers had wanted, with the exception of the recognition of the UMWA. Instead, at the urging of labor advisor William Lyon Mackenzie King, the future prime minister of Canada, Junior formed a group within CF&I that represented the workers and presented grievances. The Rockefeller Plan, as it came to be known, has been described as a sort of "company union," but that term seems to me oxymoronic.

In the end, the only guardsman to be punished in the aftermath of Ludlow was Monte Linderfelt, who was found guilty of abusing a prisoner in his treatment of Tikas. Hundreds of strikers were indicted on various charges, but the indictments resulted in only two convictions, both for murder, which were later overturned.

Rockefeller Junior was among the three thousand in attendance when the Ludlow monument was unveiled on Memorial Day in 1918. Presumably, he watched as Mary Petrucci pulled a cord and a silk American flag rippled down to reveal the towering granite monument. With Junior was his labor advisor, the Canadian Mackenzie King. Their presence at the dedication was the end of the beginning of a public relations campaign for the Rockefeller family that would, ultimately, culminate in Nelson Rockefeller (Senior's grandson) serving more than ten years as New York governor and being appointed vice president of the United States in 1974 by Gerald R. Ford. By the time Nelson was elected governor, the Rockefeller family was known more for its philanthropy and progressive policies than its bloody and rapacious past.

After the dedication, Mary Petrucci and her husband, Thomas, seldom spoke of the events of April 20, 1914. They lived in a house on a small plot of land near the former tent colony, where they raised chickens, and Thomas went back to work for CF&I. They had seven more children— including three they named for the children who had died in the fire.

"The Ludlow Tent Colony Site is significant as a place of memory," its National Historic Landmark Nomination reads, "one of the few sites of violence and tragedy immediately commemorated by a union with a substantial memorial." The designation was granted in 2009.

Martelle, in *Blood Passion*, declines the popular designation of *massacre* in connection to Ludlow. While the tent colony fire was the result of criminally negligent acts, he argues, there is no evidence that a mass loss of innocent life was intended. It is my belief, however, that the actions of the Colorado National Guard and the mine operators were not merely negligent, but intentional, and today would qualify as terrorism. Deploying a privately controlled army with machine guns against a tent colony of displaced families who were regarded as racially inferior was a strategy with sadly predictable results.

But on the rainy day in June when I stood in the shadow of the Ludlow monument and regarded the unlocked metal door covering the death pit, I hadn't yet focused my thoughts. Instead, I was debating on whether I should open the door and look beneath.

Impulsively, I swung the steel door open, revealing a row of steps leading down into darkness. The odor that rose from below was that of earth and moisture in an unventilated space. *Damp.* The walls and steps of the pit were reinforced with concrete, decades old, whitewashed, and road-mapped with cracks. As I crept down, the smell became thicker, with a bit of rotting organic material mixed in. It was surprisingly dark at the bottom, and I took a penlight from my pocket and twisted it on, the brilliant beam dancing over the gravel floor.

The room was eight feet square. Wooden 4x4s had been knocked into place to support the roof, and around the base of one of these posts someone had left a few plastic flowers, a spray of prairie sage, and a small figurine. I had to drop to one knee to get close enough to see that the four- or five-inch figure was of a child in prayer, or perhaps an angel. A pair of tiny plastic wings was on the gravel nearby. Had a child left this bit of kitsch as a token of remembrance for other, long-dead children? It was surprisingly disorienting and claustrophobic in the hole, and I imagined flames and the stutter of machine-gun fire. I thought of my own three children.

Above, thunder echoed from the mountains and rattled the plain.

There would be more mine strikes in the two decades after the Ludlow Massacre, until the administration of Franklin Delano Roosevelt granted miners and others nationwide the right to unionize. The things that most of us take for granted today—the eight-hour workday, a paycheck every two weeks, the right to safe working conditions, and a choice in where we live and shop—are things we owe to pressure from organized labor, whether we belong to a union or not. But the conflict between Capital and Labor continues, with the pendulum having swung relatively far to the right, with Ludlow remaining just far enough off the interstate of national politics for most of us to breeze past.

That does not lessen its relevance, however, and Ludlow is a monument awaiting rediscovery in popular culture. If we're lucky, it will come in the form of a blockbuster movie, a premium cable miniseries, or a plaintive ballad by a new Woody Guthrie. If we're unlucky, our memory will be jogged by another bloody confrontation in which tons of granite are later erected to the memory of the innocent dead.

Whatever form it takes, it *will* come.

Buy and Dry
Elevation: 4,692' (Pueblo)

In their efforts to provide a sufficiency of water where there was not one, men have resorted to every expedient from prayer to dynamite. The story of their efforts is, on the whole, one of pathos and tragedy, of a few successes and many failures.

—Walter Prescott Webb, The Great Plains, 1931

One morning in June a genial man named Raymond Fuertes took me from the bottom of the Pueblo Union Depot to the very top, offering me a panoramic view of the heart of the historic district below. I had met Fuertes, who is the maintenance supervisor for the privately owned depot complex, only an hour before. I had climbed up from the river and just crossed over from the Union Avenue Bridge, where I had been taking photos of what had once been the world's largest mural, a series of panels painted on the slabs for three miles of the concrete levee that protects the city from flooding.

With a population of 108,000, Pueblo is the largest city through which the river flows in Colorado. Fifteen or so miles upstream of the city, the river begins to widen and eventually helps fill Pueblo Reservoir, created by an earthen concrete dam with a concrete spillway that was completed as a flood control and irrigation project in 1975. It's the last reservoir in the Frying Pan–Arkansas diversion project, which uses a series of tunnels to divert water from the western slope of the Continental Divide near Leadville, fill some man-made alpine lakes, and eventually use the river as the channel to bring the water to Pueblo Reservoir. Because the reservoir has submerged miles of the original river bed, I was uninterested in paddling any of its 10,000 acres of water; I had paddled, fished, and dove a dozen or so man-made lakes in the Midwest, especially Melvern Lake near my home in Kansas, and Table Rock in Missouri, and they all have the same generic US Army Corps of Engineers feel (although the water is clearer in the Ozarks). So, I was satisfied skirting the edge of the Pueblo Reservoir in my Jeep, following the river as it comes out of the spillway below the dam. For the few miles from the spillway into the city proper, the trout fishing is some of the best in Colorado.

The Pueblo Reservoir dam changed the topography of not only the

What was once the world's longest mural on the levee below Union Depot.

Arkansas River but also one of Colorado's oldest water diversion ditches, the Bessemer Ditch. The reservoir submerged the ditch's original headgate, up where Salt Creek flowed into the Arkansas, and to solve the problem a new gate was built into the dam.

Originally called the Big Ditch when it was dug in 1874, it was built by a real estate firm in service to the Denver and Rio Grande railroad, and was meant to irrigate the area south of Pueblo to make family farms possible. In the 1880s, the ditch was expanded to bring water to the Colorado Fuel and Iron steel mill.

The Bessemer Ditch still goes to the old CF&I complex, near Interstate 25 on the southeast side of the city, but the company—which went through several bankruptcies—is now owned by EVRAZ, a steel-making and mining multinational whose largest operations are in Russia. The imposing Spanish Mission–style CF&I administration building has since been purchased by the Steelworks Center of the West, which operates a museum there. Talk about Pueblo to out-of-staters, and there are three things they're likely to have heard of: the CF&I mill, the US Government

Publishing Office, and the world's longest mural, painted over the years on the flat concrete walls of the flood-control levees.

Because of repair work that has already begun, the mural is no longer the world's longest. The top thirteen feet—about a third—of the levee has been removed to make repairs to the buckling concrete. The removal decapitated one of the most famous panels, "The Corn Maiden" by local Cynthia Ramu, which some regarded as the spirit guardian of the river. The panel was meant as a memorial to Pueblo artist Judith Pierce, who died in 1995, and Pierce's ashes were mixed into the paint. Even though the other murals may soon be gone forever, the Corn Maiden may live on. Before removing the top of the levee, workers had carefully removed the concrete that bore the face of the maiden, and other panels, in the hope the artwork could someday be reassembled. What was left above the water was her flowing green robe and the psychedelic cornstalks.

Looking upstream from the bridge, I could see the city's Whitewater Park, a series of drops and chutes below the mural, and towering just downriver from the park, Union Depot. Drawn by the stately brick structure, topped by a clock tower, I had been photographing the depot's main entrance on B Street while Fuertes was watering the grass. He asked why I was taking pictures, and I told him what I was working on, and he beckoned me to follow him.

During the tour, he showed me the plaque on the river side of the depot, placed at the high-water mark—ten feet, six inches—of the devastating June 3, 1921, flood. It began with an ordinary cloudburst, according to the National Oceanic and Atmospheric Administration, which dumped half an inch of water on the city in a few minutes. Upriver on the Arkansas, rains had swollen the river and burst reservoirs. The city's recently "improved" flood levee failed, and while a flood alarm warned people to move to high ground, the city's poorest residents lived near the railway tracks in an area called "Peppersauce Flats" and were hardest hit. By 6 p.m., most of the city was submerged, and scattered fires broke out. "Burning piles of timber from a blazing lumber yard drifted through the streets of the city, lodging momentarily against frame buildings and setting them on fire," said a federal report published on the flood in 1922. "It was almost impossible to fight the fires, as the buildings were surrounded by water, which prevented the fire department from reaching them."

The flood killed hundreds and destroyed the city's downtown, leaving ten feet of water over Union Avenue. It also cut transportation and communication lines, isolating the city from the rest of the world. Over the next three days, another six inches of rain would fall, sometimes sending walls of water into the already terrified city. The flood stretched from thirty miles west of Pueblo to the Kansas line, destroyed 600 homes, caused $25 million dollars in damage, and may have killed as many as 1,500. When the water finally receded, it left a foot of mud on the ruined streets of Pueblo. It also changed the course of the Arkansas River, moving it a half mile south.

By 1926, Pueblo had completed a rechanneling and flood control project, including new levees, paid for by municipal bonds. The city's business district had moved from devastated Union Avenue to Main Street, two blocks to the southeast. As Union Avenue's fortunes fell, it became known for its taverns and red-light district. In recent decades, it has been renewed as a historic district with family-friendly shops. The river, too, has been returned, at least in part, to its original path through the city. The Historic Arkansas Riverwalk is a "32-acre urban waterfront experience" created around a new channel filled with Arkansas River water. I was not much interested in the riverwalk because it was too new and just seemed, well, too commercial.

At Union Depot, Fuertes took me down into the boiler room, which he said was completely filled with mud in June 1921. Then he led me on a tour of the rest of the complex, which is owned by Pueblo businessmen Jim and Joe Koncilja. The depot originally served five railways: the Denver and Rio Grande, the Texas and Fort Worth, the Rock Island, the Santa Fe, and the Missouri Pacific. In the coach yard near the depot is the Colorado Railway Museum exhibit of engines and rolling stock, including the Santa Fe 2912, a massive 4-8-4 Northern steam locomotive, built in 1944. The 2912 was a fast engine that ran from La Junta to Los Angeles.

After leading me through the cavernous passenger areas and the renovated office spaces of the depot, Fuertes unlocked several doors that led to a passage into the clock tower. We climbed stairs part of the way, and then narrower stairs, and finally a ladder, and arrived at the top. A hand-painted message on some slats in the tower proclaimed that workmen (or *a* workman) named Miller McDow completed the copper work on the tower on January 1, 1924. There were no hands in the clock face, as the mechanism is awaiting restoration, so our view of downtown Pueblo was unimpeded. Practically everything we saw had been shaped by the flood of nearly a century ago.

Control of the Arkansas River became an obsession during the twentieth century, driven in part by the desire to prevent the kind of catastrophic damage that resulted from the 1921 flood. It was complicated by the dramatic variation in the natural flow of the river—along much of the Arkansas, water could be reliably expected only in the spring—and by the system of reservoirs and irrigation ditches that proliferated in attempts to irrigate the otherwise nonarable soil.

There are hundreds of miles of canals in eastern Colorado, watering thousands of acres, and they are invariably called "ditches" by the locals. One of the earliest ditches was built in the spring of 1864, by Army engineers under the direction of the Bureau of Indian Affairs, for the use of the Cheyennes and Arapahos on their reservation, to fulfill one of the promises of the Fort Wise Treaty. But after the events later that year, including the Sand Creek Massacre, the agricultural experiment ended. The ditch originally meant for the Indians was bought by a pair of local ranchers and operated from 1868 to 1883, when a Denver real estate developer bought it to "rent" water to farmers. The scheme collapsed because of mismanagement. The system was sold and reformed as the La Junta and Lamar Canal Company, which eventually would include 110 miles of ditches. More ditch companies would come. The water in the Arkansas River was treated as a commodity to be exploited for "beneficial" purposes, which was interpreted as serving the needs of agriculture and industry. In the semi-arid climate of southeastern Colorado, crops will not grow without irrigation. Those in the valley believed they were engaged in the conquest of nature, and with the right technology, they expected to win.

On the Kansas side, farmers needed water, too, but in a somewhat different way than those on the Colorado side. There was more rainfall on the high plains of Kansas, but drought was an ever-present worry, and irrigation was needed to sustain the field during the dry times. A series of ditch companies were formed around Garden City (four or five of these still exist, depending on how you count them). But Kansas farmers and the ditch companies depended primarily on water that flowed from

Colorado. Inevitably, Kansas felt that the state upstream was unfairly holding water that it needed.

In 1901, Kansas brought the first interstate water suit before the US Supreme Court, asserting that it had the right to all of the natural flow of the Arkansas, without human interference. Colorado said it had the right to divert the entire flow of the river, if it chose. Six years later, in rendering its opinion in *Kansas v. Colorado,* the Supreme Court established the doctrine of "equitable apportionment" of benefits. This doctrine said the court must apportion water in an equitable fashion, considering the interests of all parties involved.

"What is so plain and yet so significant about this case is that it failed to deal with the environmental and social reality of the situation," writes Jim Sherow in *Watering the Valley.* "Instead, it considered only the economic or commodity aspects of the dispute. The decision simply provided a yardstick to measure the diversion of water between contending states."

Neither state was satisfied with the 1907 ruling, and a century of litigation followed. The water dispute between Kansas and Colorado is the *Jarndyce and Jarndyce* of Supreme Court cases. It has been thought settled several times, only to come back in some form. The midcentury Arkansas River Compact was the closest the issue has ever come to being resolved.

The 2.6-mile earth and concrete dam that created the John Martin Reservoir, on a portion of the river downstream from Pueblo, between Las Animas and Lamar, was started by the Army Corps of Engineers in 1939. It wasn't completed until 1948, however, because of the intervention of World War II. The reservoir, which is about sixty miles from the Kansas line, is named for the congressman who advocated it, and is the largest body of water in southeastern Colorado. Like the reservoir at Pueblo, the John Martin has destroyed the topography of the original river, and I was similarly disinterested in launching my kayak there.

Designed as a flood-control and irrigation project, and as a seasonal water storage facility, it is essential to the Arkansas River Compact of 1949, which is a federally ratified agreement to "equitably divide and apportion between the state of Colorado and Kansas the water of the Arkansas river and their utilization."

But urban growth along Colorado's Front Range, and increased agricultural pressure and new irrigation technologies, disrupted the compact's delicate balance. In 1985, Kansas went back to the Supreme Court, alleging that Colorado was violating the rules of the compact. The case dragged on until 2001, when the court found for Kansas. It established a "hydrological-institutional model" to bring Colorado into compliance, and awarded $34 million in damages. Kansas objected, because the award was in cash—and not in water. Some aspects of the dispute limped on until 2009, when the Supreme Court ruled that Colorado didn't have to pay $9.2 million that Kansas claimed its consultants in the case were owed (they received about $200,000 instead). It was the only decision in the history of the dispute that clearly favored Colorado.

Both Colorado and Kansas use the doctrine of "prior appropriation" in determining water rights, which means that the first to use or divert water for a beneficial purpose owns priority water rights (Kansas, however, until 1945 had used the riparian doctrine common to eastern states, in which land ownership only *along* a river confers a water right). Prior appropriation rights—often understood as "first in time, first in right"—may be sold, and as the need for water increases, the water rights often exceed the value of the property it benefits. Aging farmers, when there are no offspring to leave the farm to, are increasingly cashing out their shares. This is known as "buy and dry," in which agricultural water rights are transferred to cities, or increasingly, to speculators. More and more, the Arkansas River water that irrigated thousands of acres of farmland now flows in city taps, and vast swaths of southeastern Colorado have again become barren. The situation is not expected to ease anytime soon, as urban growth in the Front Range is expected to exceed the available water by 2030. The controversy over water rights has become so intense that it took a 2016 state law to make clear that household rain barrels were legal and did not violate the doctrine of prior appropriation.

An environmental and agricultural historian at Kansas State in Manhattan, Sherow published his book on the Arkansas River valley in 1990, but his observations are increasingly relevant.

Sherow likens the human population of the Arkansas Valley to an invading organism, and the ditch companies, the dams, and the reservoirs to the means by which it attempts to establish ecological niches. "When any invading organism assumes a niche in an environment," he writes, "it may make alterations to that environment. Quickly or slowly, the changes produced could then destroy the environment and share a symbiotic relationship with its natural surroundings. What makes a particular organism adaptable or maladaptable depends on its own nature." He was talking about the different natures of the various ditch companies, but he might as well have been talking about us.

Despite expectations, Sherow concludes, neither the John Martin Reservoir nor any other project added a single acre of farmland to Colorado. The unintended consequences of the irrigation and water diversion and storage systems included increased salinity of the river, the spread of the invasive saltcedar plant, increased sedimentation, and alteration of the original river channel. The residents of the Arkansas Valley had seldom acted as stewards of the environment, but had acted in vested self-interest to commodify the water and dominate the river.

"When their aspirations fell short and their water systems failed, as was wont to happen during drought," Sherow concludes, "the road to conflict opened. Occasionally people fought one another with guns. . . . Far more often, people responded with hired assailants or protectors (depending on their relative position in litigation) called water lawyers."

The phrase *water lawyers* sends a chill down my spine.

What chance does the average Kansan or Coloradan have of their interests being protected when legions of water lawyers and speculators are vying for a limited public resource? One may have a keen interest in protecting the wild, but the state laws are largely concerned with protecting the right of privileged individuals and entities to commercially exploit the wilderness. The doctrine of first appropriation, which comes from an age when water was regarded as an unlimited resource, has created a protected water class and made paupers of the rest of us.

Dan Gordon, a La Junta resident and veteran journalist, may have said it best in a 2012 opinion piece on the state's water crisis for the *Denver Post*. "In the semiarid west," he said, "water flows toward money."

Next morning they decided to throw a stick into the air and proceed in whatever direction it happened to fall. . . . Two days later they descended in the Arkansas valley and after many mishaps forded the icy roaring torrent. They moved up the river to Cache Creek, where all staked claims. They found much fine gold, but so mixed with a heavy black sand it could not be extricated with the means at hand.

—George F. Willison, Here They Dug the Gold, *1946*

The peacocks are the most puzzling thing at Bent's Old Fort, the castle-like adobe outpost on the Santa Fe Trail on the north side of the river between La Junta and Las Animas. The brilliantly colored and surprisingly large birds have the run of the courtyard and the nested maze of corridors and walls surrounding it, and their raucous cries are alarming. It's not something you would expect to find in a fort at the very edge of the American frontier in the 1840s, but the National Park Service has painstakingly recreated the complex from old drawings, archaeological evidence, and eyewitness accounts—and has placed the appropriate livestock in and around it, including the peacocks.

The Bent family, majority owners of the fort, apparently tried their hands at raising peafowl, perhaps because they saw the birds as good watch animals—they tend to shriek when visitors approach. Or, the family may have simply longed for a touch of color within the monochromatic sand-colored walls. The shimmering blues and greens of the bird's plumage and the eye-spangled tails astonished the Cheyenne and other tribes who came to trade, George Bent recalled years later, while their harsh voices startled them.

One day in June, a couple of years ago, I had most of a day to kill while waiting for Kim to arrive on an Amtrak passenger train from Kansas. I had driven up from a writing conference in Texas, and the plan was for me to pick her up at the Amtrak depot in La Junta, and from there we'd go up into the mountains to pan for gold. But heavy rains in Illinois had delayed her train, so that it was eight hours behind schedule by the time she boarded at Newton. I spent a few of those hours touring Bent's Old Fort.

From 1833 to 1848, this adobe fortress with its screaming peacocks

Quaking aspen near the Colorado Trail.

was the most important military and trading outpost in the American Southwest. It was located along the mountain route of the Santa Fe Trail, which linked Independence, Missouri, with Santa Fe. Mexico won its independence from Spain in 1821, following a war, and the trail was the primary artery between the two countries. From atop the rounded towers of the fort, where the swivel guns were mounted, you could see Mexican territory—it was just across the river to the south.

William Bent, his brother Charles, and their partner Ceran St. Vrain had established the outpost in 1833 to trade for buffalo hides, primarily with the Southern Cheyennes and their allies, the Arapahos. The fort was key to their expanding empire, which sold goods imported from Missouri and sent back hides and fur. Although privately owned, the fort became increasingly important to the US Army, was a social center for travelers and trappers, and was for most of its time the largest white settlement in the Southwest. William Bent had originally planned to locate the fort closer to the mountains, but the Cheyennes suggested it would be better for trade if it were located on the river. Bent had a close relationship with the tribe and later married Owl Woman, the daughter of White Thunder, and with her had four children, including George.

Late in the year the fort was built, White Thunder, a Cheyenne chief and sacred arrow keeper, saw a spectacular meteor storm from near the fort. There were tens of thousands of shooting stars per hour, and the shower was witnessed across North America; today we know that the November 13 display was the peak of the Leonid cycle, as the earth passes through tons of tiny particles left in the wake of a periodic comet. Many plains tribes, such as the Lakota, recorded the event in their pictorial calendars called winter counts as "The Year the Stars Fell." White Thunder believed the celestial display was a sign promising good fortune in trading with the whites at Bent's Fort—and also in recovering the tribe's most important possession, the sacred arrow bundle, which had been lost in battle to the Pawnees.

The four medicine arrows represented safety and subsistence to the tribe, according to Donald J. Berthrong in *The Southern Cheyennes*, and were received by a prophet called Sweet Medicine from a supernatural being. Ceremonies associated with the arrows are among the tribe's most sacred and solemn, and the arrow bundle is kept by a single family, and the rites traditionally descend from father to son, or perhaps a brother. It was the custom to carry the arrow bundle into battle, and the arrows were lost in 1830 when the Cheyennes attacked the Pawnees along the Platte River. White Thunder managed to negotiate the return of one or two of the arrows from the Pawnees following the meteor storm.

The Cheyennes had occupied the plains between the Arkansas and Platte Rivers only for a generation or so. They had originally dwelled along the shores of the Great Lakes, and they ventured west and south, displaced by other tribes and lured by the horse culture of the plains. They went from the Great Lakes area of Minnesota to the Dakotas and then present-day Wyoming, where Lewis and Clark encountered them on the Yellowstone and Cheyenne Rivers. By the 1830s they had dropped down to Colorado, and bands could be found from the Platte down to the Arkansas River Valley. They were, or had been, at war with many other tribes, including the Pawnees, Utes, Kiowas, and Arikarees. Chief among their few allies were the Arapahos, a smaller tribe that typically traveled and camped with the Cheyennes. In the year or so before Bent established his fort, the latter tribe had split into two groups. The Northern Cheyenne remained along the North Platte River, near the Black Hills, and the Southern Cheyenne found a new home along the north bank of the

Arkansas River in what is now Colorado and Kansas. The sacred arrows stayed with the Southern Cheyenne, while another important ritual object, the medicine buffalo hat, was kept by the northern group.

According to Cheyenne religion, Sweet Medicine performed several miracles—including one involving a beautiful bird with shining feathers of all colors on its wings and neck—and foretold the coming of white people, the horse, and the demise of the buffalo.

And although Sweet Medicine admonished his people to remember the things he had told them, he said he knew they would forget. "Your ways will change," he prophesied, according to John Stands in Timber in his book with Margot Liberty, *Cheyenne Memories*, published by Yale University Press in 1967. "You will leave your religion for something new. You will lose respect for your leaders and start quarreling with one another. You will lose track of your relations and marry women from your own families. You will take after the Earth Men's ways and forget good things by which you have lived and in the end become worse than crazy."

At Bent's Fort, the Cheyennes and others camped in the cottonwoods along both sides of the river, sometimes in the thousands. The buffalo robes they brought would be traded for goods, typically ten prime robes for a Navajo-type wool blanket. The exchange rated worked out to about thirty cents per robe. The Indians could also trade for food, beads, gunpowder—or spirits. In 1835, an army lieutenant with an expedition to Bent's Fort seeking to establish relations with the Cheyennes noted that many were drunk on liquor obtained from "Mexican" traders. "They are very fond of whiskey, and will sell their horses, blankets, and everything else they possess for a drink of it," the lieutenant commented. The introduction of alcohol to native cultures, unconditioned socially or psychologically by centuries of drinking, spawned generations of misery.

The buffalo robes were squeezed by a wooden press into 100-pound bundles, then shipped to St. Louis, where they were sold at a considerable profit for use as blankets. In addition to the buffalo robes, white trappers and mountain men sold the company beaver pelts, which were also pressed into bundles and shipped out. There was an enormous demand for beaver felt for European hats, and a prime beaver "plew" was worth a princely six dollars. Compare that to the average wage for a farm laborer in 1830, which amounted to only six or seven dollars a month.

The period of peace and prosperity at the fort came to an end in 1846, with the advent of the Mexican War. The conflict was sparked by the annexation of the Republic of Texas, which Mexico considered part of its territory, despite the declaration of Texas as independent ten years earlier. The war sent thousands of soldiers down the Santa Fe Trail. Bent's Fort became a convenient staging area for General Stephen W. Kearny's "Army of the West," comprising about 1,700 soldiers bound for the Mexican state of California. A topographical engineer named James Albert who had become ill during the march spent several weeks recovering at the fort, and to pass the time he made sketches and drew plans of what he saw; more than a century later, these would prove crucial in recreating the outpost.

The brief war resulted in an American victory and the ceding of California and vast swaths of territory north of the Rio Grande; the result was, with the land already gained through the Louisiana Purchase, a largely unimpeded course for American empire all the way to the Pacific.

Despite the influx of military traffic, the war was an economic disaster for the fort. Commerce with New Mexico collapsed, and fur trading with the Native Americans diminished. The demand for beaver pelts dropped dramatically through the 1840s, as fashions changed and materials such as silk replaced felt. Charles Bent, who had been appointed governor of New Mexico, was scalped alive and then shot full of arrows during an uprising of Pueblo Indians. St. Vrain withdrew from the business venture and turned to other interests, and William Bent was left as the sole owner. In 1849, a cholera outbreak spread like fire down the trail from back east, leaving several thousand dead in its wake. At Bent's Fort, the disease killed half of the Cheyenne tribe. William's wife, Owl Woman, had died in childbirth two years earlier.

William Bent entered into talks to sell the fort to the army, but no deal was made. In frustration, Bent may have set fire to the fort; whether he was responsible or not, the fort was partially destroyed by fire under mysterious circumstances. In 1853, William Bent ventured about forty miles downriver and established a new fort, on some bluffs in a bend of the river called Big Timbers, just west of present-day Lamar, Colorado. This fort was also on the north bank of the Arkansas River, but instead of adobe, it was built of stone, with sixteen-foot walls.

The Fort Laramie Treaty of 1851 had granted the Cheyennes and Arapahos all of the territory between the North Platte and Arkansas

Rivers, an area that ranges from present-day Wyoming and Nebraska down to the southern plains in Colorado and Kansas. The Oglala and Brulé Sioux and other tribes were given lands that ranged from the north bank of the Platte into the Dakotas. The tribes agreed to stop fighting one another, give travelers on the Oregon and other trails safe passage, and allow the United States the right to build roads and military posts. At the treaty signing, each tribe received mounds of gifts, from calico to knives to copper pots. The chiefs each received a uniform of a general in the US Army. Under the terms of the treaty the Indians would receive, for the next fifty years, the protection of the United States and fifty thousand dollars in goods annually. But the treaty lasted only a few years. Many of the Indians believed they weren't bound by it, because it was approved by tribal representatives rather than consensus; also, the United States unilaterally shortened the length of the treaty to just ten years. In 1859, gold was found on Cherry Creek, near Denver, and tens of thousands of fortune hunters streamed onto land that belonged to the Cheyennes and the Arapahos.

Because the quest for gold is such a large part of the history of the Arkansas headwaters, I wanted to know what it was like to prospect for gold in the mountains. With the exception of using plastic gold pans instead of metal ones, prospecting—at least for the individual treasure hunter—hasn't changed much since the days the first miners struck it rich at California Gulch. After getting some advice on where to go at the Rock Doc, a gem and mineral shop between Salida and Buena Vista, Kim and I headed for Cache Creek, a Bureau of Land Management area, and the site of one of the area's first gold strikes, in 1859.

Before going to Cache Creek, we had a couple of stops to make. We wanted to visit a ghost town, and on the other side of the river, at the end of a long four-wheel-drive road in the Mosquito Range, we found the ghost town of Futurity. The town was notable because the gold mine was in the middle of town, and miners had only to walk a few steps to get to work. What is left now is a few buildings, a large tailings pile, and swarms of mosquitos. Actually, *swarm* doesn't do the sheer number of mosquitoes there justice. Kim proposed a new name: *a panic* of mosquitoes. We also found plenty of bear scat, which made me nervous, so we didn't stay long. On the way back, we saw a few bighorn sheep standing on the mountainside.

Then we went to Ruby Mountain, which is on the east bank of the Arkansas River about six miles below Buena Vista. This is an easily accessible and well-known spot for rock hounds, and we spent a couple of hours scrambling over the rocky cliffs on the west face and searching the talus at the bottom. We collected a plastic pail of rocks we found interesting and a handful of obsidian nodules called "Apache Tears." Ruby is named because of its abundance of garnet, but that was something we didn't find.

Then we set off for Cache Creek.

At Granite, you take a hard turn west off Highway 24 onto a winding county road that leads you to a meadow high above the valley. From there, you follow the dirt until you reach the turnoff to Cache Creek, which is to the south. But on our first attempt to find the creek, we missed the turn and ended up climbing toward the Continental Divide. We found a turnout where the Colorado Trail, a hiking trail between Durango and Denver that was established in the 1970s, crosses the road. Just past the turnout, we rounded a curve and found ourselves in a stand of quaking aspen.

The sensation was surreal.

The slender trees, with their pale trunks and dark markings, represented not just a single tree, but a single living organism. While aspens and birch trees look similar, the leaves of aspens are creased and more slender. In the summer, the leaves are green, but in the fall they turn a brilliant gold. Found at elevations between 6,500 and 10,000 feet, they reproduce asexually and produce identical clones in any given colony.

We parked the Jeep at the turnout, walked up the road, and remained for a while in the shelter of the trees. When the wind blew, it made a sound as if the aspen were gently breathing. Then we returned to the car, retraced our steps, and found Cache Creek.

Here, during weather good enough to allow passage along the access road, you can prospect for gold for free among the tailings left by previous gold-mining operations. At least, you could when we were there; the Bureau of Land Management now charges $5 a day, has closed all but 25 acres of the 2,161-acre property to prospectors, and prohibits any method other than hand panning.

On the day we were there, we encountered only a half dozen other people, and most of them were, like us, working with hand tools that could be carried in a five-gallon plastic bucket. There was, however, evidence of more serious digging in pockets along the property, including deep "coyote holes" that undercut some trees. The gold found here is placer gold, washed down from the mountains and concentrated in alluvial deposits of sand and gravel in ancient streambeds. Commercial gold prospectors use panning as a way to scout for gold along creeks before bringing in the heavy equipment, while hobbyists are often satisfied with and sometimes legally limited to just what they can find in their pans.

After walking a quarter of a mile or so into the woods, we found the meandering creek, and followed it downstream to an area where commercial mining in decades past had left mounds of tailings, as well as some rusted cables and other metal trash. I took a GPS reading with my Garmin, in case we wanted to return to this spot, and noted the elevation: 9,230 feet. Then I muscled some basketball-sized rocks for better access to the pile, and Kim dug with her scoop at the base, seeking the darker material beneath. Soon she had filled the bottom third of our orange plastic bucket, and it was time to start panning.

I filled one of our green plastic pans with material from the bucket, picked out the larger chunks of rock, then kneaded the material to break the rest of it up. Squatting at the edge of the creek, I dipped the pan into the chilly water, and shook it vigorously to let the water carry away the lighter stuff. I stirred it with my fingers, and shook it again. This was repeated many times until what was left was the darkest and heaviest material, consisting mostly of black sand. Then as I gently swirled the water about, the black sand formed a crescent from which emerged a few flecks of gold.

"Color," I told Kim.

Gold shines in an unmistakable way, a kind of dull yet warm yellow, with a texture that seems hammered. Rather than trying to separate all of the black sand from the few grains of gold, I took a soft plastic sniffer bottle and sucked up the gold from the pan.

The thrill at the moment the color was revealed in the pan was oddly similar to that of catching a fish. We had found gold by following the common wisdom among treasure hunters: look in the place where others had found it. We repeated the process of digging and panning many times

over the next few hours, and while we added to our cache in the sniffer
bottle, we never exceeded the amount of color in that first pan. There's
a knack to panning and, while it doesn't take long to describe, it does
require some muscle memory to get the tipping, rocking, and swirling
motions right. What you end up with is a spoonful or two of black sand
concentrate, which is magnetite or hematite, and maybe some gold.
When we finally knocked off, my back ached, my knees hurt, and my
fingers were numb from dipping them in the creek.

As we walked back to the parking area, with our single bucket
containing all of our gear, we met a couple from Wichita loading a dozen
or more five-gallon buckets of material into the back of their pickup. They
asked us how we did, and we told them, and then we asked about their
luck. They wouldn't know, they said, until they got home and processed
their material through their motorized gold pan.

Even though we were leaving with gold, it wasn't worth enough to
make me consider gold prospecting as a sideline. It was serious work.
Gold was selling at $1,200 an ounce that week, and what we had found
was just a gram or so, enough perhaps to pay for the dinner we had that
night (there are 31.1 grams in a troy ounce, so one gram of gold is worth
about $38). But, its sentimental value was worth much more. As I write,
the gold is on a shelf behind me, in a small plastic vial of water with a
black screw top. It is strange to think that gold is a symbol of the best and
the worst of us—love and greed. A wedding band, a gold coin.

Ghosts of Sand Creek
Elevation: 4,001' (South Bend, Big Sandy Creek)

When I was at Sand Creek, after I left, I told my wife they were talking. I can see them, they could see me. If I was there with them and we could see each other, why did they have to talk? They could have signed to each other. I told my wife, Indians don't do that, they should have been signing. After being at the site, it's like they were trying to teach me something. Like "hey don't forget us, we're still here. The old ones and the young ones doing battle and the babies, we're still here."

—Robert Toahty, Kiowa-Arapaho, Colony, Oklahoma

In 1860, William Bent found himself dealing with the US Army again, which was charged with protecting the gold seekers. The army first used Bent's fort as a commissary. Then, it began its own fortifications downhill from Bent's and refused to pay rent, because it considered Bent a squatter. The army christened its structure Fort Fauntleroy, after a colonel of dragoons, which may be the worst-sounding name in the history of US military installations. In 1861, at the outbreak of the Civil War, Fauntleroy joined the Confederacy, which prompted the army to change the name to Fort Wise, after the governor of Virginia.

As relations with the plains tribes deteriorated, settlers in Denver began to have jitters because the Indians were angry about the influx of whites into their buffalo hunting territory. The Cheyennes and Arapahos signed a new agreement, the Treaty of Fort Wise in 1861, which reduced their lands to about a thirteenth of what they previously had, and it located them near the Arkansas River in southeastern Colorado Territory. Chief Black Kettle was the principal negotiator in the Fort Wise treaty, who believed resistance would only bring misery and was continually attempting to broker peace with the United States. But many within the tribes refused to accept the new treaty, again claiming that it was not adopted by consensus, and refused to cede their hunting grounds. Particularly resistant to white incursion were the Cheyenne Dog Soldiers, a military society that had been active since the 1830s, and they ranged with the bison herds along the Smoky Hill River in Kansas. Following the Fort Wise treaty, they began to burn homesteads and attack wagon trains. Raids continued sporadically through 1862, and while the residents (and

Monument on the bluff above Sand Creek.

politicians) in Denver anticipated that the Cheyennes and Arapahos
were gearing up for an all-out war with the whites, there is no evidence to
support such a coordinated strategy. By 1863—a pivotal and bloody year
in the Civil War, which saw both the battle of Gettysburg and the siege of
Vicksburg—the tribes in western Kansas and eastern Colorado remained
largely quiet.

Fort Wise did not keep its name for long. When the Virginia governor
threw in with the Confederacy, the name of the fort was again changed,
to Fort Lyon, for Nathaniel Lyon. He'd been killed in August 1861 at
Wilson's Creek in Missouri—the first Union general to die in the war.
By a coincidence, George Bent, the son of William and Owl Woman,
and a nephew of Black Kettle, was at the battle in which Lyon was killed.
George Bent had been schooled in Missouri, had joined a troop of
Confederate cavalry at the outbreak of the war, and had fought at Wilson's
Creek. He was captured in 1862, but was released after signing a loyalty
oath to the Union. He returned to his father's ranch near Fort Lyon in
Colorado Territory, but because of anti-Confederate sentiment decided it
was safer to live with his mother's side of the family. By November 1864,
George Bent was encamped with a group of Cheyennes and Arapahos

about thirty-five miles northeast of Fort Lyon, at a place known as the South Bend of Big Sandy Creek.

History has shortened the name to Sand Creek.

By 1864, Colorado Territory was free of any military challenge from the Confederacy, but insurrection among the plains Indians had consumed the attention of civilian and military authorities. In the old buffalo hunting grounds that had been taken away from the tribes, a series of stock thefts, skirmishes, and occasional bloodletting had shocked eastern Colorado and western Kansas. The Indians who fought for the old way of life were fierce, and some adhered to a standard of tribal warfare that allowed mutilation of enemy dead, the murder of children, and the rape and enslavement of women. It would be unfair to characterize these actions as representative of all Native American combatants, in the same way it would be unfair to characterize the actions of all US Army officers by the actions of William Calley. In 1968, Lieutenant Calley was in command of a company that killed as many as 504 unarmed civilians in the My Lai Massacre. After an initial military cover-up, Calley was charged with 109 counts of murder, and eventually convicted of the premeditated murder of twenty-two villagers. The parallels with Sand Creek are striking. "I was ordered to go in there and destroy the enemy," Calley said in a statement. "That was my job that day. That was the mission I was given. I did not sit down and think in terms of men, women and children. They were all classified as the same." After three and a half years of house arrest at Fort Benning, Georgia, Calley was released when a federal judge found his trial tainted by prejudicial publicity and other legal problems.

Perhaps I'm being naïve, because the nature of war is brutality, whether hurling a stone or a nuclear weapon, but I remain disheartened by the massacres at Sand Creek and My Lai, and the torture of prisoners at Abu Ghraib. Americans must be held to a higher standard of conduct than our adversaries, or we will become the things we profess to hate. The wonder is that anybody emerges from combat with their humanity intact.

The brutality of the plains tribes was only sometimes visited upon white soldiers and settlers, but when it was, the news rolled like thunder over the prairie. Earlier in 1864, the First Colorado Cavalry had confronted a band of Dog Soldiers believed, perhaps mistakenly, to have been involved in raids on the South Platte; after a skirmish, the Cheyennes decapitated a sergeant killed in the fight. In other incidents, soldiers shot, without provocation or after goading them into a fight, chiefs and Dog Soldiers, and sometimes killed their women and children. Grievances multiplied on both sides, and hostilities increased. As the year wore on, diverse bands of plains Indians drew blood from the Platte to the Cimarron, far below the Arkansas.

But it was the Hungate killings that drew the most white outrage.

In June, a ranch hand named Hungate and his family were killed on Box Elder Creek, thirty-five miles outside Denver. No surviving whites saw the killings, but because the bodies were mutilated and there was some evidence of rape, it was assumed the Cheyennes were responsible. The bodies of the family—father, mother, and two young daughters— were loaded into wagons and hauled to Denver for public display. Although the Cheyennes were blamed for the killings, it now appears the violence may have been committed by a few Arapaho warriors with a grudge to settle.

Territorial Governor John Evans used the Hungate killings to press for troops to defend against "a powerful combination of Indian tribes, who are pledged to sustain each other and drive the white people from the country." As the Indian raids continued into the fall—at least forty white settlers were killed, and a half dozen women and children taken captive— Evans called for homegrown "patriots" to kill the hostiles. The *Rocky Mountain News* advocated a few months of "active extermination."

Evans received permission from Lincoln's secretary of war, Edwin Stanton, to raise a regiment of 100-day volunteers to protect the white settlements. This became the Third Colorado Cavalry Regiment, placed under the command of Colonel John Chivington. He was a veteran of Glorieta Pass, where he had displayed uncommon skill, and was the chief military officer for the district of Colorado.

Chivington stood six feet, four inches tall, weighed around 240 pounds, and was called "the fighting parson." Born in Ohio, he'd been a firebrand abolitionist and Methodist preacher back in Kansas, and he harbored a desire to be a US senator. But he badly needed another battlefield win to secure his political ambitions. The mission to lead the Third Colorado against the Indian insurrection presented that opportunity—but the clock was ticking on their 100-day enlistment. The

Third Colorado, nicknamed the "Bloodless Third" by detractors, spent two months loafing in camp while Chivington waited for an opportunity.

Meanwhile, Black Kettle had attempted to negotiate a peace. From his camp at the headwaters of the Smoky Hill, he sent word—via a letter written by George Bent—that he would accept peace if it also included the other rebellious plains tribes, and that he was willing to exchange seven white captives. They had been taken during raids on August 7 and 8 along the Oregon Trail in southwest Nebraska Territory.

When an army detachment arrived at Black Kettle's camp at the headwaters of the Smoky Hill River, they found themselves outnumbered by several hundred Indians encamped there. The detachment was led by Major Ned Wynkoop, commander of Fort Lyon, and a man who respected the leadership of Black Kettle. But the various tribes could not agree on peace terms, and Black Kettle was able to deliver only four of the seven prisoners: sixteen-year-old Laura Roper and three younger children, Isabella Eubank, Ambrose Usher, and Danny Marble. Black Kettle, according to Cheyenne custom, had to buy the prisoners in order to exchange them. Two of the children, Isabella and Danny, were ill, and died within months of their release, at Denver. Of the remaining three captives, Nancy Morton was released first, when she was ransomed on the Upper Powder River in Wyoming. Lucinda Eubank, who said her person had been repeatedly violated, and her infant son were finally freed the next May.

At the urging of Wynkoop, Black Kettle agreed to move his band to the protection of Fort Lyon, where Evans had promised "friendlies" would be protected. In September 1864, Black Kettle and six other Cheyenne and Arapaho chiefs agreed to a council with civilian and military authorities at Camp Weld, located at what is now the intersection of Eighth and Vallejo in Denver. The ranking white authorities in attendance were Evans, the governor of Colorado Territory, and Chivington.

Black Kettle said he had come at the urging of Wynkoop.

"We have come with our eyes shut, following his handful of men, like coming through the fire," the chief said, through an interpreter. "All we ask is that we may have peace with the whites; we want to hold you by the hand. . . . I have not come here with a little wolf's bark, but have come to talk plain with you. We must live near the buffalo or starve. When we came here we came free, within any apprehension, to see you, and when I go home and tell my people that I have taken your hand . . . they will feel well."

Evans was little interested in Black Kettle's peace overture, however, and pressed the Indians to admit their guilt in starting a war. He was also keen for the Indians to cede what little lands they had, by treaty, left. Chivington said little, but as the council was nearing its conclusion, he announced that his rule for fighting white or red men was to "fight them until they lay down their arms and submit to military authority." When they were ready to do that, he said, they could go to Wynkoop at Fort Lyon. The Indians left with the impression that peace was at hand, but Chivington was preparing for war. While the Black Kettle delegation was on its way to Denver, Chivington had received telegraphed instructions from Samuel R. Curtis, the major general in charge of the Department of Kansas, that the ringleaders be imprisoned, restitution paid for stock losses, and all captives delivered. For now, Curtis said, "I want no peace."

George Bent recalled later that Black Kettle moved his band to the Big Bend on Sandy Creek at the urging of Wynkoop, who promised that they would be protected if they camped near Fort Lyon. Wynkoop also shared rations with the Indians, believing that it was better to have them close, where any hostility could be closely observed. But Wynkoop's superiors declared these actions to be unauthorized, and replaced him as commander of Fort Lyon. The new commander, Major Scott Anthony, suggested the Indians withdraw from the fort to Sand Creek.

Meanwhile, Chivington had earlier moved the Third Colorado about sixty miles outside Denver. Late in November, he marched them through the snow to Fort Lyon, where he ordered all traffic along the Arkansas halted, for fear that someone would report his movements to the "hostiles." Along with the Third Colorado, there were also five companies of the First Regiment of Colorado Cavalry. In all, Chivington had more than 700 troops under his command, and a battery of four howitzers. The latter were twelve-pounder mountain Model 1835 howitzers, light field pieces with stubby barrels used in rough terrain, and they had a range of 800 to 1,000 yards, depending on whether they were loaded with shot or shell. The soldiers carried an assortment of weapons: muzzle-loading, single-shot rifles in .69 and other calibers, .36-caliber navy percussion revolvers, .44 army revolvers, .52-caliber Starr carbines, and many other firearms. There were sabers, knives, and bayonets. Chivington himself carried one of the most advanced small arms of the Civil War, a .56-56 caliber Spencer repeating rifle, which was fed from a magazine tube inserted into the stock, and could fire seven shots in less than thirty seconds.

They arrived at Sand Creek just before dawn. It was Tuesday, November 29, 1864.

From a ridge overlooking the Big Sandy, it was probably light enough for the soldiers to make out the grove of trees and the village stretching before them to the north. This was a remote and peaceful place well-known to the Cheyennes, a place that had good water and pleasant camping and was marked by the furrows of an old lodgepole trail that crossed the creek. There were more than a hundred Cheyenne lodges here, and a few Arapaho, and more than a few of the conical buffalo hide–covered structures that would have been illuminated from within by early morning fires. The total number of inhabitants likely did not exceed five hundred, and it was estimated later that two-thirds of them were women and children. Those who were awake must have been reluctant to leave the warmth of their homes. In one of the lodges, perhaps still asleep, was George Bent. His brother, Robert Bent, had been forced to lead Chivington to the camp from Fort Lyon; the old black mountain man Jim Beckwourth, nearing seventy, had also been pressed into service as a guide, but had been allowed to turn back because of the bitter cold. Whatever Chivington was thinking when he gazed down on the sleeping village, it did not soften his heart; instead, he readied his plan of attack, with the Third Colorado in the middle, and units of the First flanking. A detachment or two were instructed to cut the village off from the pony herds, and some of the women mistook the sound of hooves and the approaching dark forms as a buffalo herd running through the village.

Then the shooting began.

Eyewitness accounts of the events that followed are ambiguous and at times contradictory. I have chosen from among what I believe are the best sources, including the letters of George Bent and material prepared by the National Park Service.

The Cheyennes and Arapahos streamed out of their lodges to be cut down by crossfire from the First and Third. When the soldiers began advancing on the village, many Indians were shot dead even though their hands were raised in surrender. Black Kettle stood waving an American flag at the end of a lodgepole, pleading for the soldiers to stop, and later added another, white, flag. George Bent was shot in the hip. Some of the Indian men and boys resisted the attack, primarily with bows and arrows, as most of the inhabitants of the village fled along the creek, to the northwest. They hid beneath the low bluffs or clawed pits in the sand to try to get beneath the bullets. Cheyenne chief White Antelope, wearing a peace medal around his neck that had been given to him by President Lincoln, attempted to parlay, but when he saw it was useless he began his death song: "Nothing lives long, only the earth and the mountains."

White Antelope was shot down.

At some point, the howitzers were brought up and their fire was directed at the village, and later at the Indians hiding along the creek. If there had been a plan for the attack, it fell apart as the Bloodless Third made an uncoordinated advance, haphazardly shooting men, women, and children. Soldiers pursued the retreating Indians over several square miles. With discipline gone, the soldiers became a mob. Along the river, trapped in the bluffs or the pits, or running across the prairie, the Indians had few guns and fought mostly with knives and stones against mounted troopers with revolvers and rifles, and sometimes supported by artillery. The killing went on for hours, until the soldiers were too weary to continue, when they returned to the camp Chivington had made on the remains of the village.

They camped for two days, purposely crushing all evidence of the village into the sand—and posing an ever-present threat to those Indians still hidden on the cold prairie. When they left, many of the gruesome trophies they had gathered from the dead went with them to Denver.

But not all of the soldiers under Chivington's command participated in the killing and subsequent mutilation. Among those refusing was Captain Silas Soule, an abolitionist with a reputation for daring who had come to Lawrence, Kansas, with the New England Emigrant Aid Company. Soule had expressed reservations at Fort Lyon about moving on a group of Indians that were regarded as peaceful, and in command of Company D of the First Colorado, ordered his men to stand down the morning of that attack. In a letter to his friend Wynkoop, written shortly after the massacre, Soule said that hundreds of women and children had been on their hands and knees pleading for mercy, and found none.

"The massacre lasted six or eight hours," Soule writes. "It was hard to see little children on their knees have their brains beat out by men professing to be civilized. One squaw was wounded and a fellow took a hatchet to finish her, and she held her arms up to defend her, and he cut one arm off and [she held it with the other while he] dashed the hatchet through her brain. One squaw with her two children, were on their knees begging for their lives of a dozen soldiers, within ten feet of them all, firing—when one succeeded in hitting the squaw in the thigh, she took a knife and cut the throats of both children, and then killed herself. . . . The [dead] were all horribly mutilated. One women was cut open and a child taken out of her, and scalped."

And this: "Squaw's snatches were cut out for trophies."

At least 150 Indians were killed, and two-thirds of them were women and children; another 200 or so had been wounded but escaped. About 16 soldiers were killed, and a few dozen wounded. At least some of the federal casualties appear to have been caused by friendly fire.

In 1865, Soule would testify before federal investigators, although under questioning he admitted to not having directly seen all of the atrocities he had previously described. Chivington would offer a vigorous defense, repeating claims that the engagement was a battle, not a massacre, and exaggerating the number of Indians killed to 500 or 600; he said fresh white scalps were found in the camp, that his troops were outnumbered, and that the Indians had put up fierce resistance throughout, and especially from the rifle pits that had been previously prepared.

"My reason for making the attack on the Indian camp was, that I believed the Indians in the camp were hostile to the whites," Chivington testified. "That they were of the same tribes with those who had murdered many persons and destroyed much valuable property on the Platte and Arkansas Rivers during the previous spring, summer and fall was beyond a doubt. When a tribe of Indians is at war with the whites it is impossible to determine what party or band of the tribe or the name of the Indian or Indians belonging to the tribe so at war are guilty of the acts of hostility. The most that can be ascertained is that Indians of the tribe have performed the acts."

Chivington, who had resigned his commission a few months before the inquiry, was condemned for his conduct by the Joint Committee on the Conduct of the War, but would face no criminal charges. As the newspapers reported the testimony and the public grew disgusted, his political ambitions were dashed. He died of cancer in 1894.

Soule lived only days after his testimony damning Chivington. On the night of April 23, 1865, near the corner of Fifteenth and Arapaho Streets in Denver, he was ambushed by two soldiers of the Second Colorado Cavalry. Soule managed to draw his revolver and wound one of them before being shot—fatally—in the face. The assassins fled, and neither stood trial.

George Bent, who had managed to escape from the creek bank, recovered from his wound. He joined the Dog Soldiers and participated in several attacks against whites, including the Battle of Platte Bridge Station in July 1865 near present-day Casper, Wyoming, where a thousand warriors from various plains tribes burned a wagon train and killed twenty-two soldiers.

Black Kettle, still attempting to make peace, signed the Treaty of the Little Arkansas, at a location near Sixty-First Street and Seneca in modern Wichita, Kansas. William Bent was there, as was Little Raven, a chief of the Arapahos. Black Kettle told the government representatives that his "shame was as big as the earth" in having trusted the whites. This new treaty guaranteed "perpetual peace," limited them to a reservation south of the Arkansas River, and admitted that at Sand Creek, the army had attacked and killed peaceful Indians under protection of the American flag, and promised reparations. Three hundred and twenty acres of land were to be given to various chiefs, including Black Kettle, and six hundred and forty acres—one full section—to some of those related to the Indians by blood, including George Bent, and Amache, the wife of John Prowers and the daughter of One-Eye (also known as Onichee), another Cheyenne chief killed at Sand Creek. The treaty lasted less than two years, collapsing under grievances on both sides.

At the Washita River in Oklahoma Territory in November 1868, the Seventh Cavalry under George Armstrong Custer attacked Black Kettle's camp and killed as many as 140 Indian men and up to 75 women and children. Other women and children were taken captive. And Black Kettle was among the Cheyenne dead.

The Sand Creek Massacre sparked a decades-long plains Indian war that whites had feared all along. Typically, the Cheyenne and other tribes had the advantage in the summer months, while the US Army had the upper hand in winter, by virtue of better rations, arms, and equipment. Custer and most of his command were wiped out at the Battle of the Little

Bighorn in Montana in June 1876, with about 300 army dead. Although the Little Bighorn was a clear and decisive victory for the Indians, it only postponed the inevitable. The plains wars came to a final, bloody end with the Wounded Knee Massacre in 1890, in which the Seventh Cavalry killed more than 150 Indian men, women, and children. Chief Spotted Elk (known also as Big Foot), a devotee of the Ghost Dance religion that had swept the plains and promised to rid the land of whites, was among those who died in the snow. After Wounded Knee, there was no more large-scale organized military resistance.

George Bent, who had given up arms and returned to his role as interpreter by the time of the Medicine Lodge Treaty of 1867, fought continued bouts with alcoholism, but in 1901 emerged as a Cheyenne historian, writing many letters about the history of the tribe, and his witnessing of Sand Creek and other events, that were collected into book form. He died in 1918, at the age of seventy-five, in Washita, Oklahoma.

The army returned to Sand Creek in 1868, just four years after the massacre, when Lieutenant General William T. Sherman, the famous Civil War general who was now in charge of all operations in the West, undertook a tour of sites of military importance. With him was Second Lieutenant Samuel Bonsall, who, according to regulations, prepared a map of distances traveled and important features during the tour, and he labeled the Sand Creek site as "Chivington's Massacre." Sherman had his men search the site for relics to bring back with him to Washington, and they collected a wagonload, including arrows and knives and many skulls, including some from children. The crania were later used in two ways: first, in studies by anthropologists to "prove" that Indians were inferior to whites; and second, as the subject of military ballistics examinations to determine better ways to kill.

While the Sand Creek Massacre lingered in the collective memory of the nation, in Colorado the reaction has been somewhat different. Just a few miles south of Sand Creek is the tiny community of Chivington, founded in 1887 as a whistle-stop on the Missouri Pacific Railroad. Now, it consists of just a few houses along US 96. One night long ago, while driving back from a Western Writer's Conference in Wyoming, I took a wrong turn and became lost in sparsely populated, eastern Colorado. Taking the first road that led east, back to Kansas, I was shocked to find myself passing through the community and realized the Sand Creek site was nearby.

Like many Americans, I had first learned details of the Sand Creek and Wounded Knee massacres in Dee Brown's *Bury My Heart at Wounded Knee*, which I read as a kid not long after it was published in 1970. The book presents the Indian's point of view in describing the loss of their West, but has been criticized for emphasizing story over the careful presentation of history.

"Scholars greeted *Bury My Heart at Wounded Knee* with skepticism bordering on contempt," historian Ari Kelman wrote in 2013 in his own book on Sand Creek. "Most professional historians damned Brown's work with the faint praise reserved for well-told tales that do not rise to the academy's analytical standards: he had produced a gripping narrative." Kelman notes that part of the book's popularity lay in its timing: it was seen as an allegory for the Vietnam War, describing events appallingly similar to the actions of Lieutenant Calley at My Lai, and it was contemporary with the rise of the American Indian Movement.

Brown, a librarian who pounded out his books after he had put his children to bed, was passionate about the history of the American West. His best seller is undoubtedly one of the most influential books on American Indian history, following in the mold of Helen Hunt Jackson's *A Century of Dishonor*, published in 1881. What historians miss, I think, is that despite the errors in *Bury My Heart at Wounded Knee*, the narrative is substantially correct. It changed the way generations of Americans think about the Indian wars. That it came from outside the academy seems to be its unpardonable sin.

I spoke with Kelman, who is the McCabe Greer Professor of the American Civil War Era at Pennsylvania State University, about his own book, *A Misplaced Massacre: Struggling with the Memory of Sand Creek.* The book weaves together three distinct threads: the history of the massacre itself, the frustratingly long struggle to have the site designated as a National Park Service unit, and the surprisingly robust controversy over exactly where Black Kettle's village was located. Kelman joked that the book is the "story of the longest committee meeting," because he attended every important meeting that led to the establishment of Sand Creek as a national historic site. But the book is well-written and compelling, if not a "gripping narrative," placing Sand Creek in the context of the Civil War and making clear that the soldiers involved were US troops and not some ragtag militia, as has often been claimed. Some of the detail I've used above, especially about Bonsall and the collection of human remains, have been drawn from Kelman's book, which asks uneasy questions about how we should remember an atrocity committed by American troops.

In writing the book, Kelman said, he did not attempt to evaluate the relative merits of "truth claims" about aspects of the battle, but tried instead to acknowledge the depth of the conflict between otherwise credible sources. There was considerable tension between the oral traditions of the descendants of the Cheyennes and Arapahos killed there and some of the historical and archaeological evidence uncovered. The Bonsall map, for example, proved to be a breakthrough for historians, but the descendants believed it was a record of grave robbery. Indian traditionalists insisted that the massacre had taken place at South Bend, just below the bluff that contains a decades-old monument. In 1978, the tribe's Sacred Arrow Keeper conducted a ritual there and declared it was where the village had stood, and where their people had died, and he consecrated the ground as Cheyenne earth.

In the end, the Sand Creek Massacre National Historic Site was dedicated in 2007, and it was the result of a balancing act between a strict interpretation of events, based on empirical data, and the stories and traditions of the tribes who were the descendants of the dead. The exact location of the village was left to interpretation. One of those who spoke at the dedication was US Senator Sam Brownback of Kansas, who was then a Republican primary candidate for president. "You can sense the woods still ache," Brownback said, as reported by the *Denver Post*. "I acknowledge and admit wrongs were done by the federal government or tolerated by the federal government here and across the nation. I deeply apologize and I'll work to right this wrong."

Yet, despite our most heartfelt promises, we always seem to forget the past.

The parallels between the Sand Creek and Ludlow massacres are too powerful to ignore. In both cases, communities in crisis were living in temporary fashion, under the protection of the American flag, only to face the guns of Colorado soldiers; the violence was encouraged by bigotry, women and children bore the brunt of the assaults, and both communities were leveled; finally, after congressional hearings, no real punishment was handed down.

In 1999, a Kiowa-Arapaho by the name of Robert Toahty was interviewed by a National Park Service employee on a mission to gather oral histories of Sand Creek for a site study. Toahty said he was descended from survivors of the massacre, but had never visited until one afternoon three years before, when he and his wife camped there in their tipi.

"I sat there by the trees facing north, about three or four o'clock in the afternoon, and could hear about a dozen children up in the trees. You could hear them giggling. Once in a while you could hear a word, but it was inaudible, you couldn't really understand what they were saying, but you knew they were saying something. Sometimes you could tell if it was a girl or a boy. Later on when it started getting dark, I went on down and you could hear old women talking around the trees."

Sometimes the spirits knew he was there and at others, they didn't, as if it was in another time. As he walked north, along the riverbed, he said he could feel the eyes of the warriors. He stayed there until long after it was dark, and he finally withdrew to his tipi not because of the spirits, but because he was afraid of the band of coyotes gathering about a mile to the southeast. Toahty explained that he had artificial legs and supported himself with crutches.

"I know they're scattered all up and down there," Toahty said. "Because a lot of them were taken before their time and their bones are scattered. The children were just killed out of cruelty and the old people, for no cause. It was a genocide, plain and simple. . . . When I close my eyes while walking, it's like a light that's on top of the earth that's illuminating, but you can't see it. You can feel it, but you can't see it." It was like, he said, an illuminated dome or a halo that covered the earth.

During a cold day in winter, Kim and I stood on the bluff overlooking South Bend at Sand Creek where, in 1950, local white residents had placed a red granite monument. It's still there, and looks much like a tombstone. Beneath a generic image of an Indian chief with a full headdress are the words SAND CREEK BATTLE GROUND. Visitors are in the habit of leaving objects on and around the monument, little gifts for the dead, bits of sage or ribbon or coins. On the afternoon of my visit, I left a handful of pipe tobacco.

Beyond the interpretive signs and the split-rail fence, the creek and the few trees and the broken terrain below must look much as it had in 1864. There is a desperate loneliness to the vista, a kind of melancholy that comes from knowing the tragic past. Chivington must have stood on this bluff that morning, before sending most of his troops down the hill to the right, to attack the village. Was Black Kettle's village just below the bluff, as the oral histories and tradition suggest, or was it a mile or so along the river to the northwest, as the historical and archaeological records indicate? It mattered much to the living, I knew. But I wondered if it would matter to those buried in the repatriation area nearby, where the bones of some of those killed at Sand Creek—including the skulls that had been used in the weapons studies—had been retrieved from museums and other institutions, under force of a federal law that requires the divestiture of Native American remains. But my desire to identify and label, to fix things in times and space, and to rationalize, betrays my own biases. I make no claim to understand the nature of revealed truth to native peoples, but I can testify to brushes with the uncanny that give me pause. The light I experienced on my first float on the Arkansas River near Leadville is an example, and was weirdly similar to Toahty's account of the unseen dome of light covering Sand Creek. Spiritually, I'm an agnostic. I know what I've seen and felt, but I don't claim to know what any of it means.

There are no living witnesses to the Sand Creek massacre, except perhaps the oldest cottonwoods along the banks of the creek. These are plains cottonwoods, which under ideal conditions can live up to 200 years or more, but historic floods have taken their toll on the stands. The oldest of these rugged, gnarled trees, according to researchers who studied tree ring data, were probably alive at the time of the massacre as seedlings or saplings.

As we walked the ridge that leads to the northwest and dips low toward the creek bed, I half expected to hear spirits in the trees, as Toahty had described. I walked carefully, as one walks between the stones in a cemetery, but I heard nothing except the wind sighing through the grass. I could feel no illuminating light. But the knowledge of what had happened was a weight on my shoulders that threatened to drive me down into the enduring earth.

The ABCs of Internment
Elevation: 3,602' (Camp Amache)

*"What does America mean to you?" I hesitated—I was not sure of my answer. I
wondered if America still means and will mean freedom, equality, security, and justice
when some of its citizens were segregated, discriminated against, and treated so
unfairly. I knew I was not the only American seeking an answer.*

—*Marion Konishi,* Commencement Speech, *Granada Relocation Center High
School, June 24, 1943*

This is the story the archaeologist asked me not to tell.

One bright morning last June, on a hilltop of grass and scrub
overlooking the Arkansas River valley in southeastern Colorado, a high
school student named Halle Sousa found a wheat penny in the dirt. While
this event may seem unremarkable, consider that the hilltop was the site
of a World War II concentration camp for Americans of Japanese heritage.
Consider also that Halle, the sixteen-year-old girl, was participating in
a summer archaeology program, and was the granddaughter of a man
who had been removed from California and imprisoned at this very
camp, and that she found the coin inside one of the dozens of concrete
foundations where the cold and cramped barracks once stood. Consider
that the penny, marked with a pair of bright pink flags and left in situ on
the ground by the girl for the archaeologist to examine, was found heads
up, with the date visible. It was tarnished, but probably had not been
in circulation for too long, because it showed only light wear: Lincoln's
profile, the date, and the mint mark were well-defined. Finally, consider
this: the year on the coin was 1941, and the mint mark was *S*, for San
Francisco.

The hilltop is the location of Camp Amache, one of ten World War II
concentration camps administered by the War Relocation Authority.
Most historians use the term *internment* in referring to these camps, but
that word is legally inaccurate and gives a comforting blush to a brutal
practice. But, more on that later.

Beginning in 1942, the WRA removed more than 120,000 persons of
Japanese descent from their homes on the West Coast and imprisoned
them, under armed guard, in rural America. Of the camps, Amache was

Reconstructed water tank at Camp Amache.

the smallest, with a population never exceeding 8,000. The camps were isolated and living conditions were harsh. The most well-known of these camps is Manzanar in California, photographed by Ansel Adams and Dorothea Lange, which is now a historic site run by the National Park Service, but there were also camps in Arizona, Arkansas, Idaho, Utah, and Wyoming.

There isn't much left of this camp in southeastern Colorado, which occupied a square mile of hilltop and surrounding area, just outside the town of Granada. There are acres of concrete foundations hidden by scrub, lots of junk piles, and at the top of the hill, a recently reconstructed guard post and a water tower that has been rebuilt. The original tank was reclaimed after being used since 1947 at a local ranch to water stock. The tank has been repainted in its original colors, a checked red and white, and the massive tower on which it perches is bright yellow. The tank and tower can be clearly seen for miles along nearby US Highway 50, which follows the river and leads into town. From the hilltop, you can glimpse the green water tower of the town below, population 640.

≈ ≈ ≈

The archaeologist directing the summer field study, Dr. Bonnie Clark from the University of Denver, granted me permission to spend a couple of days with her group, composed mostly of college students, as they did some preliminary survey work in preparation for the summer's dig. I stayed with the ten-member group at their crew house at Granada, where the lights went out for a couple of hours amid a fierce thunderstorm. The rain probably had much to do with uncovering the penny, making it a little easier to find. Clark, a serious woman who's been a professional archaeologist since 1990, praised Halle for her sharp eyes, but was worried about my reporting the find. The penny wasn't worth much—similar coins could be had for less than a dollar on eBay—but she feared that reporting the find would draw treasure hunters to the hilltop. But metal detectorists would have very poor luck, because coin finds here are rare (the internees did not have many coins to lose, possibly) and also because the area is littered with tin cans, nails, wire, and other debris that is the bane of detector hobbyists. Some of the metallic detritus came when the barracks were dismantled for their lumber after the war, and much of it is the result of the site having been used as a trash dump. Also, there are buried pockets of pull tabs and beer cans from past drinking parties. The coin itself, Clark said, is unusual, but of little archaeological significance. More important, she said, are the abundance of artifacts that represent daily life in the camp, such as the ubiquitous one-gallon water cans that had been refashioned into coal scoops. Couldn't I just use one of those as an example of an artifact from Camp Amache?

But to me, the finding of the coin spoke of something that approached the numinous. The synchronicity was so profound that, crouching over the penny with my camera in my hand, the thought of it made a shiver dance along my ribs. Here was a coin that may have been carried in the pocket of an internee all the way from California. To witness it being found seventy-four years later by the granddaughter of one of those internees was to be swept along by the irresistible undercurrent of history.

In 1939, following the Nazi invasion of Poland, Franklin Delano Roosevelt asked the FBI to begin gathering intelligence on those suspected of domestic subversion, potential spies and saboteurs. On the West Coast, he directed the army and navy intelligence to begin watching those deemed suspicious. The result was a master list, maintained by the Justice Department, called the ABC list. The A and B categories were for those deemed immediately or potentially dangerous. The C category, however, was for possible Japanese sympathizers. The rounding up of Japanese nationals began on the evening of December 7, 1941; on February 2, 1942, Executive Order 9066 established the military areas for the War Relocation Authority camps. The order also gave Secretary of War Henry Stimson nearly unlimited power in determining who would be held in the camps, and summarily revoked the civil rights of those selected. Of the 120,000 persons of Japanese ancestry sent to the camps, about two-thirds were American citizens. Their homes and businesses had to be sold or held in trust by others.

On the days designated for relocation, families were ordered to assemble, with only the personal effects they could carry in two suitcases, at designated times and places, and were first held in open public places, such as the Santa Anita racetrack. They were later transported to the camps, which in physical appearance were indistinguishable from prison camps: overcrowded tarpaper shacks, barbed wire, armed patrols, and guard towers with searchlights. Conditions inside the barbed wire were harsh, especially in winter, particularly for those accustomed to the mild climate of Southern California.

The Granada Relocation Center was renamed Amache, in an attempt to relieve the confusion created for the local post office at nearby Granada by receiving mail intended for the imprisoned. The name was chosen (apparently with no hint of irony) for Amache, the wife of John Prowers, Indian agent for the Upper Arkansas Agency. She was the daughter of Onichee, a Southern Cheyenne killed at Sand Creek.

The work at Amache, according to a research design and methodology written by Clark, has three goals: to provide expertise in the practice of archaeology, to create an educational environment, and to advance scholarly research. "At the heart of the Amache field school lies an ethical commitment to true engagement with communities of concern," Clark writes. "Archaeology is particularly suited to address the quotidian, as habitual acts are often the ones most evident in the physical remains of the past." Much of Clark's work has been devoted to the study of things that allowed the internees to keep a sense of identity. Cooking in the barracks was prohibited, for example, but shards of Japanese ceramics indicate that the women cooked anyway.

The camps were called concentration camps during the war, an accurate description of what a nation does to its own people. After the horrors of Auschwitz and Dachau were revealed, however, there was a shift away from the term to create distance between our prisons for Japanese Americans and the Nazi death camps with their grim ovens.

My terminology was influenced by Roger Daniels, in a 2005 essay entitled, "Words Do Matter: A Note on Inappropriate Terminology and the Incarceration of the Japanese Americans." Daniels, a professor of American history at the University of Cincinnati, is an author and expert on immigration and ethnicity.

Daniels points out that internment is an understood aspect of declared wars, and is applied to nationals of an enemy nation. In World War II, only about 8,000 Japanese were legally handled as internees, and they were treated lawfully, in accordance with the Geneva Convention, and received something resembling due process. What happened to the vast majority of West Coast Japanese Americans in 1942 was outside the framework of law, and they suffered the loss of their property and their constitutional rights.

"There has been a long history of using euphemistic language about the wartime atrocity that was wreaked upon the Japanese Americans of the West Coast during and after World War II," Daniels writes. "Begun with malice aforethought by government officials, politicians, and journalists, it has been continued, largely in thoughtless innocence, by scholars."

Clark knows the arguments, but prefers language that she sees as less divisive, even if it is technically inaccurate.

"I sometimes call it a prison," Clark said in an interview, "I will call it an incarceration camp, I will use internment camp—it depends a lot on the audience—but here's the thing . . . concentration camp is so freighted. [But] by the Geneva Convention of what that word means, yes, they're concentration camps, they were designed to separate out a portion of your populace based on ethnic or racial background. And they've done so without due process."

But, Clark said, there's a need to open a dialogue about Amache and the other camps, and for that dialogue to be as inclusive as possible. "You know, three of those kids [this summer], those crew members working with our local kids, they have to live with this in their backyard. And when you say you live next to a concentration camp . . . even more troublesome for me is that we want to work with the children of people who worked here. You know, if I consistently called it a concentration camp, I don't think these white daughters of a [Camp Amache] teacher who've been back two years in a row—well, to tell them their mom worked in a concentration camp creates a space that I don't want here."

Clark has been leading the field school since 2008, and she was originally drawn to the location because of a set of questions she wanted answered: "What do people do when their world is turned upside down?" she said. "How do they reclaim their sense of self, how do they protect their children, how do they recreate their community?"

After the camp was closed in October 1945, most of its buildings were dismantled for lumber for the nearby town. What was left was in and on the ground: the foundations, of course, but also the detritus of everyday life that, to a veteran archaeologist like Clark, began to reveal surprising patterns of optimism among an imprisoned population. They found, for example, civic landscaping that included raised walkways along the busiest streets in camp, well-tended common spaces, traditional Japanese baths, ceramics and other crafts, and the transformation of the landscape through the planting of trees and the maintenance of well-tended gardens.

"For me, because I'm interested in how people make places and how they modify the landscape, it's the depth of investment in things like making the soil better [that fascinates]," Clark said. "So you're in a prison and you crumble up eggshells, you compost, you spot water. We find consistently in the gardens that the soil chemistry has more of the nutrients that you need to grow crops than in our off-garden patches. That to me was really quite surprising when I first saw it and I just keep seeing it. Also, the variety of plants they were able to grow in this really harsh environment is surprising. We have canna, which is a tropical plant that's common in Hawaii, but also cattails, dogwood, so we find a lot of evidence of plumb and prune, so people are growing fruit trees out here."

Once, Clark said, the crew was working at a garden site, and an older gentleman came out from town and watched for a spell. Clark asked him if he remembered what the camp was like when he was a kid.

"He said it was beautiful. Just think of that, that it was this scraped raw earth when they got here, but by the time they left, it was beautiful," Clark said. "When you look at the pictures, there are certain spots that absolutely were: city parks, flowers running all the way up to the front of the barracks."

Visitors to the Amache site, Clark said, should be careful to leave it the way they found it. Something like one of those modified tin can coal scoops may seem like a nifty souvenir, and worth little else, but its value to the archaeological record is considerable. What visitors can take with them, she said, are the lessons that Amache offers about our shared history.

"Racism and fear are a very, very dangerous mix," she said. "We all have to stand up for each other's civil rights. You know, if there hadn't been this preexisting racist climate in California in particular . . . in some ways, Pearl Harbor was an excuse for people to do what they'd been wanting to do for a long time, which was keep out the Japanese. So people use certain situations as a cover for bias, and so this is a chance to say, well, what happens when that runs unchecked? Where do we end up? We end up with three-year-olds being behind barbed wire."

It is no exaggeration to say that the Japanese Americans imprisoned in this concentration camp (I will use the term, because it is the only honest and accurate way to describe what happened here) left it a better place than they found it. Part of the success of the camp no doubt owed to the compassion and fair play of the local population, but that does not excuse the racism and brutality of forced removal and imprisonment without trial.

Later, I visited the Amache Museum in downtown Granada, which is open during the summer months. In addition to the expected exhibits—photographs, poster, the luggage the internees carried—in the center of the small museum was a cubicle where Amache survivors and their families could tack index cards describing their experience. "I am writing for my mother, Jane Kuboto, who is now ninety and unlikely to be able to make the trip," read one. Another: "My grandparents, Frank Sato and Edna 'Fudge' Nimura, met in camp. Frank was known as a great dancer and played guitar and ukulele in a Hawaiian band. Fudge was active in many of the Amache High School activities from drama club to student government." At the museum, I met Rebecca Cruz, a graduate student working to organize some of the exhibits. When I asked her what impressed her most about the field work, she replied without hesitation: "The tangibility of it all."

Halle Sousa, the girl who found the wheat penny, lives in California, and was one of five high school students chosen by the National Japanese American Memorial Foundation for a digital storytelling project about the camps. Halle narrates the completed four-minute, twenty-two-second video.

"When I first set foot in Amache in June 2016," Halle says over images of the Amache hilltop, "I felt as if I was in the middle of a barren wasteland. What I saw was in stark contrast to the pictures I had painted in my mind, after doing so much research and listening to the stories of my grandfather. I felt as if people had forgotten what he and his family had gone through, and I couldn't help wondering if this wouldn't simply become another forgotten story."

The video uses excerpts of interviews with Halle's grandfather, eighty-seven-year-old Asa Yonemura. At the age of thirteen, Yonemura—who was born in California and had never been to Japan—was sent with his family to Amache. "So they just thought that if they isolated us, there's nothing that we can do," Yonemura says. "We were everyday normal citizens. . . . For one thing, I think we were fortunate that the area where Amache was, we had farmland. Being the people from the Central Valley (in California) were basically farmers, we could support ourselves."

Halle concludes the video by talking about her archaeological internship with the University of Denver, "in which we surveyed the camp for artifacts and excavated areas outside of the barracks. . . . We recorded hundreds of artifacts, such as modified tin cans, sake jug bases, and porcelain fragments. Each little thing we found restored hope, hope that this would not be forgotten, hope that with this evidence of what happened here, we could work as a community to keep history from repeating itself."

In 1943, the same year Asa Yonemura and his family were living in Block 11E, Barracks 3, the valedictorian of the Amache Senior High School graduating class delivered a commencement address titled, "America, Our Hope Is in You." Marion Konishi was eighteen years old, and her speech—to a graduating class of a school that caused a national controversy, because many Americans believed money should not be spent on educating the children of internees—is remarkable for its cautious optimism and its honesty.

"One and a half years ago I knew only one America—an America that gave me an equal chance in the struggle for life, liberty, and the pursuit of happiness." Back then, she said, if someone asked her what America meant to her, she would have unhesitatingly answered freedom, equality, security, and justice. But in 1943, she wasn't sure what her answer would be. "I wondered if America still means and will mean freedom, equality, security, and justice when some of its citizens were segregated, discriminated against, and treated so unfairly. I knew I was not the only American seeking an answer. So unmindful of the searchlights reflecting in my windows, I sat down and tried to recall all the things that were taught to me in my history, sociology, and American life classes," she said.

For 167 years, she said, America had been the only hope for the common man—to make a home, earn a living, and to worship, think, and act as he pleased. She invoked Valley Forge, George Washington, Thomas Jefferson, Gettysburg, and Abraham Lincoln.

"Sometimes America failed and suffered," she said. "Sometimes she made mistakes, great mistakes, but she always admitted them and tried to rectify all the injustice that flowed from them. I noticed that the major trend in American history has been towards equality and fair play for all." She cited the treatment of the Native Americans, and the slaves, and the German Americans who were persecuted during World War I.

Although she was "as much embittered as any other evacuee," she said, there was reason for hope. She had found "faith in the America that is still alive in the hearts, minds, and consciences of true Americans today . . . [to] judge citizenship and patriotism on the basis of actions and achievements and not on the basis of physical characteristics."

Now ninety-one, Marion Konishi Takehara returned to Amache in May 2016, for the first time since the 1940s, for the Amache Pilgrimage, held on the first Saturday before Memorial Day. She read her commencement speech for the second time.

Despite their imprisonment, many young men from the camp volunteered for service, and were typically sent to the European theater. Some of them did not survive, and are buried in the well-tended cemetery that is found at the end of a muddy lane at the southwest corner of the camp.

In 1976, the cemetery was in disrepair, but a group calling itself CARP (a nickname for the Asian American Community Action Research Project) began repairs and landscaping, in conjunction with the first formally organized Amache Pilgrimage to honor internees and their descendants. CARP was a "Yellow Power" organization composed of former concentration camp prisoners, community members, and students from the University of Colorado, according to the Amache Preservation Society. When CARP became too radical for community comfort, the Denver Central Optimist Club took over the care of the cemetery. A local high school teacher, John Hopper, and his students provided for trees and landscaping. In 1983, the Optimists erected a granite memorial inscribed with the names of thirty-one Amache internees who died in uniform while serving their country.

On a visit to the cemetery, I saw the coins that had been left at the base of the memorial and on some of the headstones. Both American and Japanese coins were left at the memorial, and on some nearby headstones. I happened to have in the Jeep a few hundred yen left over from a trip to Hiroshima nearly a year before, when I gave a lecture on the seventieth anniversary of the bombing. From the car I retrieved a handful of ten-yen pieces and left the coins on the stones. Each of the copper coins was worth, at current exchange rates, about an American cent.

Child of Calamity
Elevation: 7,652' (Hecla Junction)

But here, 800 miles from the frontiers of our country, in the most inclement season of the year—not one person clothed for winter—many without blankets, having been obliged to cut them up for socks, etc., and now lying down at night on the snow or wet ground, one side burning whilst the other was pierced with the cold wind—such was the situation of the party, while some were endeavoring to make a miserable substitute of raw buffalo hide for shoes, etc.

—Zebulon Pike's journal entry for December 25, 1806

At dusk on a gloomy Christmas Eve, with bruised and bloody fingers, I poured a generous shot of bourbon from a plastic Nalgene flask into a steaming cup of instant coffee and made a toast to John Sparks and Thomas Daugherty.

"To the sons of calamity," I said.

I asked Butch if he wanted a shot in his coffee, but he declined. He was already cold and all he wanted to do was to go back to his tent, wrap himself in his bag, and go to sleep. I asked him if he was feeling all right, and even though he said he was, I could tell he wasn't. I couldn't see his face because of the scarf wrapped around it, but I could see his eyes, and they were sunken and bloodshot. I asked if he wanted to go back and sleep in the back of the Jeep, but he shook his head. Then he had better eat something, I said, because that's one of the things the expert on winter survival told me was important: keep eating to stay warm. I gave him one of the half dozen eggs I'd boiled in a pot of water on the camp stove. He took off his gloves and picked away the shell, then lowered the scarf that had covered most of his face, and took a bite. He was wearing an allegedly Russian military surplus jacket and pants in a digital woodland camo pattern that he'd gotten somewhere at next to nothing, but they seemed to be doing little to turn the wind.

He asked me what time the moon would rise, and I said 4:29. It was already a few degrees above the horizon, but we couldn't see it yet because of the mountains to the east. It would set at 7:09 on Christmas morning, and I said I hoped the sky would clear enough for us to see it.

He nodded and whistled a bit.

Christmas Eve above Hecla Junction.

Then: "Tell me about the bones again."

John Sparks and Thomas Daugherty, I said, were members of the Zebulon Montgomery Pike Expedition, and they spent Christmas 1806 along the river, in miserable weather, not too far from where we were camped. They had been close to starvation, but by luck they had shot some bison on a nearby plain. They feasted on buffalo meat for Christmas Eve, and enjoyed a rare day of rest on the holiday. There was a full moon in 1806, just as there would be tonight. After leaving here and going south, the party became soaked crossing a stream, and Sparks and Daugherty soon found that their feet were too frostbitten to continue. They were left behind as the main party forged ahead, and when Pike sent scouts back to check on them, they were still too sick and could only hobble about. But they sent their commander a plea not to leave them to die in the wilderness and, to emphasize their point, they removed some of the bones from their dead toes and sent them to Pike.

Butch shivered.

"Eat some chocolate," I suggested.

No, he was going to sleep.

"Sleep in the Jeep," I said.

He shook his head, and began to whistle softly under his breath. Soon, he told me goodnight and trudged down to his tent. He hadn't used the tent in years, and when he tried to erect it, a couple of the fiberglass poles had snapped clean from the ferrules. I'd helped him tape up the broken poles with the emergency roll of duct tape from my pack, and the tent was upright but listing badly. He'd also hauled with him an antique propane camp heater that took two 14.1-ounce canisters ordinarily used for torches, and even though he'd bought new canisters, he couldn't get the heater to light. Everything he had reminded me of the stuff that my father had used in deer camp in November in the woods of southwest Missouri; it all smelled of waxed canvas and metal and oil, with a touch of mold thrown in.

Butch was having a rough time, owing primarily to equipment he hadn't touched in years that he'd dragged out of his Fibber McGee's closet of a garage. He'd also experienced what is euphemistically called a "cardiac event" the year before, and a couple of years before that he spent several hours unconscious on a roof after a tree limb fell on his head, and a year or so before that he had fallen backward from the seat of a tractor and hit his head on a concrete floor. After hitting his head, he'd started to whistle and talk to himself. The whistling consisted of little nonsense tunes, and he did it unconsciously, and he was embarrassed by it. He asked me to tell him when he was whistling without knowing it, and I did so as gently as I could.

Despite having these recent troubles, Butch was one of the toughest men I've ever known. As a young man, he spent much of the winter of 1962–1963 in a canvas pup tent along Bear Creek in Colorado, seeing few other people and subsisting mostly on venison and snowshoe rabbits. Ask him and he can still remember the dates: November 28 to January 15. Years later, he survived a motorcycle crash from which he wasn't expected to live, and it left him with a scar that looks like congealed bacon grease that snakes from one ankle up to his torso. I've never known him to be without a large-caliber handgun somewhere on, or near, his person. He's been a bail bondsman for the past thirty years, and I wouldn't want him after me for skipping bail.

But Butch was seventy-two, and I had tried to talk him out of returning to the mountains with me. I told him I was afraid that he'd have a heart attack, and that I'd be responsible for his death.

He'd laughed.

"We're all going to die," he said. "I'd rather die looking out over snow-capped peaks than staring at the tile on the ceiling of some hospital room."

After Butch retired, I sat on a blue plastic tarp in front of my nylon dome tent and sipped from the insulated mug. While it wasn't the best Irish coffee I'd ever had, at least it was hot, and provided a bit of cheer to an otherwise gray holiday. It was not a comfort that Pike would have allowed himself, because he was a confirmed teetotaler.

The river this winter is stark, with floes in the middle and ice layered like crepe against both banks, and six to eight inches of snow blanketing the red rock slopes. Above, the sky was a dishwater mix of clouds, and the sun was a white disc sinking in the west. It all was unnaturally quiet, in that muffled way of winter days. The only sound was the hissing of the white gas MSR stove as I heated more water, and the ticking of the aluminum pan as it heated. I would pour the warm water into a couple of quart-sized widemouthed Nalgene bottles, and then slip the bottles into insulated sleeves, to take into the tent with me for one of the longest nights of the year.

It had been unusually mild in Salida, with sunny days in the 30s, even though there was six inches of snow in town and a foot or more up in the mountains. The National Weather Service forecast low for Christmas Eve night was 24 degrees. I despise the cold, and hated it during those deer camps, and have long harbored an apparently futile ambition to live someplace tropical. On this trip to the mountains, I had already decided that if the forecast was 10 or below, I would scrub the plan to experience Christmas along the river and get a motel.

This was the off-season, and without the tourists Salida had reverted to a sleepy little mountain town. Many of the motels were closed for the season, and those that were open had about run out of rooms, because an avalanche had closed US 50 at Monarch Pass to the west, forcing motorists to find sudden lodging.

On December 23, we had stopped at the Arkansas Headwaters Recreation Area Visitor's Center in downtown Salida, and asked about places to camp along the river. I was told there were six fee-charging campgrounds in the recreation area, with 101 campsites. Day passes and a parking permit, amounting to around $24 per day, were required.

There was an additional no-fee campground, Salida East, with twenty spots, owned by the Bureau of Land Management. But, I was cautioned at the AHRA headquarters that Salida East was the only free campground available to the area's homeless, and the crime rate there was high. Summers in Salida are typically easy for the area's homeless, but winters can be understandably brutal. The AHRA had a pending proposal to lease Salida East from the BLM, in order to charge fees and increase law enforcement, but no decision had yet been made.

Salida East was too far south for my research purposes, so I didn't consider it; besides, I didn't want to take one of the free spots that might otherwise be used by a homeless individual. Hecla Junction, then, was the only access that might suit my purposes. It was a bit north of where I wanted to be, but it was about the closest to the spot I knew I wanted to be without trespassing on private land: the site where Zebulon Montgomery Pike and his men had spent Christmas 1806. I didn't tell the nice people at the visitor's center that I planned to park the Jeep at Hecla Junction campground and hike at will to someplace along the river where we wouldn't be constantly reminded of civilization. With luck, we wouldn't have to trespass.

As we left the visitor's center, we noticed a trio of transients huddled on the walking trail that passed by the center and led down to the river. They were all men, in frayed clothes, and their hair was wild. Two of them had school-type backpacks that had been worn slick. They joylessly passed a jug of whiskey from man to man.

Once we turned off Highway 285, the drive to the campground at Hecla Junction was four slow miles of snow-packed, low-geared four wheeling. Once we reached the self-pay station at the entrance, I dutifully stopped and filled out a permit, wrote a check for the requisite $24, and shoved it into the slot in the collection tube. I stuck the day use permit on the inside of the windshield. Then we drove on, through a deserted river access area and campground, to the loop on the far north side of the area. From a high spot, I could see the river below us, and the red rocks stretching into the canyon to the north, and at a suitable spot I parked the Jeep and killed the engine. A short distance to the north of the designated campsite, we pitched our tents. By noon, my campsite was complete. The

Walmart stuff I'd had earlier was replaced with a three-season REI Half Dome Plus tent, with my backpack and assorted other gear stored inside a vestibule; inside, a couple of sleeping bags, an inflatable air mattress, an insulated pad, and a clothes bag for a pillow; and a leveled cooking area outside with the white-fuel MSR stove with an all-purpose aluminum pot. The full list would include an additional couple of dozen essential items, such as toothpaste and toilet paper and a first-aid kit. Stowed into my red Deuter ACT 40 pack, with a couple of liters of water and food and extra winter clothes (including several pairs of wool socks), the rig weighed in at thirty and some-odd pounds. And that's not counting the snow pants and my three-layered jacket and the snow boots.

I'd had expert advice on what to pack from Alan Apt, who teaches winter survival at Colorado REI stores, is a member of the National Ski Patrol, and is the author of *Snowshoe Routes: Colorado's Front Range*. Apt told me that winter camping takes a special skill set, knowledge, and equipment. But, he said, survival could be boiled down to a few principles, which included not getting lost, eating to stay warm, and having a change of dry clothes and socks. He was also quite keen that I stay on top of the avalanche forecasts, and advised me to be prepared for unexpectedly sudden and dramatic weather changes. He wasn't thrilled that I only had a three-season tent, but said I'd be okay if there wasn't a heavy snow.

There wasn't much chance I'd get lost because I wasn't too far from civilization, and if I did, all I had to do was follow the river. Still, I had an old-fashioned Silva compass in my pack, several maps of the area, and a new-fashioned Garmin GPS receiver.

At eleven in the morning, it was 19 degrees, the sun was shining, and there was no wind. As I worked to set up camp, I became uncomfortably warm so I stripped off some layers, and worked in my fleece pullover and down vest. Afterward, when I stopped working, I had to put the jacket back on. With camp made, I decided to take a walk down to the river. As if on cue, a bald eagle came soaring up the river, headed north. It was low enough that I could see the individual feathers fanning out from the tips of its wings. I thought the bird might be hunting, but I never saw it dive or otherwise waver from its course upriver. Bald eagles typically winter across the continental United States, and return to Canada in the summers to breed. I wondered where this eagle called home, and how much territory it had seen in just one day.

I walked cautiously among the evergreens along the river bank, and gazed out across the cold water to the deserted railway line that serpentined along the base of the rocky spires opposite. I found a flat rock, brushed off the snow, and sat. Not bad weather for the last week of December, I thought. The coming night—from sundown at 4:47 to sunrise at 7:21—was one of the longest nights of the year, at 14 hours and 24 minutes, but the weather didn't seem so bad. The sky had clouded up a bit, and there was some wind now, but it was still quite pleasant. I saw no other animals during my reconnoiter, except for the eagle again, flying the same straight course, but downriver.

I took off my gloves and fished a notebook out of my inside jacket pocket to jot down some thoughts, and was surprised to find that the middle finger of my left hand was bleeding. My wedding ring was still on my finger, because fearing losing it in the snow when I removed my gloves, I had again Band-Aided it on. On my other hand, I had split a fingernail. It had taken some digging and scooping of snow to set the aluminum snow stakes while pitching the tent, and my bare hands had taken more of a beating than I thought. If my hands looked this rough after just a few hours here in winter, I could only imagine what Zebulon Pike and his men, lost and near starvation, had endured. I had made winter camp in the upper valley of the Arkansas, to be amid the snow and to feel the cold, and to gain a better understanding of the headwaters in winter—and to taste just a bit of what the Pike expedition had experienced firsthand.

With luck, I would avoid the lost and starving part.

When Zebulon Montgomery Pike and his men feasted on bison as their Christmas dinner more than two hundred years earlier, they may have thought the worst was behind them, but their troubles had just begun. Pike was an ambitious young army captain who, through a combination of bad luck and arrogance, had led them into the valley of the upper Arkansas in the jaws of winter. Simply put, they were lost. Pike had been charged with finding the source of the Red River (and secretly, perhaps, to spy on the Spanish), but inaccurate maps and bad judgment had brought them to a Donner Party near-catastrophe. The sixteen men in the expedition were not expected to winter in the mountains; they were outfitted only with cotton summer uniforms, and in the days leading up to the Christmas encampment, they were near starvation, risking frostbite, and low on ammunition. While the men's clothing had been reduced to rags, and they were spending the night in the open and cutting up their wool blankets for socks (actually an excellent idea), their twenty-eight-year-old commander was sleeping in a tent and hauling a trunk of his favorite books around with him. I could certainly understand the desire, if not the need, to haul a traveling library.

Pike was obsessed with improving his character and he devoured popular texts, according to biographer Jared Orsi, and one of the most influential books he read was *The Economy of Human Life*. Published in 1750 and probably written by the Englishman Lord Chesterfield, the curious book purported to be a translation of an ancient book of Eastern wisdom. "Its almost certainly fallacious introduction narrated a fantastic tale of a Chinese emperor who sent a scholar to recover documents archived in Tibetan monasteries," Orsi recounts. "One of these texts so enthralled a British traveler in China that he translated it into English and sent it to an unnamed nobleman, who passed it on to [Robert] Dodsley." Although it was published anonymously, it was thought during Pike's time to have been written by the aforementioned Dodsley. The book offered advice on self-discipline and sacrifice, family life, and happiness in general. It prescribed fortitude as a panacea, stressed the importance of honor, and said the only path to wealth was through introspection and long hours of hard work.

"Perils, and misfortunes, and want, and pain, and injury, are more or less the certain lot of every man that cometh into the world," the book advises in the chapter on fortitude. "It behoveth thee, therefore, thou child of calamity, early to fortify the mind with courage and patience, that thou mayest support, with becoming resolution, the allotted portion of human evil."

In another chapter, "Misery," is this instruction: "Thine entrance into the world, is it not shameful? Thy destruction, is it not glorious? Lo! Men adorn the instruments of death with gold and gems, and wear them above their garments. He who begetteth a man, hideth his face; but he who would killeth a thousand is honoured."

We don't know if Pike carried his copy of *The Economy of Human Life* with him to the upper Arkansas, but he certainly carried with him in practice the precepts he had learned in his faux biblical-sounding pages. Orsi believes the book provides a key to an important part of Pike's character, his loyalty to superiors who were obviously corrupt. It seems to me the book helps explain Pike's willingness to rush blindly into situations, with little regard for the safety of himself or the men under his command, in the pursuit of glory—and ultimately, death.

During the expedition, Pike would have ample opportunity to pursue both.

Orsi, an associate professor of history at Colorado State University at Fort Collins, seems admiring of Pike in the biography. His thesis is that Pike exemplified a kind of nationalism that was tested body and soul by the rigors of the American West, and that the highest honor was corporal sacrifice to the republic. Pike left behind him a voluminous journal of his expedition, which I have at hand, and between the literary conventions of the day and Pike's failure to command the English language, it's a tough read. Whatever his men were feeling during the expedition we can only guess, because they left no firsthand accounts.

The United States proper, in 1806, extended no farther west than the Mississippi River, but the Louisiana Purchase, acquired three years earlier from France, had provided room to grow, a great swath of western territory for expansion—much of it ruled by the Comanche nation, and unexplored by whites. The French had little idea of the boundaries of the land they had sold for $15 million dollars, and there were ongoing territorial disputes with Britain and Spain. The legal description for the purchase was for all lands that drained to the Mississippi River, including its tributaries, the Arkansas and the Red among them. The purchase's western limit was agreed to be the Continental Divide, but nobody involved in the deal knew much about it. There were a couple of prevailing theories, however, including one suggesting that continents were symmetrical, so the divide should be found in roughly the same terrain and elevations as the Appalachian range in the east. In reality, the highest peak in the Appalachians is less than half the height of any of the fifty-three tallest peaks in Colorado alone, all of which are above 14,000 feet. Another wrong-headed assumption came from a German mining engineer, Baron Alexander von Humboldt, who had never visited the American West but made a map anyway. Humboldt's map put the sources of both the Arkansas and the Red Rivers in the mountains of Colorado, and he shared his theory with Thomas Jefferson, who was eager to explore the new territory.

About the time Lewis and Clark were homeward bound from their expedition, Pike was given orders to ascend the Mississippi, find the headwaters if possible, find locations for forts, and make alliances with Indian tribes or, failing that, impress them with American might. Within days of returning to St. Louis from this first expedition into the Louisiana Purchase, he was given a second: he was to go west, spread American influence among the Comanches, and perhaps find the headwaters of the Arkansas River, and return by way of the Red River. Exploring the Red River was important, because Spain was disputing the boundaries of the purchase, and the Red River—to the American mind—constituted a good portion of its southwestern boundary. He was to scout an overland route to Santa Fe. And, among other things, he was asked to survey the natural resources of this newly acquired area, so that the growing country might exploit them.

Unlike Lewis and Clark, who received orders directly from Thomas Jefferson, Pike received his instructions from General James Wilkinson, who seems to have been a scoundrel and, possibly, a traitor. There's evidence that Wilkinson was a spy, and that he fed the Spanish information on the nature of the Lewis and Clark Expedition and other matters. Curiously, Pike was absolutely loyal to Wilkinson.

Pike set out again from St. Louis, and his first task was a complicated diplomatic trip. He was to escort some Native Americans back to a Pawnee village along the Republican River in south-central Nebraska, following their Jeffersonian tour of the United States. On the way, he probably crossed very close to Emporia, where I live, and somewhat west he encountered some "very ruff flint hills," a name that stuck; the rugged Flint Hills extend from near the Nebraska border into north-central Oklahoma. Pike left the Pawnee village in October and picked up the Arkansas River near Great Bend and followed it west. There was plenty of bison and other game to eat, the weather was mild, and in spite of having their baggage stolen by a Pawnee war party, the prairie traverse was uneventful. In mid-November, when the party got their first glimpse of the far blue Rockies, Pike—who was familiar only with smaller, eastern mountains—believed they would reach them in a day or two. But they were still more than a hundred miles away, a distance it would take more than a week to cross. The biggest peak seemed, to him, the Grand Peak—now called Pikes Peak, near Colorado Springs—and he futilely attempted to climb it without food, blankets, or spare socks (an aside: there is no apostrophe in Pikes Peak because, since 1890, it has been the policy of the United States to expunge them, in an effort to avoid the suggestion of private ownership of a public place). The mountains could not be more than 3,500 feet or so, he may have thought, because that was about the height of the peaks he was familiar with back east. He made it as far as Mount Rosa, a nearby but lower pinnacle, where they spent the night in a cave. But Pikes Peak—one of the fourteeners—must still have seemed as remote as when they began climbing. At the end of November, in heavy snow, they resumed their trek up the Arkansas, and into the range Pike called the "Mexican Mountains," which were claimed by Spain.

As the weather steadily grew worse, they trudged through the snow and over frozen ground, while magpies picked the flesh from the raw backs of the horses. One of the horses was driven out of its head with fear, and bolted for the prairie back to the east, never to be seen again. In the first week of December they camped near present-day Cañon City, where several streams ran between narrow canyon walls to join the Arkansas River. Here, Pike heard a report from a couple of his men that they had followed the Arkansas up a narrow canyon until it had disappeared. Believing they had found the headwaters of the Arkansas, he then chose to lead his men to the north in search of the Red River. This made little sense, because even the most casual familiarity with the geography of the region would have called for a turn to the south or southwest. In his journal, Pike confided that his decision was influenced by his desire to follow some Spanish soldiers he thought he had spied in the distance. At several earlier points, they had discovered the remains of what Pike believed had been Spanish encampments. So Pike drove north, eventually finding—and correctly identifying—the headwaters of the South Platte, which he followed as far as present-day Fairplay. There, on December 16, with his men hungry and shivering, he decided that perhaps he had not been following the Spanish at all, and he turned the group to the southwest, crossed the Mosquito Range, and emerged near what is now Johnson Village, below Buena Vista. At the bottom of a valley he found a river about twenty-five yards wide, and running swiftly over rocks—and mistook the Arkansas for the Red. With renewed ambition to find the headwaters, he took two riders and ascended the river as far north as Leadville, where the river was only a brook, and then returned. They were running out of food, as were the men back in camp, but luck came in the form of eight bison that were killed on Christmas Eve, four of them by hunter John Sparks. The recombined force made camp somewhere between Salida and Browns Canyon, on or adjacent to a meadow or plateau where they discovered the bison that saved them. There's a turnout up on Highway 285 that has a state marker and some other interpretive material about Pike and the Christmas of 1806, and many historians believe the camp was close to the turnout, near the mouth of Squaw Creek. But nobody really knows where the camp was; it might have been anywhere along the ten-mile stretch from Salida to Browns Canyon.

"We spent the day as agreeably as could be expected from men in our condition," he noted in his journal. "Caught a bird of a new species, having made a trap for him. The bird was of a green color, almost the size of a quail, had a small tuft on its head. . . . We kept him with us in a wicker cage, before leaving him with an interpreter on the Arkansaw." The bird probably was not a new species, but a Carolina parakeet, whose range extended to eastern Colorado and across the eastern United States. The only parrot native to the United States, regarded as a pest by farmers and prized by milliners for the feathers, they were hunted to extinction. The last Carolina parakeet died in captivity in 1918. It is unclear why Pike included the entry on the bird on Christmas Day, unless he was feeling morbidly retrospective: "We at one time took a companion of the same species and put them in the same cage, when the first resident never ceased attacking the stranger until he had killed him."

Now reprovisioned with meat, they were on the march again by the next day, and made more than seven miles downriver. But that night Private Thomas Daugherty, Pike's personal attendant, fell ill, as did another man. Pike allowed the men to sleep in his tent, while he spent the night outside. Still, they continued down the river, which became so narrow in some places, and the canyon walls so steep, that they were forced to sometimes wade the ice-choked river. The passage was hard on the men, and hard on the horses, which often fell on the ice. They made sleds to relieve the packhorses of their burdens, but the sleds broke. They tried to climb out of the river bed, but the cliffs proved too formidable, and once a horse stumbled and fell. Pike was forced to kill it. Two others went berserk and had to be abandoned. They were running low on food again, but refused to eat horseflesh. This decision has confused some historians, but I believe it may reflect a particular cultural taboo: the eating of horsemeat, in the Anglo mind, smacked of paganism or even cannibalism, because a horse was a companion. The United States was among the world's leading producers of horsemeat, but the majority of it was sold elsewhere; in 2006, federal funding for inspections of horse slaughter houses was cut off, and the export business shifted to Canada and Mexico.

Pike and his men had no choice but to press to the south, down the treacherous passage we now know as Royal Gorge. Pike bent the barrel of his rifle in a fall and found the weapon he considered his greatest asset would no longer shoot straight. The hardships that Pike and his men endured as they followed the frozen canyon downriver are almost beyond modern imagining. To Pike's regimented mind, the upper Arkansas in winter must have been a landscape right out of nightmare, rocks and water threatening ever-present death, the natural world turned to hell. They were poorly equipped and poorly informed, but Pike made their situation worse at nearly every opportunity by making decisions that appear inexplicable, unless he were operating on secret orders. Finally, they managed to climb out of the canyon, and to their dismay found themselves back at the spot where they had camped in the first week of December. They had made a circle, and found themselves back at the place they had mistaken for the headwaters of the Arkansas, but which obviously was not. While his men built a small stockade in which to weather the next few days, he went through his journal and crossed out the word "Red" in his earlier descriptions of the river and replaced it with "Arkansas."

Meanwhile, his mentor, General Wilkinson, was in hot water. He had been a key conspirator in Vice President Aaron Burr's apparent plan to establish an empire in the middle of the country. The plan had been developing since 1804—the same year Burr killed Alexander Hamilton in a duel—but by October 1806 Wilkinson, either from cold feet or in an attempt to save his own skin, ratted Burr out to Jefferson. Burr was tried in 1807, but acquitted because the key piece of evidence collapsed under examination. The evidence—indeed, the only evidence—was a coded letter that allegedly outlined Burr's plan to steal lands in the purchase, but the case collapsed when Wilkinson admitted it was in his own handwriting, saying he had lost the original. Wilkinson was somehow exonerated by a court martial after the Burr affair and went on to serve as a general officer in the War of 1812.

In the mountains of Colorado in 1806, however, Pike knew nothing about the letter that Wilkinson had handed over to Jefferson. Instead of political survival, Pike was confronted by actual life-or-death decisions. He and his men could either attempt to spend the winter there, at the blockhouse at Cañon City, and hope they could shoot enough game for subsistence, or they could again push on. Pike chose the latter, and on January 14 they hefted their seventy-pound packs and set out for the massive mountain range to the south and west, the Sangre de Cristos. He did not know it, but he had chosen a range dotted with many of those 14,000-foot peaks.

Three days later, calamity struck.

Crossing the appropriately named Wet Mountain Valley and approaching the Sangre de Cristos, Pike spotted some trees and a stream at the base of the mountains. There was only an hour of daylight remaining, but Pike believed the trees were not so far away, and they set out across the valley. Again, he had underestimated distances, and the expedition found itself struggling for hours in the dark. The temperature dropped dramatically during the crossing, and in the middle of the valley they sloshed across Grape Creek, soaking their boots. "Here we all got our feet wet," Pike notes in his journal. By the time they made camp, they had marched twenty-eight miles, and the temperature had dropped to 10 degrees below zero.

Orsi, the biographer, describes what came next: "Frostbite first grips the extremities of the circulatory system—fingers, noses, and toes—sometimes within as little as thirty minutes. After fording Grape Creek and hiking for several more miles, the men would have first felt stinging and burning. Then they would have begun to lose sensation in their extremities. By the time they reached camp, they probably were hobbling on feet they could no longer feel."

Pike, Orsi notes, wrote far less frequently in his journal about his men's health than did Meriwether Lewis, so he may not have had the medical knowledge to deal with emergencies. Lewis had treated frostbite in 1805 by placing the men's feet in cold water, which presaged modern treatment. Pike—and his expedition's doctor, John Robinson—probably pursued, or at least allowed, the worst practice in dealing with frostbite. The fourteen men likely clawed off their boots and shoes and shoved their feet toward the warmth of the newly kindled fires. Their feet thawed, but then swelled and blistered. Unable to get their footwear back on over their hard and grotesquely swollen feet, they probably froze them again, in a cycle that would do the maximum damage to the fragile flesh.

By morning, nine of the men were unable to walk.

In addition to the frostbite, the men were also facing starvation and probably dealing with hypothermia. Following the Christmas Day feast, their routine had consisted of gorging and fasting, resulting in an inability to replenish muscle and fat. Before the Grape Creek disaster, they had not eaten for three days. They would have had trouble concentrating, their memories would have been impaired, and they were probably prone to bouts of apathy and violent anger. As their core body temperatures fell, hypothermia would have worsened these symptoms. Pike and the doctor went out to hunt, but succeeded only in wounding several bison they were unable to track. It was at this point that Pike apparently decided to die there, rather than return to camp and face the anguish of his ill and starving men. "We were . . . determined to remain absent and die by ourselves rather than return to camp and behold the misery of our poor lads," he wrote.

But then, another group of bison presented itself.

"With great exertions I made out to run and place myself behind some cedars," Pike noted, in his characteristically tortured style. "By the greatest of good luck, my first shot stopped one, in which we killed in three more shots; and by the dusk had cut each of us a heavy load."

Once more, the expedition was saved by the prevalence of bison.

After three days of rest, seven of the nine men who had been made lame by frostbite were able to continue, some on crutches. But Daugherty and Sparks still could not walk, and Pike made the decision to leave them behind at the Grapevine Creek camp. While it may have been more prudent to return to the blockhouse on the Arkansas River, Pike decided to cross the Sangre de Cristo Mountains as intended.

By February, he had reached the San Luis Valley, in what is now Great Sand Dunes National Park. There he found a river, which he mistook for the Red, and ordered his men to fell cottonwood trees and build a blockhouse. When it was finished, he raised the American flag. He also sent a rescue party back to check on Sparks and Daugherty across the mountains near Grapevine Creek, who were found alive, but still unable to travel. They had lost—or had amputated themselves—some of their gangrenous toes, which they sent back to Pike with the plea not to abandon them.

Before Pike could decide what to do about the stranded, his stockade was visited by a force of a hundred Spanish soldiers. They must have been amused at the ragged condition of the American soldiers—and their ignorance. Their commander told him that he was not camped on the Red River, but the Rio Conejos—the River of Rabbits—a tributary of the Rio Grande, in what is now extreme southern Colorado. Pike and his men were arrested as spies, and taken to nearby Santa Fe. What followed was a burlesque of intrigue.

The Americans were treated more as guests than prisoners, and Spanish officials welcomed Pike as an equal, perhaps to win his confidence. The contrast with their suffering on the upper Arkansas could not have been more sharply drawn, as the Spanish fed and clothed them and granted them every freedom except to leave. Pike was treated to rounds of banquets, refined discussions, and $21 for travel expenses—a debt the US government was expected to repay.

The Americans were marched south to the capital of Chihuahua, more than 500 miles from the cottonwood stockade on the Rio Conejos. Along the way, at a stop in Albuquerque, Pike met an old priest who took him into his home and offered him the companionship of young women the cleric called his "adopted children," many of whom he had bought from slavery, apparently from the Comanches, as children. A pair of white women, perhaps American although they had no recollection of their past lives or nationality, were bid to sit and treat him with affection, but Pike doesn't make it clear if sex was being offered or only patriotic companionship. Then the priest took the young officer into a room with black silk curtains, where the old man donned a black gown and miter, and showed him images of various saints and Jesus crucified. He attempted to pull him down by the hand to pray, but Pike rebuffed the invitation, reacting with what seems to have been indignation. All the while, Pike was making notes about the sizes of the cities and villages they encountered, and a wealth of other intelligence.

At Santa Fe, he met the governor and the two conversed in French.

"You come to reconnoiter our country, do you?" his excellency asked.

"I marched to reconnoiter our own," Pike replied.

"In what character are you?" the governor asked.

"In my proper character, an officer of the United States army."

The contents of Pike's locked trunk proved an endless fascination for the Spanish, and there was much business about the key Pike held to it, and once it was opened, about the contents, including the journal. For reasons that remain unclear, the Spanish kept Pike in a sort of diplomatic limbo, never charging him as a spy but not quite trusting him, either. During this time Pike was entirely dependent on the benevolence of his captors, who must have been puzzled by his wild appearance and rough ways. But Pike regarded himself as superior, and considered the Spanish to be morally and politically corrupt—or at least that's the way he played it in his journal. After months of captivity, the velvet confinement ended with banquets and toasts to goodwill between New Spain and the United States, and Pike and most of his men were returned to American territory in July 1807.

As a gift to President Jefferson, Pike sent ahead two grizzly bear cubs he had purchased in New Mexico during the return trip. Pike noted in a letter that they were of a species considered "the most ferocious animals on the continent." Jefferson kept the growing bears in cages and then for a time penned on the lawn at the White House. But, the president confided in a letter, "These are too dangerous and troublesome for me to keep." He gave them to a Philadelphia museum owner who, after exhibiting them for a time, was forced to shoot one of them after it broke free and terrorized his family. The other was shot as well, and both were stuffed and mounted for display.

~ ~ ~

By sundown on my Christmas Eve, the weather had worsened. After finishing the Irish coffee, I crawled into my tent, like a bear into his cave, and made ready for the night.

By flashlight, I unlaced my boots and left them just outside the tent door, beneath the nylon vestibule, then zippered the tent door tight. I stuffed the down sleeping bag inside the synthetic one, made sure whatever I needed during the night was close at hand—water, snacks, iPhone—and plumped a stow bag of clothes as a pillow. I stripped down to my socks and insulated underwear but kept my watch cap, and twisted my way down inside the bags. I looked at my watch.

It was 6:30.

Six hundred miles and a time zone earlier in Kansas, I imagined Kim sitting down to a lonely Christmas Eve dinner. *An aside:* Kim later corrected this impression. Not only did it portray her as pathetic, she said, but it was also inaccurate. For the record, on December 24 she was busy assembling bookcases and forgot to eat any dinner, lonely or otherwise.

My children, all grown now, were probably getting ready to open presents at their mother's house in southeastern Kansas. I had no idea what my brother, who retired to northwestern Arkansas, was doing.

I must have napped, because I awoke an hour later to the sound of snow, or perhaps ice crystals, falling on the tent. It was a whispering sound, like a drummer drawing a whisk on a snare, and it was underscored by the gentle rhythm of the wind rippling the nylon. Except for the glow of the luminous hands of my watch, it was eerily dark inside the tent, a dark as substantial as that of a cave. I fumbled for the headlamp, knocking my carefully arranged things around like bowling pins. After I found the light, I sat up and drank some water from one of the Nalgene bottles, had a square of chocolate, and took a bite or two of a Clif bar. I tapped my phone to bring up the screen, and saw that it still had an 87 percent charge. I'd had a cell signal earlier in the day, when I walked down along the river, but I had none now. I darkened the screen and put my head back down.

It seemed colder now, but I assumed it was because I had been still for so long. I should be fine, I told myself. I was in a down bag, and that was inside a synthetic bag. The ratings on the bags were 20 degrees. Still, my face and hands were cold. I tried zipping the bags up, but I hated the feeling of my head and shoulders being confined. So I snapped the headlight on again and rummaged through my things until I found the sleeve of my heavy coat, and pulled it to me. I draped it over me like a cape, so that my hands and most of my face were covered, but with a space to breathe through.

Then I slept.

I dreamed of my children when they were small, and the Christmases we had, and then my dreams turned to my own childhood, and what a rotten kid I had always been during holidays. I dreamed of my father, coming home from work at Sears and Roebuck on Christmas Eve with his arms laden with presents. There was one record I listened to over and over on our Silvertone console stereo, "The Little Drummer Boy." I had been a lonely kid, even surrounded by people, and I grew to be a lonely adult, and distant from my family. I had even separated myself from my own wife—Kim, of the fictional lonely Christmas Eve dinner—in a sort of strange working exile, camping along the river in the mountains in the dead of winter, although I despised the cold.

Nobody is that committed to their work, I realized.

What drove me to put time and territory between myself and the people I loved? I didn't know, and yet I did it every time. There hasn't been a holiday during my adult life without some sort of professional deadline lurking in the background, and when there wasn't a work deadline I created a relationship crisis to obtain the relief of requisite distance. It was selfish, but not in the sense that I was profiting, materially or emotionally; instead, I was like some kind of addict who had to scramble just to approach normal, and received no joy from the vehicle of addiction, only release.

The people who might have been able to offer the best insight, my mother and father, are long dead. My mother died young and has been gone for thirty years, and my father since 1998. My father died suddenly, after suffering a brain aneurism, but while he was still conscious he asked a neighbor to call me. There had never been much distance between us, at least not for long. But my mother, who went into the hospital on Thanksgiving and died a week before Christmas—that was a different story. I had been punishing myself and everyone else over it for years.

When I opened my eyes, the interior of the tent was clearly visible, illuminated from some source outside. I could see the crossed poles and pockets of snow on the roof. *Who would be shining a light toward me, I* wondered with some alarm. I threw off the coat and crawled out of the bags and went to the door, which I unzipped, and peered through the screen. It had stopped snowing, although it was still overcast, but the full moon was high in the sky, and bright enough that even through the clouds it gave enough light to walk around by. I could see the snow-limned hills and the evergreens and my own half-covered tracks in the snow. There was no wind now, and there was no sound, not even the burble of the river.

There was no hint of the two centuries that had passed.

Pike and his men had seen something very similar, if not identical, beneath the winter moon. Had they dreamed of home and woken to private grief? Or were they too tired and footsore even to dream, much less reflect? Pike had taken the time to note their hardships in his journal but, as was expected of an officer, gave no indication of private thoughts. Was he homesick? Did he miss his wife? Had he been embarrassed by any of his mistakes? Did he yet see Spaniards on the foggy horizon?

I was shaken from my reverie by a cry that pierced the night. It went from a kind of low growl and rose swiftly in pitch to an unearthly screech with a nerve-rattling quaver. It sounded like something a sound effects artist might create, given the assignment to make a banshee or the last shrieks of a woman being murdered. The sound wasn't close, perhaps somewhere on the opposite bank of the river, but it gave me gooseflesh. It wasn't a human being, I knew, but was some kind of animal, perhaps a loon or an owl. Loons have an eerie, mournful call that can sometimes sound like a woman's voice, and some kinds of owls have calls that sound like raw-throated screaming. This wasn't exactly either of those, and it was more intense. I suddenly found myself reaching for my pack, where I keep a Buck knife with a three-and-one-half-inch drop-point blade sheathed in a side pocket. Not as deadly as Butch's 9 mm Smith & Wesson, but it was the only thing at hand.

Then I stopped, knowing I was just spooked. Whatever was making the sound probably wasn't a threat, and even if it was—well, what was I going to do with a knife that had a blade shorter than my index finger?

Encountering something in the wild you can't identify is an unnerving experience, and it first happened to me when I was around ten years old, in a small boat with my father and brother on a river at dawn, in late summer, approaching a trotline we had set the night before. There was something splashing on the surface above the line, caught on one of the hooks, perhaps, flopping and flashing white, seemingly larger than any flathead or blue we had ever caught. There was a heavy fog on the river that morning, which obscured vision and muffled sound, and I remember being somewhat afraid until I saw the alarm in my father's face. Then I was frozen with fear, unable even to speak. The thing on the line suddenly took on supernatural significance for me, some horror that men were not supposed to see. My father and my brother, who must have been twenty or so at the time, exchanged a few low words about how odd it was, and then my father shook off whatever he was feeling and said it had to be something natural. As the bow of the jon boat glided through the fog toward the trotline, the fog suddenly parted and we saw what was making the sound: a green branch that had floated down, had been snagged by the line, and was now animated by the current. The water would tug it downstream until there was no more slack in the line, and then the branch would snap back, its leaves shaking and throwing water like some kind of animal trying to escape.

Whatever was in the night along the snow-covered river in Colorado was equally natural, even if I couldn't identify it. There are only two types of animal predators that are threats to humans in the Colorado Rockies: bears and mountain lions. Attacks from both are uncommon, and fatalities are rare. During Pike's sojourn, grizzlies were abundant in Colorado, but this fiercest of continental American bears has been driven out of the state, along with the wolf, largely by a campaign of extermination by ranchers in the late nineteenth and early twentieth centuries. There are probably only about 1,500 grizzlies left anywhere, experts say. Weighing as much as 900 pounds, and an apex predator at the top of the natural food chain, its scientific name is *Ursus horribilis*— terrifying bear—and it was revered by the mountain men as "Old Ephraim." The last confirmed grizzly sighting in Colorado was in 1979, when Ed Wiseman, a bow-hunting guide in search of elk, encountered a 400-pound female near the Continental Divide in the San Juans. The grizzly knocked the bow from his hands and seriously mauled him, but Wiseman managed to grab one of the fallen arrows and kill the bear by stabbing it with a razor-sharp broadhead.

Black bears are common in Colorado; although I never saw one, at least not outside a park, I found plenty of tracks and scat along the river and in the mountains. They are mostly considered a nuisance instead of a threat, as many have become habituated to unnatural sources of food found in trash bins or at campsites. Campers are advised to keep their food in a bear sack, which is hoisted into a tree away from their shelter, or in an impregnable bear keg. The typical male black bear weighs 275 pounds, can smell food from five miles away, and is smart and incredibly strong. Black bears are not as aggressive as their brown cousins, but they can be dangerous and occasionally kill. In 1993, twenty-four-year-old logger Colin McClelland was killed by a black bear that dragged him from his camping trailer on Waugh Mountain, north of the river town of Cotopaxi.

Mountain lion attacks are even rarer than bear attacks, and the total number of humans killed by cougars in the last century is likely no more than a dozen. In Colorado in the past decade, hungry cats displaced by land development or climate shifts have been encroaching on the suburbs, where they sometimes snack on household pets. In the 1990s, mountain lions killed two people in Colorado, an eighteen-year-old high school student on a jogging trail in Idaho Springs, and a ten-year-old boy at Rocky Mountain National Park. In June 2016, an Aspen-area mother rescued her five-year-old son, whose head was in the mouth of a cougar, by prizing open its jaws with her hands.

The Colorado Division of Wildlife offers the following advice for avoiding trouble in lion and bear country, according to a couple of brochures I just about memorized: don't hike or jog alone, make plenty of noise, and if you are threatened by a mountain lion, make yourself look bigger by waving your arms, maintain eye contact, and don't turn your back. For bears, the best advice is to keep your campsite clean and avoid bringing food or other attractants into your tent. If you see a bear on the trail, stay quiet, don't run or climb a tree, give it space for an escape route, and use bear spray if you have it. If you're attacked, by either a bear or a mountain lion, be prepared to fight back with whatever is available.

While wild animal attacks are the stuff of our ancestral nightmares, they are so rare now that you are at greater risk of being fatally struck by lightning in Colorado than being killed by a wild and hungry creature. From 2004 to 2015, the state ranked third in lightning deaths, according to the National Weather Service, averaging two deaths per year (Florida leads in lightning death, with about ten killed annually). More common outdoor deaths are caused by drowning, falling, and assorted misadventures.

But death by wild animal—bears, especially—is firmly rooted in our collective subconscious and woven into a tangled tale of misbelief. The closest of domestic animals, the dog, poses a far greater threat, with about 1 in 70 Americans bitten each year, according to the Centers for Disease Control; of those mauled by dogs each year, twenty to thirty will die. But a dog, perhaps because of its familiarity, does not invoke the terror that a bear does.

In popular culture, the story of mountain man Hugh Glass continues to resonate. Glass was mauled by a grizzly bear in 1823 in present-day South Dakota and left for dead by his companions, who took his Hawken rifle. He lived, however, and crawled the 200 miles to Fort Kiowa on the Missouri River. The tale has inspired writers and filmmakers, who keep reimagining it every generation or so. As part of his research for *Lord Grizzly* (1954), novelist Fred Manfred walked and sometimes crawled some seventy miles across the Dakotas to know what it felt like, and occasionally ate bugs. Richard Harris did the crawling when he starred in 1971's *Man in the Wilderness*. The story was told again, with a new revenge twist, in *The Revenant*, released in 2015 and directed by Alejandro G. Iñárritu. Glass is played by Leonardo DiCaprio, and there's a fictional half-Pawnee son called Hawk who is murdered. The film is notable for its vistas, attention to authenticity, use of natural light, the hardships endured by the cast and crew—and, of course, the two-minute bear attack sequence, which was made using a combination of live action and CGI.

But the most horrifying bear attack on film is one that is unseen, when director Werner Herzog listens to the death of Timothy Treadwell in the 2005 documentary *Grizzly Man*. Treadwell, an oddball who wanted to become as close as possible to the bears, was killed and partially eaten by one in Alaska, while the audio of the attack was being recorded by a fallen video camera. It is Herzog's reaction as he listens to the attack that is so disturbing.

Although I don't know for certain what the scream was on Christmas Eve night, a colleague later played recordings of mountain lion vocalizations that seemed very similar. But I can't say for sure it *was* a big cat. A bird is still a possibility, but that seems less likely now.

Whatever the source, the cries lasted only a few minutes. They had been animated by my imagination into something threatening, and after they stopped my mind remained on alert. Gradually, I relaxed.

I sat cross-legged at the door of the tent and stared into the darkness for a good long while. I pulled my coat over my shoulders and bunched some clothes under me, because the floor of the tent, beyond the edges of the foam sleeping pad, was cold. Finally, shivering, I zipped up the door, crawled back in my bags, and went again to sleep.

There came another cycle of dreams, and this round recalled other times in my life when I was cold: November deer hunts with my father, wading through dark water duck hunting with my brother, diving on a New Year's Day at a Midwestern quarry in a wetsuit that was much too thin, camping on an island in Spring River during a cold snap in March when I was thirteen, wading into a stream on my walk home from Washington Elementary School one October and changing out of my clothes at my grandmother's house and being towel-dried by her and being embarrassed by my erection.

Then things got weird.

In my dream, the cold was an animal in the tent with me, circling the sleeping bag, probing to find a weakness. The cold nipped at my face and hands with fox teeth, and I squirmed to avoid them. Now awake, I saw that I had knocked the coat to the floor in my sleep, and had come halfway out of the bags. This time I did burrow down into the bags, readjusted the coat, and zipped the inner bag up over my head and shoulders. In a moment I was back in the dream, and the cold was now water that came rushing into the tent, swirling around me and soaking the sleeping bags, and I couldn't extricate myself. The torrent of ice-cold water kept coming, and still I couldn't free myself from my bedding.

I woke gasping for breath. My hands and face were stung by cold.

My wristwatch said it was 2 a.m. exactly. Suddenly awake, I compulsively reached for my iPhone to see if there was a signal. The screen flickered weakly, then went dark. I cursed, then searched for the headlamp. When I found it, I pressed the switch, but it too was dead. It was the same with the AA battery mini-flashlight I carry in the side pocket of my pack.

It was a bad sign that my phone and lights had failed, because it meant the night was colder than had been predicted. I had a thermometer clipped to a zipper on my pack, but without a light I couldn't read it, so

I had to guess how cold it was. In the past, I'd had cameras and phones suddenly fail at around 15 or 20 degrees, so I guessed it must have been about that cold. I had been chilly, but not shivering. Things felt a little damp to the touch inside the tent, and I knew that was because of the moisture in my breath. At least I'd known enough not to breathe inside my down bag—thanks, Alan Apt—because that would have been miserable. Also, the temperature ratings for sleeping bags are calculated not for comfort, but for the lowest temperature at which it will probably protect the average individual from hypothermia.

Outside, it was snowing heavily, and there wasn't much light coming from the moon now. The snow had piled up on the tent so that the roof was depressed, and I shook a tent pole to dislodge some of it. Enough of it slid down the sides that I figured I didn't have to actually go outside and brush it away. But, if it continued to snow heavily, I would have to pull on my boots, go outside, and start brushing. It was another five hours and twenty minutes until dawn, and I would just have to stick it out. I ate some more chocolate and tried to drink some water, but discovered that the water in both of the Nalgene bottles had frozen, despite being in insulated sleeves.

When it stopped snowing, I tried to get some sleep, but without luck. You can only sleep so long during a fourteen-hour night, and I'd reached my limit. Without light, there wasn't much to do except stare into the darkness and think. There was an emergency candle in my pack, but I didn't want to have an open flame in the tent. It was too early to go outside and fire up the stove and make breakfast. So I burrowed as deeply into my bags as I could, breathed through my coat, and decided to spend the time coming up with a plan to make holidays more bearable for myself and those I love. The answer I came to, there in the darkness in the highest valley of the Arkansas, was what I had known I should do all along, but kept from thinking about by burying it inside me: *I'd tell people what they meant to me. I wouldn't allow myself to rationalize the distance I put between myself and others by saying it was work—which in my case means writing on deadline—or some other unavoidable obligation. And, I would not spend another Christmas alone by choice. I would make peace with the holidays, attempt to repair my relationship with my children, forgive those (living and dead) for whom I harbored anger, and ask those whom I had hurt intentionally or otherwise to forgive me.*

It was eight o'clock before it was light enough to see inside the tent, and I was surprised to see the interior was caked with frost from my respiration. It was like waking up in a freezer. I dressed slowly, because my body ached from spending such a long night in a space where I couldn't stand up. My snow boots had turned into concrete, or at least they felt that way, and it took some time to soften them up enough that I could jam my feet into them. When I finished dressing I went to the MSR stove and removed the pot, which I had turned upside down to protect it from the weather, and pumped up the fuel reservoir. I had to take off my gloves in order to run the fuel valve, light a match, and adjust things until it started generating on its own, and the cold stung my fingers. Without water to pour into the pot, I walked out behind the tent and scooped up several pans of clean snow, and melted that to make coffee. Once I had some coffee, I went down to check on Butch. I woke him up and, after a long time spent dressing, and much coughing and hacking, he finally crawled out of his tent and took the coffee I gave him.

"How'd you sleep?"

He mumbled something noncommittal.

I asked him if he'd been cold.

"No," he lied. "You?"

"Not much," I allowed.

Sitting with a steaming cup of coffee, with the snow coming down heavily, and with camp left yet to break, I paused long enough to take a notebook from the breast pocket of my coat and jot down the following:

The truth hides in lonely places.

Later, after throwing the gear in the back of the Jeep, but before turning the key in the ignition, I had an anxious thought: what if the car battery is dead, too? But the Jeep started on the first try, and the glowing green digits in the dashboard displayed the temperature.

It was 6 degrees.

This felt brutal to a flatlander like me, and while it was much lower than predicted, it was close to an average December low temperature for Salida, which is 10 degrees Fahrenheit. Compared to the state's record historic low, it was downright balmy. The low of 61 degrees below zero was recorded at tiny Maybell, in northwest Colorado. It was so cold there wasn't enough natural gas pressure to heat the schools. Only Alaska, Montana, Utah, and Wyoming have recorded colder temperatures. The lowest temperature ever recorded in Kansas was –40 at Lebanon, in the north-central part of the state. That was in 1905.

After breaking new snow on the road out of Hecla Junction and regaining the highway, we passed the roadside marker to Pike and the expedition. It's on 285, and there's a wayside turnout with some covered picnic tables and a good view to the west of the divide skipping from peak to peak. A weather-beaten wooden marker erected by the state historical society commemorates Pike's 1806 ordeal. The marker concludes:

ON CHRISTMAS EVE TWO HUNTING PARTIES SHOT EIGHT BUFFALO
AND CHRISTMAS DAY WAS SPENT NEAR THE MOUTH OF SQUAW
CREEK (ONE-HALF MILE TO THE SOUTH) FEASTING ON BUFFALO
AND REPAIRING EQUIPMENT. EARLY IN 1807 PIKE CROSSED INTO
THE SAN LUIS VALLEY AT THE GREAT SAND DUNES AND BUILT A LOG
STOCKADE (RECONSTRUCTED AS A STATE HISTORICAL MONUMENT)
ON THE CONEJOS RIVER NEAR PRESENT LA JARA, WHERE HE WAS
TAKEN PRISONER BY THE SPANISH.

The marker does not mention Daugherty or Sparks.

By the War of 1812, Zebulon Montgomery Pike had been promoted to brigadier general. He died the hero's death he claimed to have longed for on April 27, 1813; in preparing to take the principal defenses of a British fort near Ontario, he sat on a stump and interrogated a British prisoner. Pike did not know that even while the Union Jack still flew over the fort, the redcoat commander had abandoned it—and fired the powder magazine. When it blew, it killed about forty Americans and an equal number of British, including the prisoner being questioned. Pike's back and ribs were smashed by stones, but the ultimately fatal blow probably came from a projectile that struck his forehead. He lived long enough to be informed that his men had taken the fort, and was rowed out to an American ship, where he died. His body was embalmed for the voyage home in a casket of rum, which, as biographer Orsi notes, was consumed by "a few thirsty soldiers" before burial.

Pike was thirty-four.

Thomas Daugherty and John Sparks, the pair who had sent Pike their frostbitten and disarticulated toes, never did catch up with their commander. They did recover enough to travel, and after being retrieved by a detail on horseback, were taken to New Spain, where they and four others from Pike's expedition were held separately from the rest of the company, and not released until 1809.

Their rhetoric and their speech have revealed a hatred for Muslims, Somalis, and immigrants. They chose the target location based on their hatred of these groups, their perception that the people represent a threat to American society, a desire to inspire other militia groups, and a desire to "wake people up."

—Affidavit filed in relation to the alleged plot by three white supremacists to bomb a Somali apartment building in Garden City

At the African Shop at 911 W. Mary in Garden City, Kansas, the most common phrase is *Assalamu alaikum,* a common greeting among Muslims. It means "Peace be with you." I hear it spoken softly in the background as customers pass through the doors, while I sit drinking a cup of black Kenyan tea with sugar. The shop is one of the mainstays of the 600-member Somali community here, along with the apartment complex just down the street, where one of the rooms has been repurposed as a mosque. At the shop, the shelves are filled with brightly colored Somali clothing and ethnic ingredients like Ethiopian chili powder that are scarce elsewhere in Garden City. The local planning and zoning commission regards the shop as a convenience store, but to me the shop seems more like an old-fashioned general store, where one gets the staples: food, clothing, a little gossip, and a sense of community.

The shop was among the targets considered in a bomb plot by three men, militia members, who considered it their patriotic duty to rid the community of the Somalis, according to an affidavit filed in the case. They finally settled on using fertilizer bombs to destroy the apartment complex on November 9, the day after the presidential election. The plan was thwarted in mid-October by the FBI and other agencies, relying on a confidential informant in the group.

When I came to the African Shop that morning, one of the owners, Adam Keynan, greeted me warmly and in competent English, but asked to call someone to translate. I apologized for my lack of Somali or Arabic—and for the intentions of the three men who were my race and about my age. The co-owner of the shop, a confident Somali woman named Halima Farrah, insisted that I have a cup of tea while I wait. When

The African Shop at Garden City.

she asked if I wanted sugar or cream, I said no, black would be fine. I would want the sugar, she said.

The customers at the African Shop are refugees and mostly employees of Tyson, the local meat-packing plant—as is the young man who appeared within a few minutes to translate. His name is Mursal Nameye, and his job at Tyson is training new employees in the demanding, and often hazardous, knife-wielding job of processing beef. Many of the Somali refugees speak little to no English, and twenty-seven-year-old Mursal shows them how to do the job safely. Since the bomb plot, because of his excellent English and with the trust of his people, he's also become a spokesman for the Somali community.

"I used to see bombing, killing people," Nameye says when asked about his life in Somalia, which he left seven years ago before seeking refuge in the United States. "Vicious acts all of the time. But here in America, I haven't seen it before. Never thought things like that would happen here. But when I hear about [the plot], I remember what it was like back in my old country. That is the reason I left. Now people want to bomb and kill us here?"

For most Americans, any concept they have of Somalia likely comes from two things: *Black Hawk Down*, the Ridley Scott film based on the Mark Bowden book about the rescue of the crew of a downed American helicopter during the Battle of Mogadishu in 1993, and *Captain Phillips*, the 2013 movie in which Tom Hanks portrays the real-life captain of a container ship kidnapped by Somali pirates.

The story of Somalia's quick slide into anarchy and its long road back to marginal statehood is a complex one, but the abbreviated version is this: Somalia, a country of 6 million on the Horn of Africa, and known as "the nation of poets" for its literary heritage, had been ruled since 1969 by Dictator Mohamed Siad Barre. It was the last year for democratic elections in Somalia. Siad Barre came to power through a military coup, ruled through a cult of personality, and imposed a doctrine that blended the Quran with Marxism. Clan membership is vital to Somali culture and politics, and there are more than a dozen competing clans; the dictator exploited clan rivalries to consolidate power and distract opponents. He was forced to flee in 1991, when opposition clans seized the capital of Mogadishu. The government of Somalia collapsed as the nation plunged into civil war. In 1992, the United States led—and chiefly manned—a United Nations–sanctioned effort to provide humanitarian relief. Several UN programs followed, but peacekeeping efforts were clearly doomed and American troops withdrew in the year following the Battle of Mogadishu. The last peacekeepers left Somalia to its fate in 1995.

Somalia was declared a failed state by the UN.

Without a government, and with much of the country ruled by warlords, Somalia slid into bloody anarchy, creating a global refugee crisis. The conditions also gave rise to a culture of modern piracy along the Gulf of Aden, a vital passage to the Suez Canal. In Mogadishu, business could only be conducted by paying tribute at various checkpoints controlled by militias aligned with various clans. In spite of the lack of government, and the difficulty of conducting business in a war zone, telecommunications startups grew rapidly, because phones were a lifeline to the outside world. Somalia soon had the best and cheapest cell service in Africa.

Nameye, the young translator at the African Shop in Garden City, told me that his father had been in telecommunications. But on his way to work one day, Nameye said, his father was dragged out of his car and shot by one of the country's many militia factions, apparently without provocation or reason. Nameye was a student studying medicine in Egypt, where he learned English, but he was forced to give up his studies and help his family. His uncle was also attacked on his way to work but

survived, and together they joined the Somali diaspora. They settled
in Minneapolis, which has the largest Somali population in the United
States. His uncle still lives in Minneapolis, but soon Nameye was on the
move, looking for a job that would pay enough to send money back to
family members still in Somalia. He worked for a time at a meat-packing
plant in Dodge City, and then came to Garden City. The work was hard,
but it paid better than anything else he could find.

Today, Somalia is no longer described as a failed state, but as a "fragile
recovering country" that has a weak government and is rife with security
concerns. A return to democratic, one-person, one-vote elections was
promised for 2016, but the promise was broken; instead, a complex
system was adopted in which clan elders select delegates to an electoral
college. All told, less than .02 percent of Somalis have a voice in choosing
members of parliament, or their president.

An Islamist militant group, al-Shabab ("the youngsters" in Arabic),
which is allied with al-Qaeda, is battling the UN-backed government. Al-
Shabab controls most of the rural areas in southern Somalia, surrounding
Mogadishu, and often launches attacks into neighboring Kenya. In
April 2015, 147 people were killed during an assault on a university in
northeastern Kenya.

In terms of refugees' country of origin, Somalia currently ranks third
globally, behind Afghanistan and Syria. These three countries account for
half of the world's 21 million refugees, according to the United Nations,
and most of the displaced are sheltered by host countries nearby. Turkey
shelters more refugees than any other nation in the world, owing to the
millions pouring across the Syrian border. In 2016, the United States
admitted 84,995 refugees, according to the State Department, and those
refugees included nearly equal numbers of Christians and Muslims. Most
of the Muslims were from Syria and Somalia.

To be resettled in the United States, refugees face a complicated
process that begins once they leave their home country. In a mass exodus
situation, such as exists in Somalia or Syria, they typically travel hundreds
of miles on foot to reach a camp operated by the United Nations High
Commissioner for Refugees (the UN refugee agency). Once there, they
may wait for months outside the camp to be vetted for admission.

As of the end of 2016, according to the UNHCR, 4 million people
live in refugee camps. There are more refugees and displaced persons

now than at any time since World War II, and more than half of them are children. The world's largest refugee camp is called Kakuma, in Kenya in East Africa, and it shelters 185,000 individuals primarily from South Sudan and Somalia. Overcrowding contributes to malnutrition and disease. The second-largest camp is Hagadera, and it is occupied by 105,000 refugees, largely from Somalia; it is part of the Dadaab refugee complex in southeastern Kenya, which is also home to the world's third- and fourth-largest camps.

At the camps, the UNHCR interviews individuals and collects personal and biometric information, and in 2016 began taking iris scans of Syrian and other refugees, which officials say help in speeding food relief. It also may be a response to European jitters about the vetting of refugees; some of the killers in the 2015 Paris attacks, in which 130 died, had used the flow of migrants as cover. After the UNHCR grants an applicant status for resettlement (which happens in fewer than 1 in 100 cases), applicants bound for the United States are taken to a federally funded overseas Resettlement Support Center. There, more biographical data is collected, and is shared with several federal intelligence agencies, including the FBI and the State Department. After multiple rounds of interviews, a medical screening, and vetting by Homeland Security, the refugee is then admitted to the United States, and required to obtain a green card within a year of arrival. The green card is proof the holder has permission to legally reside and take employment in the United States.

In November 2015, following the Paris attacks, Governor Sam Brownback issued an executive order forbidding any state agency from helping to resettle Syrian refugees in Kansas. Twenty-five other mostly Republican governors did the same, citing security concerns. In January 2016, Brownback issued an expanded order to exclude refugees from anywhere in the world.

The ban on refugees was a change of direction for Brownback.

As a US senator in 2004, he visited Sudan and called the regime-sponsored genocide in the Darfur region there the world's most pressing humanitarian problem. He encouraged the United States to begin issuing visas to refugees at the same rate as it had before September 11, divested his family's holdings in any companies that did business with Sudan, and condemned the United Nations for allowing Sudan to sit on the Commission on Human Rights (not to be confused with the UN refugee agency with a similar acronym). He urged the First Assembly of God church in Topeka to become the sponsor of the first Sudanese family to be resettled there by Catholic Charities of Northeast Kansas, according to a report in the *Topeka Capital-Journal*. Brownback was an evangelical Christian before he converted to Catholicism.

In September 2016, the Obama administration announced plans to increase the number of refugees admitted in 2017 by about 30 percent, to 110,000. Presidential nominee Donald Trump vowed repeatedly to end admission of all Syrian refugees, and to dramatically roll back the number of all refugees allowed into the country. Kris Kobach, the Kansas secretary of state and an immigration hardliner, was one of Trump's advisors during the campaign, and also helped build a GOP platform that endorsed Trump's promise to build a wall at the Mexican border.

On Friday, October 14, the US Attorney's Office in Wichita announced that three men had been taken into custody and charged with conspiring to use a weapon of mass destruction to destroy the mosque in the Somali apartment building in Garden City. The trio belonged to a militia group called the "Crusaders," which identified with the sovereign citizen movement, and the charges were based largely on information from a paid informant within the group. Two of the charged, Curtis Allen and Gavin Wright, both forty-nine, are from Liberal, seventy miles due south of Garden City, just above the Oklahoma line. The third, Patrick Eugene Stein, forty-seven, is from a small town an hour's drive to the southeast, near Dodge City.

Wright is the owner of a mobile home business in Liberal, and his Facebook page has the typical photos of family and friends, and notes that he's a graduate of Garden City High School. Stein's Facebook page is filled with anti-government rhetoric, and up to the day of his arrest he was sharing racist memes and false news stories, including one alleging the impending release of "a video of Bill Clinton raping a 13-year-old girl" and another that accused Obama of being the architect of massive voter fraud. Curtis Allen was an Iraq War veteran with extreme views and probably suffered from post-traumatic stress disorder, his family told reporters. Allen also had a history of domestic violence, and his October 11 arrest on charges of beating his girlfriend during an argument over money prompted federal authorities—who had been monitoring the Crusaders militia cell for eight months—to arrest Stein and Wright three days later.

Stein, according to the undercover informant, had earlier said that the girlfriend "needed to disappear" because she was suspected of giving information to law enforcement. After Allen was arrested by the Liberal Police Department, they reportedly found more than two thousand pounds of ammunition in his home and vehicle.

Earlier in the investigation, according to the complaint, federal authorities instructed the confidential informant inside the Crusaders to introduce an undercover FBI agent, posing as an arms dealer, to Stein. The ruse was that the confidential informant worked for the FBI undercover agent delivering money and contraband, and that automatic weapons and components for explosives could be provided. The day after Allen's arrest on the battery charge, Stein met with the undercover agent in the country to examine weapons that were ostensibly being offered for sale. In reality, the guns—including two fully automatic rifles, one in 5.56 caliber and another chambered for 7.62 x 39—were from the FBI lab at Quantico, Virginia. Stein shot both weapons, according to the complaint, asked about price, suggested trading drugs for guns, and agreed to show the undercover agent the apartment complex that was the intended target. Stein allegedly said the complex was "full of goddamned roaches."

The plan was to place four vehicles, loaded with fifty-five-gallon drums containing explosives made from ammonium nitrate fertilizer—similar to that which was used in the Oklahoma City bombing in 1995—at the corners of the apartment complex containing the Somali mosque and to detonate the explosives via cell phone. Stein, according to the complaint, had said during a militia meeting, "The only good Muslim is a dead Muslim." Another time, he said, "When we go on operations there's no leaving anyone behind, even if it's a one-year-old, I'm serious. I guarantee if I go on a mission those little fuckers are going bye-bye."

The group used an app called Zello that allowed their cell phones to be used in walkie-talkie mode, with the added benefit—or hazard, in this case—of all the voice messages being saved in a history. Some of the ideas allegedly shared during these meetings were kicking in doors of Muslim homes and using .22s with silencers to kill the inhabitants, using arrows dipped in pig's blood, obtaining rocket-propelled grenades to blow up the Somali apartment complex, burning Garden City churches that had supported the Somali refugees, targeting landlords who rented to the Somalis, and assaulting a city or county commission meeting. Stein, in particular, suggested the execution of government officials and hanging signs around their necks that read, "I support illegal immigration, I go against the Constitution on a daily basis, I do not have any care for my fellow citizens in the state or in the town that I represent."

Stein reportedly had surveilled the apartment complex on more than one occasion, equipped with a pistol, an assault rifle with several magazines, a bulletproof vest, and a night vision scope; Allen had said he could make the explosives from aluminum powder from ground soft drink cans and ammonium nitrate fertilizer. When authorities executed a search warrant at the mobile home business owned by Wright and where Allen worked, they said they found materials to improvise explosives and a copy of *The Anarchist's Cookbook*, a 1969 counterculture handbook that has remained a staple of terrorists and would-be revolutionaries at both extremes of the political spectrum.

"The only fucking way this country's ever going to get turned around is it will be a bloodbath and it will be a nasty, messy motherfucker," Stein said, according to the complaint. "Unless a lot more people in this country wake up and smell the fucking coffee and decide they want this country back . . . we might be too late, if they do wake up . . . I think we can get it done. But it ain't going to be nothing nice about it."

Allen was, according to the complaint, writing a manifesto for the group. If he completed it, authorities have not yet released it. All three men were indicted on federal domestic terrorism charges by a grand jury and, as of this writing, are being held without bond, awaiting trial.

"These charges are based on eight months of investigation by the FBI that is alleged to have taken the investigators deep into a hidden culture of hatred and violence," said acting US Attorney Tom Beall in a press release. "Many Kansans may find it as startling as I do that such things could happen here."

I was dismayed, but not particularly surprised.

Prior to September 11, the deadliest act of terrorism on American soil was the Oklahoma City bombing, and it was domestic terrorism. Terry Nichols, the bombing co-conspirator, is now serving 161 consecutive life sentences on "Bomber's Row" at the federal Supermax prison, which is literally up the river near Florence, Colorado. At the time of the bombing, Nichols was a resident of Herrington, in east-central Kansas, and he and Timothy McVeigh had mixed the explosives at a nearby lake. Nichols had met McVeigh during a stint in the military, and both were racists and rabidly anti-government.

Nichols was also an activist in the sovereign citizen movement.

"The FBI considers sovereign-citizen extremists as comprising a domestic terrorist movement," says a bulletin from the bureau's Counterterrorism Analysis Section. "Scattered across the United States, [it] has existed for decades, with well-known members, such as Terry Nichols, who helped plan the Oklahoma City, Oklahoma, bombing. Sovereign citizens do not represent an anarchist group, nor are they a militia, although they sometimes use or buy illegal weapons. Rather, they operate as individuals without established leadership and only come together in loosely affiliated groups to train, help each other with paperwork, or socialize and talk about their ideology. They may refer to themselves as "constitutionalists" or "freemen," which is not necessarily a connection to a specific group, but, rather, an indication that they are free from government control."

Nichols had attempted to renounce his US citizenship, had surrendered his driver's license, and had refused to pay about $40,000 in credit card debt because he claimed he was not bound by state or federal law.

"One prevalent sovereign-citizen theory is the Redemption Theory, which claims the U.S. government went bankrupt when it abandoned the gold standard basis for currency in 1933 and began using citizens as collateral in trade agreements with foreign governments," according to the FBI bulletin. The claim is that social security numbers and birth certificates are used to register individuals in trade agreements, and that each citizen has a monetary value—kept in a Treasury account—of between $630,000 and a few million. The movement also embraces a strategy of filing reams of court documents, often amounting to little more than gibberish, aimed at disrupting the criminal justice system or clouding issues of civil debt and ownership.

The movement has often been associated with Christian Identity, a white supremacist ideology that holds blacks and other races were "mud people" without souls. While Christian Identity peaked in the mid-1990s, the sovereign citizen movement has found new traction in the twenty-first century. The forty-one-day occupation of the Malheur National Wildlife Refuge in early 2016 was supported, in part, by those affiliated with the movement.

≈ ≈ ≈

Ryan Bundy, one of the seven charged with conspiracy in the occupation, identified himself as an "idiot" and sovereign citizen in a number of court filings, said he was a member of his own society, and claimed the government had no jurisdiction over him. The occupiers, who were heavily armed, said they were protesting the mismanagement of public land by the federal government, and wanted the area returned to local control to aid ranchers and others who depend on the use of natural resources. During the occupation, a spokesman for the militants, fifty-four-year-old Arizona rancher LaVoy Finicum, was fatally shot in the back by Oregon state troopers after he ran from his truck after attempting to evade a traffic stop. Although troopers killed Finicum—who ignored commands and insisted that officers shoot him—the first two shots of the encounter came from FBI agents, a fact that was not disclosed until an investigation weeks after. Authorities said Finicum was reaching for a loaded handgun in his pocket when the state trooper fired; supporters countered that he had been murdered while defending the Constitution.

Stein talked often about the occupation and of Finicum's death, according to an affidavit filed in support of the Garden City complaint, events that "are often cited by militia and sovereign citizen groups as a call to action against the United States government and federal authorities."

On October 27, 2016, Ryan Bundy and his six fellow defendants were acquitted of "conspiracy to impede federal officers by force, threat or intimidation" by a federal jury in Portland. "While federal prosecutors worked to keep their case focused on conspiracy, the trial quickly came to symbolize the growing divide between urban and rural America," reported Oregon Public Broadcasting on the day of the verdict. Ryan Bundy and his brother, Ammon, the leader of the occupation, remained in federal custody after the verdict, because the pair faced other charges in Nevada for an armed standoff that had occurred two years previously at the family's ranch. Their father, Cliven Bundy, was already being held, awaiting trial.

In 2004, I had the chance to study Terry Nichols in person while covering a portion of his state trial at McAlester, Oklahoma. Nichols and McVeigh had used a rented panel truck with a diesel fuel and fertilizer bomb in the back to bring down the Murrah building. They had been convicted of killing eight federal agents, and not the 160 civilians who also died in the blast, because the federal court had jurisdiction only over the eight officers killed in the line of duty. Nichols was sentenced to life in prison without the possibility of parole, and McVeigh was sentenced to death. McVeigh was executed June 11, 2001, at a federal prison at Terre Haute, Indiana. In the McAlester trial, Nichols was charged with 161 counts of murder (including one count for an unborn child) by the state of Oklahoma, and faced the death penalty.

Nichols struck me as an anxious man in a cheap suit and unfashionably large glasses who would be more at home selling insurance than making weapons of mass destruction. You would never take him for the type to plan the mass murder of innocents in the name of an ideology, but then, that's the thing: they seem like normal people. I've interviewed killers on death row in Tennessee and Texas who were remarkable only in that they seemed unremarkable, until you knew the acts they had committed against the defenseless. Nichols is of this type, a coward; he embraced a racist, religious, and militant subculture to bolster his lack of self-esteem and for a sense of belonging, and he took part in a revenge fantasy come true in which people who had done him no personal harm had died. At McAlester, Nichols was convicted on all 161 counts, but the jury deadlocked on the death sentence. He was returned to federal custody to serve out his sentence, which presumably means he will spend the rest of his life in prison.

At the African Shop, I asked Nameye what he would say to the men charged in the bomb plot, if he had the chance. "What did we do to you?" Nameye answered quickly. "Why would you love to kill us? You know, we're just people like you. You need to understand, that out of more than a billion Muslim people in the world, not even 1 percent do anything wrong. I would like to say, what did we do to you, that you want to hurt us?"

Then I asked if anyone has experienced direct examples of discrimination, and the half dozen people in the room shake their heads. No, not me, not that I know of, the men say. But later, Farrah, the co-owner of the shop, tells me that they have been looking for a new location for the shop, because the local planning and zoning commission has ordered them to vacate, saying a convenience store can't be in an industrial zone. When they go to inspect locations, she says, and the landlords see that they are Somali, the rents either go up beyond their reach or the property has just been rented. Isn't this discrimination? I ask. She does not know, she says, because she cannot see into the hearts of others. When I suggest that this may be a matter for an attorney, the owners of the African Shop say they have been to see all of the local attorneys in town, and none of them will take their case.

The city manager here is Matt Allen, a well-spoken Garden City native who is at ease answering questions from journalists and who will repeat the message he wants you to hear: the city has a long history of tolerance, it's been a home to immigrants for more than a century, residents celebrate their diversity and look to continued growth because of it. About twenty years ago Allen graduated from Garden City High School, which he describes as a melting pot of languages and cultures, both then and now. Latinos have been part of Garden City's history for more than 100 years, but after the fall of Saigon, Vietnamese became a significant fraction of the population. African and Asian ethnicities have grown the fastest in the last decade, drawn mostly by work at the Tyson plant. In 2009, the Census Bureau declared Finney County to be one of six new "majority minority" counties across the country in which changing demographics had made whites the minority. The official population, according to the 2010 census, is just under 27,000, but Allen insists that the methodology was flawed. The current population, he said, is at least 31,000. The publicity surrounding the bomb plot is a sore point with Allen, who says the city is known for tolerance and the welcoming of immigrants. He points to the way the community came together after the plot was announced, including support from an interfaith alliance, and a candlelight vigil at the apartment house for the Somali community.

"Each [of our ethnic communities] has added a flavor to our history," Allen said. "We try to celebrate it as much as we can. Because we've embraced that, we now have a very powerful labor force to support the growth in ag-related industry. We've really found a workforce just . . . being welcoming to others, whoever it is."

Allen declined to speculate on what effect a Donald Trump presidency would have on that workforce, saying that any politician would have to be judged by their actions, not their campaign rhetoric. When asked about whether he believed the African Shop owners would be discriminated against in their search for an alternative location, he said it certainly sounded like it was possible, but that would be a matter for other agencies to address, not the city. The local planning and zoning commission, he said, had been more than patient in dealing with the situation, which had lasted two years.

I asked Allen if he thought it would be the humane thing to show the shop even more tolerance, considering it had been reported by the FBI as one of the proposed targets of the alleged bomb plot.

"Is there some concern about hypocrisy of local government? I would say no," Allen said. "We had to push for a solution. Part of celebrating diversity is helping everyone understand the common set of rules and regulations we adopt that are indeed blind to differences. But in our execution of that, can we handle that in a way that shows an appreciation of the difficulties that may be there for new arrivals to Garden City?"

The answer, he says, is "of course."

When asked if he considered Garden City a sanctuary city, he said he'd heard that designation before, but that he didn't think it had any legal weight. The city never had any policies that conflicted with federal law, so he was unsure, he said, of why the city and the county showed up on some websites as being a sanctuary city.

A sanctuary city is a municipality that has a policy of protecting unauthorized immigrants from prosecution for federal immigrant laws, and guaranteeing them access to services. New York, Chicago, and Washington, DC, are examples.

The Center for Immigration Studies removed Finney County from its list of sanctuary cities following efforts by Sheriff Kevin Bascue and County Administrator Randy Partington, the *Garden City Telegram* reported in early 2017. A note on the CIS website read: "According to information provided to the Center by the Sheriff and ICE [Immigration and Customs Enforcement], Finney County now complies with all ICE detainers and requests and is fully cooperative with ICE."

Five counties in Kansas are labeled on the CIS website as sanctuaries: Butler, Harvey, Johnson, Sedgwick, and Shawnee. All of Colorado is designated a sanctuary.

≈ ≈ ≈

Four miles south of the African Shop, the Arkansas River snakes around the southern edge of the city. It's muddy and brown when it flows, but southwest Kansas is entering a droughty winter, and the little water there is in the river bed is all but stagnant. On the east side of town, in an affluent shopping area called Schulman Crossing, a new water park is nearing completion. It will be named Parrot Cove and, according to the *Telegram*, it will have 8,000 square feet of water area, four-story waterslides, and an artificial "lazy river." It will be the biggest water park between Denver and Kansas City. The newspaper story notes the "excitement" surrounding the anticipated opening, but doesn't mention where the water for the privately owned park will come from. The Parrot Cove website doesn't say, either, but gives admission prices based on height. For those 48 inches and taller, regular admission will be $30 a day.

The water for the park, I later learn, comes from the municipal water supply. The city buys its water from the Wheatland Electric Cooperative, headquartered in Scott City, about thirty-six miles to the north. The co-op was formed to provide rural electricity in 1948, but built a water treatment plant and began selling water in 2000. Wheatland has more than a dozen wells that tap the Ogallala Aquifer—and the aquifer is the reason Garden City began to flourish in the middle of the twentieth century, after decades of drought following its founding in 1878.

"In the vicinity of Garden City some 28,000 acres are irrigated with water pumped from an apparently inexhaustible subterranean supply lying from 11 to 40 feet under the surface," reports the 1939 WPA state guide to Kansas. "This water, according to geologists at the State Water Resources Board, fell in the Rocky Mountains 2,000 years ago and seeped underground until it was impounded here."

In Garden City, the imminent opening of a tropical-themed water park in droughty southwest Kansas is among the ironies I'm given to ponder. We're not so much using up the water here, as quickly redistributing it. What was once thought an inexhaustible reserve beneath our feet has been largely released back into the water cycle, where a changing climate won't carry it back to the Rockies, but will instead pour it out as rain into our rising oceans.

Half a world away, Somalia is seized by the worst drought in living memory, one that is wrecking crops, causing starvation, and ruining water supplies. The United Nations says the drought is contributing to the worst humanitarian crisis it has faced since 1945—a famine, fanned by war and climate change, threatening to sweep all of East Africa.

Millions are expected to die.

As I leave Garden City, taking US 400 as it follows the Arkansas River southeast toward Dodge City, I'm on autopilot. I've traveled this stretch of road so often during the last three years, usually towing behind the Jeep my home-built trailer with the kayak racked on top, that it all feels like my backyard. There's the wind turbine plant on the south side of the road, the regional airport, the slow curves leading into Pierceville. But I'm five hours away from home, allowing for a snack and another tank of gas.

That's a lot of time to think.

The interviews with the Somalis left me numb. I cannot claim to be startled, as prosecutor Beall suggested that many Kansans were after news of the bomb plot broke, because I've written so much about violent racists like McVeigh and Nichols. While there was an outpouring of support for the refugees from a broad cross-section in Garden City, I could not help but think that what had happened in my hometown a few years before was a more accurate representation of how deeply conflicted Kansans are.

In 2006, Emporia unexpectedly became home to a few hundred Somali refugees, when Tyson closed one of its facilities in Nebraska and offered the laid-off workers transfers to its beef-slaughtering plant in Kansas. While some community members were welcoming, and a group was formed to aid the refugees and educate the community, the level of distrust was high. As they would later in Garden City, the 400 or so Somalis tended to stick to themselves, living in an apartment building near the Ayan Café, a restaurant that catered to them. Even though Emporia already had a high immigrant population, because of the Latinos from Mexico and elsewhere who worked at the meat plant, many residents feared the Somali refugees. Perhaps it was because they were black, or the difference in their religion, or just that they were "other." By 2007, rumors fueled by emails or the *Emporia Gazette*'s online forum had accused the Somalis of a range of distasteful activity, from being dirty and spreading tuberculosis to raping women on the local university campus. Although the newspaper and civic leaders repeatedly pointed out the rumors were untrue, the animus boiled over at a standing-room-only community forum with city officials. While some residents questioned the stress the refugees placed on schools and other community services, many of the loudest voices spouted racist, anti-immigration rhetoric—they were taking jobs, they were a threat to the public health, they were being given benefits and considerations denied native Kansans. Only the concern about health had any validity, because the Somalis have a high rate of latent tuberculosis, and one worker who had died on the job was discovered at autopsy to have active TB. But the worst comments were personal, and reflected a cultural distrust. "They don't wear sanitary napkins and they're walking in Wal-Mart and I've personally seen that myself, it dropping on the floor," the *Gazette* quoted an area resident as saying. One of only two Somalis to speak at the meeting defended the hygiene of the refugee community. He also said many were thinking of leaving.

The crisis ended in January 2008, when Tyson announced it was closing its beef-slaughtering operation in Emporia and would shift its cattle operations to western Kansas. The Somalis and other workers were offered bonuses to transfer again, this time to Garden City.

Had the Somalis remained in Emporia, perhaps they would have eventually been assimilated into the community. Or, they might have been the targets of a bomb plot there instead.

The Waterscrape
Elevation: 2,637' (Cimarron Crossing)

In regard to this extensive section of country, I do not hesitate in giving the opinion, that it is almost wholly unfit for cultivation, and of course uninhabitable by a people depending upon agriculture for their subsistence. Although tracts of fertile land considerably extensive are occasionally to be met with, yet the scarcity of wood and water, almost uniformly prevalent, will prove an insuperable obstacle in the way of settling the country.

—*Major Stephen H. Long, upon surveying the Great Plains in 1820*

I'm hiking down a dry riverbed on a cold morning in winter, and with each step my boots make a sharp sound in the gravel. This is Cimarron Crossing, where travelers along the Santa Fe Trail had a serious choice. They could continue up the Arkansas on the Mountain Route, which would take them to Bent's Old Fort and then south over the Raton pass. Or, they could choose the middle crossing. They might ford the river here, or at points nearby, and follow the Cimarron ("wild" in Spanish) route, which was shorter but had less water and poorer grass—and offered more certain prospects for bandits and encounters with displeased Indians. Ahead was the roughest section of the trail, often called the "Waterscrape," and the closest source of water was the Cimarron River, sixty miles distant. Neither route was easy, hazards changed with politics and the season, and the consequences of a bad choice could mean hardship or even death.

The river today would be unrecognizable to the travelers who paused beneath the cottonwoods on the north bank and weighed their choices. With the absence of surface water, the cottonwoods that once marked the course of the river across the plain and provided the weary with a bit of shade are gone, too. The last anyone can remember seeing the river here—the real river, in which you could wade and picnic along the bank and catch catfish for your dinner—was in the late 1970s. Instead of a river now there is the bed, which is heavily rutted by the passage of ATVs and four-wheel-drive trucks. An occasional tumbleweed rolls down the riverbed, driven by the wind. But even this symbol of the Old West would have been unknown to travelers on the Santa Fe Trail, because

Harvesting wheat and wind near Dodge City.

tumbleweeds are an invasive species, Russian thistle, that came with the wheat farmers and wasn't commonplace until the twentieth century. Another invader that came late is the scrubby saltcedar, also known as tamarisk, originally imported to America from desert Africa in the nineteenth century as an ornamental bush. Its rough gray-green leaves are crusted with salt, and when it blooms, it explodes in feathery pink blossoms. As it eventually spread across the American Southwest, this "thirsty plant" was blamed for drying up rivers and killing indigenous species. The US Geological Survey coined a name for it and other species that seemed machine-like in their ability to send down tap roots and suck up water: *phreatophytes*. An eradication campaign began in the 1950s that, in some cases, saw flame throwers deployed against the plants. But the saltcedar tenaciously clung to western rivers. A study released in 2009 by the Department of the Interior and the US Geological Survey, however, suggests that hatred of the plant is misplaced. By diverting surface water and depleting groundwater stores, we have changed the ecosystem necessary to support the native trees. The cottonwood and other species are at a disadvantage when compared to the drought-resistant and salinity-tolerant saltcedar. But it isn't the saltcedar that has been killing the cottonwoods, the willows, and other native species; we have.

The Arkansas River meanders into Kansas near the tiny community of Coolidge, back at the state line, and the water there is so saline it is unfit for human or animal consumption. This change has taken place in the last few decades, and is the result not of any industrial pollution, but of the way in which we have changed the river by altering its natural flow pattern and storing water to accommodate agriculture and send water to cities along the Front Range.

"The Arkansas River is one of the most saline rivers in the US," Don Whittemore, a senior scientific fellow in hydrology with the Kansas Geological Survey, told me. For a river to be considered fresh, the upper threshold for salts is 1,000 milligrams per liter, a ratio that can roughly be understood as 1 part in 1,000. The highest concentrations in the Arkansas River are about 4 in 1,000, which is eight times the recommended maximum for public water supplies.

It was difficult at first for me to understand how the river could be so saline, when there was little or no flow in much of western Kansas. But Whittemore explained that the process was similar to what happens when you leave a pot of water heating for too long on your kitchen stove. The water evaporates, leaving a concentrated white residue behind. As we changed the way water evaporates in the Arkansas valley, we have created a system in which the water left behind also has a high concentration of solids. This saline water contaminates the shallow alluvial (river) aquifer and the deeper, High Plains aquifer system.

The common way of measuring the salinity in the river is simple and effective. Because salinity increases electrical conductivity, an electric charge is passed through the water, and the resistance measured. The lower the resistance, the higher the salinity.

"The primary sources of the dissolved constituents in Arkansas River water are from the soils and bedrock in Colorado," Whittemore wrote in explanatory material for a Kansas Geological Survey report on the salinity of the upper Arkansas River corridor. "The dissolved salt concentration in the river water greatly increases across eastern Colorado as evapotranspiration from ditch diversion and storage systems consumes water, while the dissolved salts remain in the resident water."

In conversation, Whittemore summarized it this way: "Colorado keeps the water, and gives us the salt."

Within the next fifty years, according to the report Whittemore helped prepare, water seepage has the potential to contaminate *all* 500 miles of High Plains aquifer that underlies the Arkansas River corridor to a concentration that would exceed, by a factor of four, the maximum level proposed by the EPA for drinking water.

As climate change reduces snowmelt in the Rockies and contributes to more violent storms on the plains, Whittemore said, the situation along the Arkansas River is likely to get worse. In addition to drought, flood also poses a risk. The last major flood in this part of the valley was in June 1965, when a wall of water swept down the river. While levees and spillways have been built to prevent that kind of flood, the changing environment and the deepening and narrowing of the riverbed could make it hard to anticipate the nature of the next flood.

For the first half of the nineteenth century, the land from the 100th Meridian (which passes through Dodge City) to the Rocky Mountains was generally described—and marked on maps—as the "Great American Desert." There just wasn't enough rainfall to sustain agriculture, and the broad and generally treeless plains were considered a natural barrier to population. This notion changed following the Civil War, with the doctrine of Manifest Destiny, and through the efforts of boosters like Charles Dana Wilber, who declared that "rain followed the plow." The claim, based on flawed climate analysis that confused cause and effect, was that human habitation and agriculture permanently changed the environment for the wetter.

The thing that allowed the High Plains to be successfully farmed wasn't magical thinking, but the tapping of the vast Ogallala Aquifer, which stretches from South Dakota to Texas. While farm water wells had been drilled since the nineteenth century, it took technological advances in irrigation following World War II to really exploit the Ogallala. Water from the aquifer is the foundation of a $20 billion industry that produces one-fifth of the nation's wheat, corn, and beef cattle. But while it was once thought to be an inexhaustible resource, increasing demand may result in the depletion of the Ogallala within the lifetimes of some Americans now living.

In Kansas, groundwater allegedly belongs to the public, but most of the water management districts appear uninterested in any conservation measures that would result in any significant reduction in irrigation. Some management districts have committed to cutting water usage by 20 percent a year, but it's not nearly enough. We're draining the aquifer at a rate of four to six inches every year, but the average recharge is only about half an inch a year.

Kansas has some of the best data in the country on groundwater levels, and much of the reason is that staffers from the Kansas Geological Survey have gone out every winter for decades and dropped steel tapes down alluvial and deep aquifer wells. The last ten feet or so of the ends of the tape are chalked, and when the tapes are pulled up, the amount of chalk the water has washed away indicates the level. The measurements are made in winter, when levels are relatively stable, but sub-freezing temperatures or snowy or wet conditions often pose a challenge for those taking the measurements. While there are variations among wells, the trend has been a steady decline in water wells, with the sharpest dip coming about 1986.

In his office at the Kansas Geological Survey in Lawrence, I met Rex Buchanan, the survey's director emeritus, to talk about the future of water in Kansas, among other topics. Although semi-retired, he had just returned from helping crews measure groundwater levels in western Kansas, and for years he's been assigned the same group of wells. He seemed exasperated by some of my questions—how old is some of the water in western Kansas, for example, which interested me but which seemed to strike him as silly. When I asked him how long it would take the aquifer to recharge fully by snowmelt and rainfall if all irrigation was stopped, he grew impatient, and wondered aloud why everybody was always asking him that. A reporter in Hutchinson asked him that the week before, and the answer didn't matter.

"Why not?" I asked.

"We'll never live to see it, not in our lifetimes."

I suggested that it didn't mean it wasn't important to know.

At one point, Buchanan grew impatient and started asking me questions.

"Why should you tell someone who has a water well in western Kansas that they shouldn't pump it dry?" he pressed. "What do you say when they ask what good that water in the ground is doing anybody, anyway?"

I started this as a kayak trip down the river, I thought to myself, so how do I end up being grilled about environmental policy? But I cobbled together an answer that some municipal water supplies also get their water from the aquifer, that depleting the water might have unintended consequences. He scoffed at my answer, saying that the municipal answer was partly correct, but that unintended consequences were unlikely. What, there would be sinkholes? he asked. Before I could say that unintended consequences included a much broader range than sinkholes, he answered his own question, in a manner that seemed like a tutor disappointed in a slow pupil.

"An entire ecosystem is being lost," he said, and mentioned the disappearance of the cottonwoods along the Arkansas as just one part of that collapse. "It should concern everybody that there's a major river in western Kansas that has no water in it."

Buchanan grew up on a farm in Rice County, at the headwaters of the Little Arkansas, and the more he talked about rivers in the western part of the state, the more passionate he became. He turned to the computer on his desk to call up a presentation he had recently given. One slide was of the rivers and streams in Kansas, circa 1960, and it showed waterways lacing the western third of Kansas like veins in your forearm. The next image was a map of the current rivers and streams, and it looked as if somebody had taken an eraser to western Kansas. They were just gone.

"I was measuring this well some years back," Buchanan said, "and I just asked this farmer how he did. He said he about broke even that year. And I thought to myself, here we are using a limited resource so this guy can just break even on his corn crop. Is this what we should be doing? Does that seem a wise use of water? Should we be trying to grow corn where it was never supposed to grow?"

Buchanan later said he probably shouldn't have said that last about growing corn. There were some types of corn, he said, that didn't need as much water. But still, he said, the question remained.

"Do you believe there should be water in the Arkansas River?" he asked.

"Yes."

"Then tell me how to get it back," he challenged.

Stop the irrigation, I said.

I didn't understand how complex the issue was, he said. Once, he said, he'd had a conversation along the same lines with Mike Hayden, the former Kansas governor, and Hayden said getting the river back would require buying up all of the water rights. And that would be prohibitively expensive, not to mention challenging a way of life in western Kansas.

No, I said, the solution was simple. The politics were complicated.

"What matters is what we can do now," he said. "We don't have to just stop all irrigation, we have to limit it. We're already doing that up in northwest Kansas. We don't have to stop it, just reduce it."

Although Buchanan said his legacy at the Kansas Geological Survey would likely be his response, as director, to the earthquakes in south-central Kansas, he wished it could be water conservation instead. It was the foremost environmental crisis in the state, he said, much more than the recent earthquake swarms caused by wastewater injection related to oil and gas production. He was assaulted daily, he said, by calls and emails from angry environmentalists who wanted the state to do something about the earthquakes. Yet, he had received no demands, and few public inquiries, about the water crisis in western Kansas. Because 90 percent of Kansans live in cities, most clustered in the eastern third of the state, the problem seems invisible.

I left the interview feeling that Buchanan, perhaps, was conflicted because his love for the environment wasn't matching what his experience as an administrator told him was politically possible. Perhaps I came off as some kind of Edward Abbey eco-terrorist, shouting slogans and looking for the right dam to blow. But for months I had been thinking about the disappearance of the river in the far counties—except for flooding by heavy rains, the river is mostly dry from Holcomb to Great Bend, a distance of about 150 river miles. The Arkansas River is among the greatest natural resources in the state. But for all practical purposes, the river in western Kansas is dead.

In 2013, a paper published in the *Proceedings of the National Academy of Sciences* explored some of the questions that Buchanan and I had been debating. It was titled "Tapping Unsustainable Groundwater Stores for Agricultural Production in the High Plains Aquifer of Kansas: Projection to 2110," and its lead author was David R. Steward, a professor in the Department of Civil Engineering at Kansas State University—the state's flagship agricultural school, at Manhattan.

"Eventually, the southwest and northwest (water management) districts in Kansas will realize the fate emerging in the west central district, where shallower groundwater stores have resulted in decreased well yields, well abandonment, and conversion back to dryland," the paper says. The capacity to pump water will be reduced in the 2020s, but will be offset to increase efficiency in corn and cattle production. "The future is bright in the near term but bleak beyond, and increased agricultural production may be realized before imminent reductions occur."

The problem is significant in terms of global food supply and the threat posed to agriculture in western Kansas. Corn is grown largely for use in cattle feedlots, which contributes to a congressional district (the 1st, currently held by Roger Marshall, a Republican from Great Bend) with the highest agricultural market value in the nation.

Current reductions in water usage are far short of the 80 percent needed to approach sustainability. The age of the water in the aquifer varies widely, but some recent recharge is likely added to "fossil water" that may be 13,000 years old, which is toward the end of the last North American glacial period.

"If existing trends continue to total depletion, then, depending on the district, projected replenishment times would average between 500–1,300 [years]," the report says.

As I hiked along the dry bed near Cimarron Crossing, I paused to take some photos of the massive trunk of a fallen cottonwood. This tree, I thought, may have been alive when travelers along the Santa Fe Trail forded here, or when the Cheyenne chief Dull Knife crossed the river in 1878 in an attempt to lead his people back to their homeland. But a red-tailed hawk, perched on a fencepost nearby, eyed me with cold birdlike disdain, mocking my romanticism. The hawk's russet plumage was made suddenly golden by a ray from the low winter sun.

As I raised my camera, the bird flew, an opportunity lost.

I slung the camera back over my shoulder and kept hiking. But something in the back of my mind was nagging. So I stopped, pulled a notebook from my pocket, and began to write. *We are the most invasive species.* I began. Right, but that's not very original. So what? *But unlike other species, we have the ability to choose, to sacrifice a bit now for the common good of all, or to embrace narrow and short-term self-interest—and ultimately, self-destruction. What's there left to fight for after the last of the wild is gone?* I paused, kneeling down on the bed of the river, and pondered the next lines. I touched the cold sand with the fingertips of my left hand. *Without nature, all talk is just eulogy. I began this project thinking that I was writing the biography of the Arkansas River, but I'm afraid for this middle passage, it's an obituary. We have killed the river as we once knew it and buried it beneath the plain, and it took us only 150 years to do it. We have left the wild lands worse than we found them, best suited to plants from alien climes, and made good those maps that labeled this the Great American Desert. But the river will come back one day—whether in generations or in geologic ages, it will return, perhaps long after we've abandoned agriculture here. The question is, will any of us be around to see it? Or—assuming that some living thing will survive—will the only witness be the hawks with their hard bright eyes?*

The Gun Show
Elevation: 2,493' (Dodge City)

Oh, beat the drum slowly and play the fife lowly,
Play the dead march as you carry me along;
Take me to the green valley, there lay the sod o'er me,
For I'm a young cowboy and I know I've done wrong.

—Frank Maynard, "The Dying Cowboy"

Long before you reach Boot Hill, you see his face. It's on billboards and brochures and in magazines, and his gunfighter blue eyes (the best gunfighters all had blue eyes, don't you know) are frozen in a perpetual squint. He is, as they say, ruggedly handsome. His hair is longish and frosted with gray, as is his broad moustache. He's tall and lean and wears a black hat and a red or sometimes yellow vest with a tin star pinned to the lapel, and on his hip is a .45 Long Colt single-action revolver with walnut grips. He projects an aura of strength and barely contained righteous menace, and he is the Face of Dodge City.

"Experience the history" beckons a brochure from the Convention and Visitors Bureau, "where the Marshal still roams the streets."

The Marshal is sixty-five-year-old Brent Harris, and not only does he roam the streets here, but he's also fired thousands of blank rounds through the iron on his hip, the handle of which also serves as a handy hat rack when he's leaning against a post in front of the Long Branch Saloon and watching the guests (he discourages calling them *tourists*) who come here by the tens of thousands each year and pay $10 for every adult ticket to visit the town's recreated Front Street. The question Harris is asked most often by the guests is, "When's the gun show?"

The question refers to the gunfight held twice daily during the summer. At noon and again at 7 p.m., a scripted confrontation spills out from the Long Branch Saloon onto Front Street, with thundering pistols and booming shotguns, a lot of drifting black powder smoke, some bad jokes and bloodless death scenes. This is where Harris has expended those thousands of blank rounds, in meting out mock justice in a bit of campy entertainment for guests who have come expecting to see gunplay. Harris himself, of course, never dies in these affairs, because he's the marshal.

Longhorns on Dodge City's Front Street.

The gunfight at Boot Hill is an iconic bit of American pop culture, something that everyone has a picture of in their mind's eye from westerns like *Dodge City* (1939) to *Tombstone* (1993), and especially the television series *Gunsmoke*. The hero of the series was a fictional Dodge City marshal named Matt Dillon, played with square-jawed seriousness by James Arness, and it concluded in 1975, after twenty years on the air—making it the longest-running live-action television series in history. Like the Long Branch Saloon, where you can watch a slightly racy stage show while drinking a real beer (as in 1983's *National Lampoon's Vacation*), it's something that is at once comfortable and slightly sinful. A friend, Bill Sheldon, a Kansas poet who lives and teaches in Hutchinson, had a summer job as the stagecoach driver at Boot Hill when he was a teenager, and says it was the best job he ever had.

There are other things to see at the Boot Hill Museum complex, of course, including the 60,000-plus artifacts from the early days of Dodge City that are tucked into interpretive exhibits in the city block of buildings along recreated Front Street. While the storefronts match many of those in historical photographs—the Long Branch and Saratoga saloons, Zimmermann's hardware and firearms, the Beatty and Kelley

Restaurant—things are undoubtedly cleaner than they were when Dodge City was the Queen of the Cowtowns, and Texas longhorns churned the street into a sea of mud and muck. It was also known as one of the wickedest cities in the West, a place of sudden violence where the common vices were drinking, gambling, and prostitution. The original lyrics to the most famous cowboy folk song ever written, "The Streets of Laredo," about a poor ranger who lay dying after being shot following a bout of drinking and card playing, refer not to the town in Texas, but to Dodge City. According to folklorist Jim Hoy, a Kansas cowboy by the name of Frank Maynard put new words to an old Irish ballad about a girl who had been betrayed by her lover and was dying of syphilis. Maynard used a real place in Dodge City—Tom Sherman's barroom—and changed the unfortunate girl to a young cowboy. Later versions, and most recordings of the song, changed the setting to Laredo.

Dodge City was founded in 1872, a result of converging natural, economic, and cultural forces. The location had several things in its favor: it was along the Arkansas River, on the Santa Fe Trail, in the midst of an enormous plains bison herd, and five miles west of the frontier military outpost of Fort Dodge. In the beginning, it had only one house, and one business—an outdoor whiskey bar catering to the soldiers. But the newly laid tracks of the Atchison, Topeka, and Santa Fe Railway soon made the city a railhead for the Texas cattle drives.

Cattle are still an important part of Dodge City's economy. They are no longer driven up from Texas by wild rangers who seek to slake their appetites in bars and brothels, but instead are trucked to the many area feedlots. You smell the feedlots long before you see them, and if you ask residents about the stench, they'll tell you it smells like money. Two of the country's largest meatpacking operations, owned by National Beef and Cargill, are in Dodge City. Together, they process 11,000 head of cattle every day.

Of the three towns most closely linked in popular culture to the Wild West—the others being Tombstone, Arizona, and Deadwood, South Dakota—only Dodge City continues to be supported by the economy that founded it. Dodge is also the largest of the cities, with a population of about 27,000, and each year since 2012 has hosted the "3i" agribusiness show, which draws 300,000 visitors to the city (the i's are industry, implements, and irrigation). While the economies of tiny Tombstone and Deadwood rely heavily on the tourist trade, at Dodge City tourism pales in economic importance to the shipping, feeding, and slaughtering of beef. Still, the tens of thousands who make Dodge City a travel destination each year are coming not to see Cargill or National Beef, but to visit Boot Hill and other attractions that evoke the Old West.

And Dodge City marks the spot, traditionally, where the West begins.

But for me, coming down the river, this is where it ends.

The 100th meridian, an invisible line that was once thought to divide arid western lands from the arable eastern plains, runs through the city. There's a limestone post, erected in 2007 as a community project by a local Eagle Scout, on the south side of Highway 50 between L and M Streets that approximately marks the location of the meridian.

The meridian also served to settle the dispute with Spain that gave Zebulon Pike so much trouble, because a treaty in 1819 established the boundary of the United States at this location, at the spot where the meridian meets the Arkansas River. It followed the Arkansas to the Continental Divide to the west, and went straight south down the meridian to the Red River. The boundary would remain until the lands ceded following the Mexican War would move it farther west. By the time Dodge City was founded, the United States and its territories reached all the way to the Pacific Ocean.

Modern irrigation has blurred, if not erased, the line that was thought to mark the western limit of the plow. There are now plenty of crops to be found in western Kansas, including wheat, corn, and grain sorghum, which is also called milo. But there's a price: the Arkansas River, which once was deep enough to require a ford (and later a steel bridge) at Dodge City to cross, has been pumped dry.

Although the cowboy era is indelibly etched in the popular imagination and has been a staple of American screen entertainment ever since Edwin S. Porter made the silent film short *The Great Train Robbery* in 1903, cowboys were employed on classic cattle drives for only a short period of time. It began shortly after the Civil War, when Texas cattle were driven north up the Chisholm and other trails to railheads in Kansas. The drives moved west as the railroad moved west. The notable towns include Baxter Springs (where I was born and grew up—and out), Abilene, Ellsworth, Wichita, and of course Dodge City. Although you might conclude by watching Hollywood westerns that most cowboys were white, they were in reality a diverse lot, and some historians believe that up to half of them were black, Hispanic (or the increasingly preferred and more accurate word, Latino), or Native American. The word *cowboy* comes from the Spanish *vaquero*, meaning someone who tends cows. By 1885, it was all over, due to the expansion of the railroads, and because barbed wire had tamed the West—and prevented the types of cattle drives that, by necessity, had to cross large expanses of open and unfenced range. While it's arguable that cowboy culture also existed in Australia and the pampas of Argentina—and lives on today in ranches across the West—the period of the cattle-driving, range-riding, hell-raising working cowboy lasted for little more than fifteen years.

As the railheads moved west, so did many of the lawmen who kept order in the wild and wicked sections of town that catered to the cowboys. The most famous of the lot is Wyatt Earp, who drifted into Kansas after some trouble in Illinois and Missouri. He was a sometime pimp and was once charged as a horse thief. He was a lawman in Ellsworth, Wichita, and Dodge City. In Dodge, you can't swing a cat without hitting something named for him. There's Wyatt Earp Boulevard, for example, which is the city's main drag; there's a bronze statue of him, with a detailed gun and watch chain, across the street from the Santa Fe depot; and the Wyatt Earp Inn and Hotel on the east side of town, which can charitably be described as economy lodging where you can smell the history from the nearby feedlots.

Earp's reputation, however, is mostly a twentieth-century invention, sparked by a sensational and largely fictional 1931 biography published by Stuart Lake. When the John Ford–directed *My Darling Clementine* came out in 1946, starring Henry Fonda as Earp, it framed the shootout at the O.K. Corral as the quintessential western gunfight. The Earp story would become a perennial Hollywood favorite, right to the end of the twentieth century.

Despite the exaggerations and dramatic liberties taken with Earp's story, there is some truth at its core. Being a marshal anywhere in the Old West was an inherently dangerous proposition, one that took more than a measure of courage. He really was in a thirty-second gunfight in a dusty lot called the O.K. Corral in 1881 at Tombstone, Arizona Territory.

Although Brent Harris as the official marshal of Dodge doesn't portray Earp, it's difficult to avoid comparisons. In costume, Harris looks like he could have stepped right out of *Tombstone* or *Wyatt Earp*. He is keenly aware he's playing a role in which it is impossible to match guest expectations. Harris says he has read a lot of history, and knows the stories about Earp being a pimp and a horse thief, but that he would rather not judge an individual who died nearly a century ago, when the struggle for existence was somewhat different than it is today.

One fall afternoon, when Harris was off duty and dressed instead in jeans and a sweatshirt, he met me at the Boot Hill Museum and we sat on a wooden bench in the foyer of the gift shop. He gave me a sarsaparilla, and as I sipped the syrupy drink, Harris pushed the heels of his tennis shoes across the floor to stretch his long legs. In front of us was a coin-operated pony ride, a stout metal affair of the kind that you used to see in front of grocery stores, with an "Out of Order" sign on it. Harris, who is also Boot Hill's carpenter and general handyman, remarked that he would have to get around to fixing it one of these days.

When I directed the conversations to guns, Harris chose his words carefully. Since July 2015, Kansans have been able to legally carry a concealed weapon in most public places, with no permit or training required, as long as they are at least twenty-one years old. It is the sixth state that has adopted "constitutional carry," which proponents say removes the barriers to rights guaranteed by the Second Amendment.

Some of the hottest arguments in Kansas have centered on an exemption to the law, which allowed guns to be banned on college campuses, and which is set to expire in July 2017. Although I'm a firearms owner, and have been since I took a Hunters Safety Course as a teenager, I have been deeply concerned about the proliferation of military-grade arms among the public. The current black rifle insanity was one of the reasons I allowed my brief membership in the National Rifle Association to lapse. A black rifle is the generic term for a style of weapon patterned on the AR-15, the semiautomatic and highly customizable civilian version of the US military's fully automatic M-16, and it has a distinctive profile.

I told Harris that I was worried that the expiration of the campus carry exemption would have a chilling effect on free speech in the classroom. Would students and professors be as willing to share their views on any controversial subject when it was likely that somebody in the room was packing heat? Concealed carry advocates love to quote science fiction writer Robert Heinlein, who said an armed society is a polite society, but at this moment in time—October 2016—the country has never been more armed, or less polite. The trio that planned to blow up the Somali apartment building in Garden City had stockpiled a literal ton of ammunition in preparation for their day-after-election-day attack. Some of the ammunition the trio had was for an AR-15—a black rifle.

Harris said he often feels the cultural weight of the gun on his hip.

The most uncomfortable he had ever felt when carrying the big revolver, Harris said, was when he was working a booth at the state fair at Hutchinson following the 1999 shootings at Columbine High School in Colorado. Approached by a group of middle and school students, he felt pressed to put guns in context.

"A hundred and fifty years ago, a gun was a tool," he recalled saying. "It was like a hammer or a saw; it was something you depended on for survival, whether you were a homesteader or a business owner or anyone else. It's still a tool, if you're a soldier or in law enforcement. We're blessed to have had the people before us who have fought and bled and died so we can now have a world where a gun is not a required tool."

Harris has never been in a gunfight, but he knows that the reality is far different than what is portrayed on television and in the movies or at the twice-daily gunfights on Front Street. When he talks to children at Boot Hill—which happens often—he will often kneel to be on their eye level, and tell them to be careful around strangers and to obey their parents and not to play with guns.

"I have a concealed carry permit," Harris said. "I had shot maybe ten live rounds in my entire life before beginning the reenactments here, and I got to wondering whether I was really any good. So, I took the course."

Turns out, Harris said, that all that playacting must have helped his coordination, because he turned out to be a pretty good shot. But, he says, he doesn't carry a loaded gun on a routine basis, just because it doesn't feel natural to him. I confided that I don't carry a concealed weapon because it just felt *too* natural, and I might be quick to use it.

When concealed carry without a permit went into effect in 2015, it legalized an act that formerly, and for more than a century, was a felony in Kansas. The state now has more liberal gun laws than anything that was imagined in Dodge City during its heyday. Both concealed and open carry were banned north of the "deadline" of the Santa Fe tracks, and violators were subject to a $100 fine. The ban was a measure aimed at reducing the potential for bloodshed when alcohol and passion mixed with gunpowder in the bars, brothels, and casinos of Front Street.

Some of the early victims of gun violence in Dodge City were buried in the town's Boot Hill cemetery, on the town's highest hill, overlooking Front Street and the Santa Fe tracks. It was an unofficial cemetery, the receptacle for those unfortunates who died without friends or connections; the quality were interred in the cemetery at Fort Dodge. Among the first residents of Boot Hill was Jack Reynolds, who was unlucky enough to be shot six times by a railway worker. Five buffalo hunters who froze to death on the prairie one winter were buried there, as was the only woman, a prostitute named Alice Chambers, who died of natural causes and on her deathbed declared, "Circumstances led me to this end." Chambers was the last of the thirty or so individuals to be buried at Boot Hill, which was in service only from 1872 to 1878. The bodies were removed to Prairie Grove cemetery, which was closed in 1887, and the Boot Hill bodies relocated again, to Maple Grove at the west edge of town, where they presumably remain.

City Hall was later erected on the hilly spot that was the site of Boot Hill, and in the 1920s a Dodge City dentist, Oscar Simpson, decided to celebrate the town's notorious past by casting a life-size statue of a cowboy. Simpson covered an accommodating local policeman in dental plaster, and while it set the poor man had to breathe through a straw. When finished, the statue—made of concrete, and complete with a ten-gallon hat—was placed on the city hall lawn. The old municipal building, perched just above the museum complex, is now home to the Boot Hill Distillery, which turns locally grown grain into vodka, gin, and white whiskey. You can only sample their wares, however, and not yet buy a shot, because of the county law prohibiting liquor by the drink except at restaurants.

The dentist's Cowboy statue, hand on his gun, is still out front. It is such an icon that it is inserted between DODGE CITY and DAILY GLOBE in the flag of the local newspaper, standing taller than even the font. Below is the newspaper's motto: "Covering the Old West since 1878."

Just on the other side of the fence from the distillery, in a corner of the Boot Hill Museum complex, is a mock recreation of the original cemetery, complete with grave markers and interpretive signs. This is also a legacy of the dentist's handiwork, because in 1930 Simpson created a mock cemetery for a Rotary convention, complete with concrete skulls and body parts. "The local Rotarians, infected by the spirit of Dr. Simpson's hoax, 'planted' an old cottonwood tree on the hillside and passed it off to visitors as the historic gallows tree from Horse Thief Canyon," notes the *WPA Guide to Kansas*. "It still stands—a rope, dangling suggestively from a dead crotch, draped around the dead trunk."

There's still a noose or two hanging from the tree at the museum's "cemetery." In 2010, a sixty-nine-year-old guest from Arkansas put his head through one of the nooses for a photo opportunity, and ended up passing out. He was revived, taken to the hospital, and later released when no serious injuries were found.

The last time Front Street saw a gun murder was October 6, 1996.

On that night, a fourteen-year-old gang member by the name of Rafael Flores fired six shots from a moving car into a crowd of young people who were gathered after hours in the Boot Hill parking lot, a popular hangout. Justin Mercado, eighteen, who worked at Pizza Hut and was planning a move to Arizona in two weeks to start a new life with his girlfriend, was killed by one of the shots.

Mercado had no gang affiliation.

Flores said the shooting was an accident.

Flores was tried as an adult, convicted of first-degree murder, and sentenced to life in prison. Now thirty-four, Flores was denied parole as recently as 2014, when the parole board cited his history of criminal offenses while in prison, which include fighting and participating in riots, and described him as a "habitual offender and poor parole risk." Newspaper accounts of his parole denial called him the "Boot Hill shooter."

By chance, I was interviewing Harris at Boot Hill on the twentieth anniversary of the Mercado shooting. The *Dodge City Daily Globe* had run a story that morning about the anniversary, in which Mercado's parents remembered their son. His mother, Vicki Mercado, said not a day goes by that she didn't think about Justin. "It doesn't get any easier," she told the *Globe*. "I think about what kind of life he would have had, how many grandchildren I would have had. It's hard."

The shooting changed Dodge, the story said. An alternative youth hangout called "The Alley" was created, and is mostly used by middle school or younger students. Teenagers still drag Wyatt Earp Boulevard, but they don't hang out in the Boot Hill parking lot. The community became sensitive to gang violence—as did federal authorities. Twenty-three members of the *Norteño* street gang in Dodge City were indicted on federal racketeering charges in 2012. The investigation was related, in part, to the shooting of a suspected rival gang member, Israel Peralta, at a trailer park south of the tracks in Dodge City three years earlier. *Norteño* means "northerner, north of the border," and the gang originated in Southern California, and proliferated in the state prison system there. All but one of those charged in Dodge City were convicted, and a press release from the Bureau of Alcohol, Tobacco, and Firearms said the gang used "murder, robbery, assault and the threat of violence" to protect its methamphetamine operation.

The writer of the Mercado anniversary story was Roger Bluhm, the *Globe*'s managing editor, whom I met at the newspaper offices on Second Street that afternoon. The *Globe*, a Tuesday-through-Saturday daily with a paid circulation of 9,700, is owned by the GateHouse Media chain.

Bluhm, fifty, is a relative newcomer to Dodge—he's been here just a little more than two years, after a stint in Nebraska—but he has a veteran newsman's ability to assess a community. Gangs continue to be a concern, he said, and the town "is run by the beef plants," which bring in workers to meet the demand for unskilled, low-paid labor. Latinos are now 60 percent of the population, and gained that majority in the last decade.

"I'd love to say it's wonderful," Bluhm said of race relations, "but I suppose it's as strained as it always has been."

While Latinos have been an integral part of the city's history since shortly after its founding—the Santa Fe Railroad used them as cheap labor from 1900 to about 1950—their history has been largely ignored. As with other railroad towns in Kansas, the Latinos were confined to a shanty neighborhood built south of the tracks in the Santa Fe rail yard. It was called "Little Mexico," and the segregation went so deep that Latinos were discouraged from mixing with whites or openly patronizing businesses north of the rails. The shantytown was condemned in 1955.

"There is no hot button topic in Dodge," Bluhm said. The worry about gangs continues to simmer and race relations have reached an uneasy truce, but there isn't anything prompting residents to demonstrate or write letters to the editor. What has caused some talk lately, Bluhm said, is a proposal to allow liquor by the drink, which is being lobbied for by the owners of the Boot Hill Distillery and others. Currently, a business in Ford County—like most counties in Kansas—must have at least 30 percent of its sales in food to qualify for a liquor license. But it's a local option, and about a third of Kansas counties waive the food sales requirement, while some allow no liquor sales at all.

Bluhm, who worked for a stint in the country music tourist wonderland of Branson, in southwest Missouri, said he is optimistic about the future of the city. "I know this sounds like I'm a booster," Bluhm said, "but Dodge City is on the verge of being another Branson."

As for the state's concealed carry law, Bluhm said there has been little public discussion in Dodge City about it. "It wasn't much of a concern," he said. "Most people just wore their guns on their hips anyway."

Late in the afternoon, I parked the Jeep at spacious and trim Wright Park—a few blocks south and a bit east of the Boot Hill Museum complex, and not far from where the soldiers once came to drink their whiskey at the outdoor bar—and climbed the berm that separated the city park from the river bed. The view was one not many guests at Boot Hill would likely have imagined.

It reminded me of photos of Omaha Beach.

A barrier of wire and crossed steel beams ran along the riverbank, stretching as far as I could see in each direction, like anti-tank devices. The US Army Corps of Engineers erected the levees following flooding in 1965 in eastern Colorado and western Kansas that left dozens dead and caused millions of dollars in damage. When the flood crested at Dodge City, it covered twenty city blocks here.

Passing through a gate in the riparian defenses marked "Authorized" entry only, I hiked down to the river bed, dotted with scrub, and stood with my boots planted in the sand and glad for my fleece pullover, because the wind was whipping in something fierce from the southwest. Traffic rattled above on the Second Street Bridge, the concrete pillars of which were tagged with graffiti. Far to the west, I could see the grain elevators shining in the golden light of late afternoon.

There was a rutted and potholed trail that ran the length of the river bed, and I began to hike along it. I hadn't been walking for five minutes before I heard the gasoline-powered whine of an all-terrain vehicle coming up behind me, and I stopped and watched as first one and then three neon-colored ATVs zipped by, throwing rooster tails of dust behind them. I'm not sure exactly what to call these machines, because they were bigger than the single-person, cycle-type ATVs I knew that hunters and farmers used. These had steering wheels and enough room for a driver and passenger to sit inside, surrounded by a roll cage, so I'm going to call them sand buggies. Whatever they were called, they were loud—and fast.

I watched their plumes of dust as they went perhaps a half mile down, then came roaring back. I stepped far off the trail to let them pass, alarmed at the not unreasonable prospect of being hit by them, and wondering what kind of damage they were doing to the river bed. Wanting to ask some questions of the drivers and their passengers, I attempted unsuccessfully to engage them, but all three vehicles disappeared in a rolling cloud of dust to the west.

Seven years before, a confrontation between a jogger and an ATV on the river bed in Dodge City led to a fatal shooting, a sensational murder case, and a shield law in Kansas for journalists. The story was covered by Calvin Trillin in 2010 in the *New Yorker,* and Trillin first noted the similarity of the barriers along the river to the beaches at Normandy. The lead to the Trillin piece was both expected and surprising, the kind of first sentence that journalism students like mine would be required to study: "It was the sort of showdown that might have taken place in the Dodge City of old—the Dodge City treasured by Hollywood and recalled in authentic detail in the Boot Hill Museum, just off Wyatt Earp Boulevard—except, of course, for the presence of the Chevy Blazer."

The old Chevy four-wheel-drive truck was driven by twenty-year-old Tanner Brunson, and his friend Steven Holt was a passenger. Holt was thirty-four, stood six feet, and weighed 250 pounds. He had tattoos that spelled out "Fuck You," and although his appearance was intimidating, those who knew him said he wasn't likely to start a fight. Brunson and Holt had been drinking beer.

Sam Bonilla was a part-time skip tracer for a local bail bondswoman and a full-time cable installer, and he was out jogging on the riverbed with his fifteen-year-old son, his nephew, and a dog. When the Blazer approached the trio in the middle of the sandy bed, Bonilla stood his ground. Bonilla would later say the truck nearly hit him, but others remembered it differently. What is not in dispute, however, is that some predictable words were exchanged; Holt got out of the truck, followed by Brunson; and that Bonilla produced a .22-caliber revolver. After shouting "Get back!" he shot Holt, and then Brunson.

Holt died, but Brunson would live.

Bonilla, a martial arts instructor who had an injured shoulder and leg, said he had brought the revolver as protection from mean dogs he'd encountered before in the riverbed. He said he pulled the gun against the pair because, injured, he was no match for the two men.

Bonilla had been born in Mexico and was a legal US resident, but not a citizen. He'd lived in Southern California before coming out to western Kansas to work in the meatpacking plants, but found other jobs in a year or two. At the time of the shooting, he was working as a part-time bond recovery agent for Rebecca Escalante, who owned a bail bond and tax preparation businesses. Escalante, a second-generation Latina who came from Texas, was also an interpreter for the local court system.

Bonilla was charged with second-degree murder and attempted second-degree murder, and held in the Ford County Jail with bond set at $100,000. Escalante, the bondswoman and his employer, later said she declined to post his bail, because she feared for his safety. The authorities said it was a simple case of a man who used a gun to settle an argument. Bonilla said he had shot because he feared for his life; Dodge City, he claimed, was a hotbed of white supremacists, and he wanted to talk to a reporter. Escalante contacted Claire O'Brien, the new education reporter at the *Dodge City Daily Globe* who had gained the trust of Latinos because she had lent an advocate's voice to their community.

Journalists are often some of the most unconventional members of any community, but Claire O'Brien must have seemed particularly unusual in conservative Dodge City. In a 2012 piece for the *Kansas Law Review*, Overland Park attorney Christopher C. Grenz offered a compelling portrait of the journalist who would become central to the state's biggest media law case. In an interview, she described herself as a fifty-four-year-old lesbian who grew up in San Francisco and who considered herself practically an anarchist.

"I just [do not] fit in here at all," she said.

She took the job in Dodge without even having visited the city, after being laid off by another GateHouse paper, in Illinois. She thought she knew the Midwest, according to Grenz, but she soon discovered that southwest Kansas is far from the Midwest she knew. There were powerful and compelling issues bubbling just beneath the surface in Dodge that deserved reporting. The Bonilla story was among them. Escalante escorted O'Brien into jail for her meeting with Bonilla, who talked for ninety minutes.

The way O'Brien reported the Bonilla story differed in three significant aspects from the way in which a murder case would be covered in most community newspapers: First, she was seeking the defendant's story in a criminal case, something that (unfairly) most papers would ignore, at least until trial, and rely instead on the account given by authorities. Second, she conducted a jailhouse interview with the defendant, and reported his claims of racial tension between whites and Latinos. And third, she relied on an anonymous source for a claim that Brunson, the driver of the pickup who survived the shooting, was associated with white supremacists, and was supported by a contingent of white residents armed with automatic weapons.

When O'Brien promised the source that she would protect his identity even if it meant she had to go to jail to do so, she didn't realize Kansas had no shield law to protect reporters from revealing their sources to police, prosecutors, and other authorities. Most states have shield laws, although they vary considerably in application, but generally they protect a reporter from divulging her sources, and protect her notes, photos, and other records.

There is no federal shield law, although the Supreme Court did leave room for limited confidentiality in *Branzburg v. Hayes,* a 1972 case in which four reporters were denied, 5 to 4, a constitutional right to refuse to testify before a grand jury. The majority opinion, however, carved out a slim exception: any claim to privilege must strike a proper balance between freedom of the press and the obligation of all citizens to give relevant testimony when asked about criminal conduct, and this balance should be made on a case-by-case basis.

When he read the story based on the jailhouse interview and the anonymous source, Ford County attorney Terry Malone was incensed. He could not have been surprised, because O'Brien had contacted him and asked for comment before filing the story. Malone had refused comment on the racial allegations. In an interview later with Grenz,

Malone said that he had known O'Brien for a couple of months, and that he did not consider her an "enemy," nor did he consider himself an enemy of the press. "But really, the big thing was, right there on the front page of our local newspaper was the fact that we had a guy that was alleged to be in serious harm should he ever be outside the custody of our sheriff," Malone said. "We had a duty to protect people and we had to do what we could to see if this threat was real or just imagined."

Malone filed subpoenas, one compelling O'Brien to testify at a rarely used procedure called an inquisition, and the other seeking her notes. GateHouse attorneys responded within forty-eight hours. Citing *Branzburg* and other cases, they said the county had not demonstrated the need for the information, or that it had exhausted its avenues for obtaining the information in any other way. The subpoenas amounted to a fishing expedition, they said.

GateHouse saw the O'Brien case as an opportunity to clarify the muddled Kansas law on reporter's privilege. There had only been one other noteworthy case, more than thirty years before, and the Kansas Supreme Court's decision on that case was ambiguous. Also, press freedom advocates in Kansas were eager for a case to be used as an example to encourage the state legislature to pass a reporter's shield law, because the most frequent criticism from lawmakers was that it was a nonissue; the O'Brien case could serve as a concrete example of need.

A Ford County judge declined to quash the subpoenas, finding that the information was indeed relevant to the criminal case, but that reporters had a limited privilege. In essence, it echoed the ambiguity of the Kansas Supreme Court's 1978 case. About the time of the ruling, O'Brien found out that her confidential source had lied to her about his last name, which undermined the credibility of her story and that of the *Globe*. The newspaper also concluded that O'Brien had failed to follow protocol for the use of unnamed sources in three ways: there was no second source used as confirmation, the informant's true identity was unknown to the paper, and the publisher or senior editor had not signed off on the use of the confidential source.

In spite of the deception involving his last name, O'Brien stood by her promise to keep the source confidential. After all, she reasoned, she knew his first name and his job title, and that was enough to identify him in the community.

More than 150 pages of briefs and filings were directed at the Kansas Supreme Court in the wake of the Ford County decision, Grenz notes, asking the justices to weigh in. In the end, they refused to become involved. In a two-sentence decision, the Kansas Supreme Court declined to take up the issue or comment on the merits of the case.

At that point, as the GateHouse lawyers saw it, their interests and that of O'Brien diverged. They had vigorously defended what they saw as her right to refuse to comply, but now that the Kansas Supreme Court had ruled, there was no room for appeal. If O'Brien chose to defy the order and continue to protect the identity of her confidential source, then she would have to obtain independent counsel. O'Brien remembers it differently, according to Grenz. "She contends that [a GateHouse lawyer] attempted to back her into a corner, insisting that she had to testify— divulging both the name of her source and her unpublished notes—if she were to be provided with counsel."

The lead of a *Topeka Capital-Journal* story from February 2010 described the scene when the news broke: "Reporter Claire O'Brien was smoking a cigarette outside the *Dodge City Daily Globe* on Tuesday afternoon when her editor approached and said the Kansas Supreme Court had ruled she would have to testify. She shook her head slightly and stared ahead. It had been three long months since she was first subpoenaed by the local prosecutor to hand over her notes on a story about a murder suspect and to reveal a confidential source. The stress of the situation had shown itself just the night before when she broke down talking about democracy's requirement of a robust media outside government's grasp. 'The protection of the press isn't for reporters, it's for the people,' she said through tears."

The story, written by James Carlson, included a nut paragraph that summed up what the case meant: "For the state's newspapers, the principle of an independent media is being impinged. Without protection against subpoena, they contend, reporters' ability to reveal pertinent information to the public will be stifled. And for the Kansas Press Association, the Dodge City situation has provided a real-life example for the need for Kansas to join 35 other states in passing a shield law to protect reporters."

What O'Brien did next was, as she admitted later, stupid.

She decided to skip the February 10 inquisition, a move that she was roundly condemned for. Press advocates said that even if a reporter wasn't going to answer questions, she still had to show up for court. The judge found O'Brien in contempt and ordered her fined $1,000 a day until she appeared in court and testified. In the end, however, the confidential source agreed to voluntarily reveal his identity to the prosecutor, letting O'Brien off the hook for her promise. She did testify, within a few days, and shared her notes. The judge rescinded his contempt motion and the fines.

But the relationship between the *Globe* and O'Brien would not recover. She said the locks were changed at the newspaper, and that she was the only employee without a key; that she was made to sign a statement saying she had defamed her employer; and that she was written up for minor infractions, such as turning in a story a few minutes late. She continued to be an outspoken critic of the newspaper, and a few weeks after the inquisition she was terminated, without severance pay or health insurance. At the time, GateHouse spokesmen declined comment, saying it was a personnel issue and irrelevant to the shield case.

Two weeks after her firing, Grenz notes, O'Brien won four reporting awards from the Kansas Press Association, including a first-place award for the story that led to so much trouble.

Instead of risking trial, Sam Bonilla agreed to plead guilty to reduced charges of voluntary manslaughter and aggravated battery. He was sentenced to seventy-four months, with possible time off for good behavior. During the sentencing, the judge admonished the *Globe* for stirring up racial tensions in a case where, he claimed, none existed.

While O'Brien's employment with the *Globe* was ending, a Kansas shield bill was making it out of committee. On April 15, 2010, Governor Mark Parkinson signed the bill into law, making Kansas the thirty-eighth state to shield reporters. Under the law, those seeking disclosure of confidential sources must show that the information they seek is material and relevant to their case, that it could not be obtained by exhaustive alternate means, and that it is of compelling interest. The law's definition of journalism includes online sources, in addition to legacy media.

Grenz, who wrote the definitive piece in the *Kansas Law Review*, notes that O'Brien was originally cooperative, but later made demands for notes from his interviews with his other sources. "When the author of this article declined to do so, O'Brien threatened to have the author deposed during what O'Brien promised would be a defamation lawsuit against certain individuals connected to this case."

Bonilla served his sentence and, according to the Kansas Department of Corrections, was released in November 2014 to federal authorities— presumably for deportation. At least, he doesn't show up as being in federal custody any longer, and my attempts to reach him have failed.

By the time I hiked back up the river bed, slipped through the defenses along the levee, and returned to my Jeep at Wright Park, I was thoroughly chilled and wanted a drink. I drove out to the Boot Hill Casino, just west of town, and had a glass of wine. The casino, which opened in 2009, has brought back legal gambling to Dodge City after more than a century. The casino has 584 noisy modern slot machines and a dozen table games, including poker, roulette, and blackjack. It is one of four casinos operated by the state lottery.

Rationalizing my desire to gamble in historic Dodge City by calling it research, I sat down at a blackjack table and placed a hundred dollars on the green cloth. I was only prepared to lose twenty bucks, but I didn't want to seem cheap. In exchange, the dealer shoved a couple of stacks of red checks to me. There were a couple of other gamblers at the table, both of them middle-aged men who were losing hand after hand, five dollars at a time, to the dealer's seemingly incredible run of luck. Had this been the 1870s, we wouldn't have been playing blackjack, nor would we probably have been playing poker; a card game named faro was king. It was fast-paced, played with a single deck handled only by the dealer, and offered action to many players at once who could, as in craps, place bets for or against a particular card appearing. The game was commonly called "bucking the tiger" because the cases containing the board and other pieces were commonly decorated with a drawing of a Bengal tiger. Faro was already old when it came to the West, having come from France and been played here since colonial times. But, faro—or "pharaoh"—offers only a slim margin for the houses, so casinos stopped offering it. By the end of World War II, a faro table was hard to find at Las Vegas or Atlantic City; they disappeared completely in the 1970s.

As for blackjack, the name would have been unknown in 1870s Dodge City, but you could have tried your luck at twenty-one, its forerunner. The modern name comes from 1931, when Nevada legalized gambling—and some casinos created a special payout of 10 to 1 for a hand that included either of the black jacks and the ace of spades. The payout proved unprofitable, but the name stuck.

At my blackjack table in Dodge City, after the dealer had shuffled the cards and started a new shoe, I placed a single red chip in the circle on the green felt in front of me—a five-dollar bet. I won that hand, with a nineteen against the dealer's eighteen, but then I busted on the next. I played for twenty minutes, making conservative bets and sticking to basic strategy, and hit a couple of blackjacks. The other fellows at the table kept losing, and even though I tried to strike up some light conversation, they didn't seem inclined to talk. I asked the dealer where the best place to eat was, and he said the casino restaurant could fix me up with a fourteen-ounce steak of my choice, with potato and salad bar, for $14.99. Then I was dealt a nine against the dealer's five showing. I doubled down—meaning, doubling my bet to $10—and won. On the last hand, I was dealt a pair of aces. You always split aces and eights, so I split those, and won both hands. The other guys at the table shook their heads. The shoe was done, and I was up $32 and some change. Time to call it quits before I gave it all back. After tipping the dealer, I walked away with $27.50 in profit, headed for the restaurant. It felt good to win, but I knew that if I had to depend on gambling for my dinner, I would have lost my shirt.

But for the night, at least, I was a winner—even if only a modest one. I had bucked the modern tiger in Dodge City, hiked the dry riverbed and made it back in one piece, and had a warm place to sleep. I was lucky. But why didn't it make me happy? My first thought was, just because something's legal doesn't make it moral. True enough, but there was something else. How much of my luck in general, I wondered, was really *privilege* due to the color of my skin? As a native Kansan, from a white family, I've benefited from an entitlement that I haven't thought about much, but that probably afforded me a cultural bias in education and employment that may have been denied others. I had the money to plunk down on the green cloth without worrying that, if I lost, I wouldn't be able to make the rent payment or buy groceries. The ribeye I ate that night was surprisingly good and had covered my plate, and when I was finished with it and the sides I had to loosen my belt in order to breathe. I've had some tough jobs in my life, including working for years as a newspaper reporter for relatively low pay. But never once in my life have I had to consider working in a packing plant, slaughtering beef and working in the blood and muck, in order to feed myself and my family.

River of Quivira
Elevation: 1,850' (Great Bend)

King Tatarrax! King Tatarrax!
Boughs of his forest with bells beyond number,
Golden and silvern, lull him to slumber . . .
Floats his canoe a-down the Broad River,
On through the years, Lord of Dreamland forever!

—Hartley Burr Alexander

The cottonwood trunk cracks six or seven feet up, showering rotten splinters on the riverbank. Suddenly unmoored, the skeletal branches forty feet above begin to wheel against the storm-clouded sky.

My kayak is nearly abreast of the old dead cottonwood, and the explosive sound of the bursting trunk shocks my system with adrenalin. The river was drummed by wind and rain earlier this morning, but now it's so quiet that the gentle dip of my paddle blades in the water ripples the tranquility, like the reflections in a plate glass window that gently shimmer from the air pressure of opening and closing doors. When the rotting trunk is suddenly riven, by time and gravity, there's a report and then a kind of sigh of resignation. I can judge from the way the branches are turning that it's going to fall on the bank and not the river, so even though my hands are tight on the shaft of the paddle, there's no need to scoot for safety. I've seen trees uprooted, struck by lightning, and burned by wildfires, but I've never seen one simply collapse. I watch in fascination as the tree crashes to the ground with a death shiver, branches quivering, a cloud of dust and debris blossoming.

From their kayaks, my two companions also watch the tree fall, and later we talk about what rotten luck it would be for a tree like that to come down on top of your boat. We don't know anyone that's happened to, but the Arkansas River here below Great Bend is narrow enough that a good-sized tree can easily span the width of the river channel, and we frequently encounter trees that do just that. Many of the trees that bridge the river aren't dead, like the one that just fell, but have green leaves and have fallen over because recent flooding has eaten away at the soil beneath them. When they fall, half of their roots are exposed on the bank, like broken

Vince Marshall paddling on the river east of Great Bend, Kansas.

teeth. But they are still trees, not logs, because they are—for a little while longer, at least—alive.

There's been a lot of rain in Kansas lately, and the river at Great Bend is high enough to float, which is uncommon. This is where the river emerges after its long trip underground from western Kansas, even though most of the time it appears as more of a trickle than a river.

It was raining that morning when the three of us set out from beneath the Highway 281 bridge over the river on the south side of Great Bend. Despite a forecast that predicted clear skies and temperatures that would climb to 100, the morning was cool and shrouded in storm clouds shot with lightning. The hardest part about launching at Great Bend was carrying the boats an eighth of a mile or so from the parking area, over a dike, and across soft sand beneath the bridge to the water. Vince and Kevin are veteran kayakers, and members of the Arkansas River Coalition. This is the third time I've paddled with them, and I like them more each time. Vince Marshall is in his seventies, thin as a heron, and with a back as perpetually straight in the kayak as if he were testifying in court. He seems so serious that, the day we met, he told a joke that it took me some time to get. When he is sometimes required to give presentations on the history of the Arkansas River, he said, the book he most relied on was written by "Eyeno Nuttin."

Kevin Holman is a retired Sedgwick County arson investigator and has short-cropped gray hair that he clipped when his wife lost hers to chemotherapy. His bare, muscled arms remind me of Burt Reynolds in *Deliverance*, and he is seemingly unflappable. Vince has paddled this thirteen-mile section once, but this is the first time for Kevin. We haven't seen a soul since leaving the highway bridge behind at Great Bend, and we won't see another until we emerge with our boats from beneath a similar bridge near Ellinwood. This river morning belongs wholly to us, the weather, and the wildlife.

We're paddling in Barton County, named for American Civil War nurse Clara Barton, the only county in the state named for a woman. Great Bend is well-named, because this is indeed the great bend in the Arkansas River, the lazy half-loop that meanders north out of southwest Kansas and crests just above the 38th parallel north, and reaches nearly as far north in latitude as Cañon City, Colorado. This is the same parallel that, on the other side of the globe, separates North and South Korea. Here in Kansas, the area where the river wanders north of the parallel is marked not by conflict but wistful historicism and religious fervor, which are reflected by a monumental stone cross and carefully lettered highway markers, the latter proclaiming "The Land of Quivira." This is likely where Francisco Vázquez de Coronado and his thirty *conquistadores* lingered for nearly a month before abandoning their search for Quivira, the mythical city of gold. "He had been told of a land where the king slept each night beneath a tree of golden bells that made soft music in the wind," the state historical marker near Lyons says, "and the people ate from plates of silver and gold." The marker does not mention Coronado's murderous bent. He had their guide, the Indian called the "Turk," strangled when no treasure was found.

The big stone cross that sits just west of the highway marker is yet another monument to Father Padilla, "who stood with Coronado at the erection of the first Christian Cross on these prairies" (that moment was actually a couple of hundred miles away, near Dodge City). The legend explains that the shapes and symbols on the monument stand for "Jesus Christ, Victor, and expresses the victory of faith and sacrifice. The square, quartered by the Cross, denotes the four corners of the World brought into Christian unity when Father Padilla carried the Cross of Christianity to the center of the New World." The monument, the inscription says, was a gift to the people of Kansas in 1950. Another stone says the cross was rededicated in 2000.

The reason these particular monuments are located here, alongside Highway 56 in Rice County, to the east of Great Bend, a county nearly smack in the middle of a state that is smack in the middle of the United States, goes back to another rainy season, this one in the summer of 1927. A horse being ridden across a soggy and freshly plowed field "stepped through an earthen pot of evident ancient manufacture." The quote is from Paul A. Jones, editor and owner, along with his brother Horace, of the *Lyons Daily News*, in a self-published book. "The newspaper at Lyons was notified and a story followed," Jones reports, and casts himself as a character in the tale. "The editor turned amateur archaeologist and, with a few companions, drove out and excavated the pot. Before he left the field he filled his pockets with flint arrowheads, awls, skin scrapers, drills, lance heads and knives. Into his car he threw a few stone hammers, mullers or upper millstones, fragments of catlinite pipes and potsherds of different designs." While this kind of pothunting may seem offensive today, it was common throughout the last century, and is not far removed from walking freshly plowed fields looking for projectile points. We may forgive Jones, perhaps, because in the 1920s archaeology wasn't seen as a science; most archaeology departments at the time were grouped with the arts.

Someone did summon to the field west of Lyons the state archaeologist, a genial crackpot named Mark E. Zimmerman, who believed a band of Celts came to America in 1171 and, joining forces with "Norsemen," ruled over a confederacy of Native Americans across the eastern United States. He claims these Celts, after being driven west about 1400 by an uprising, made their way down the Ohio River valley and up the Missouri River before settling in the hills of extreme northeastern Kansas. This is all according to a full-page Sunday feature about the Lyons discovery in the August 28, 1927, edition of the *St. Louis Post-Dispatch*, in which Zimmerman gives an explanation for his Celtic Kings of Ancient America theory that relies on the medieval story about a seafaring Welsh prince. Problem is, the story of Prince Madoc's discovery of America was a bit of folklore used to bolster English claims to the New World during Elizabethan times. Zimmerman also cited the eighteenth-century narrative of fabulist Maurice Griffith, a Welshman who claimed he'd been captured by the Shawnees and taken to a settlement on the Missouri River where blue-eyed white Indians spoke Welsh and had Christian artifacts. Zimmerman, who was a farmer when not pursuing revisionist archaeology, just happened to live in Doniphan County in extreme northeast Kansas, where he believed the Celtic Kings had made their redoubt.

Helping Zimmerman at the site was William E. Connelley, who had been secretary of the state historical society since 1914, an author who would become the most widely read, if not the most authoritative, source on Kansas history. Connelly is probably best remembered today for buying some bones believed to be those of the Civil War chieftain William Clarke Quantrill, who burned Lawrence in 1863. Connelley wanted to trade them for a holster once belonging to Wild Bill Hickok, as I recall the story, but ended up giving the bones to the historical society for display when the deal fell through. Connelley just happened to be from a northeastern Kansas county bordering the Missouri River, too: Wyandotte County. Photos taken in 1928 of a Rice County expedition, now held by the state historical society, show Zimmerman presiding over a party of well-dressed men digging in a field and scooping out artifacts as one would harvest potatoes.

Jones, the Lyons editor who wrote the 1937 book on Quivira, was the most scholarly of the bunch, even traveling to archives in Mexico City to gather primary material about the life of Coronado. The book stands up surprisingly well today, and leaves out the hokum that Zimmerman was spreading. That kind of thinking, that evidence of great empires in the Americas could not be accepted unless there was a corresponding theory that these kingdoms were really ruled by whites, was a common bigotry of the time. But if there were Eastern Hemisphere humans in America hundreds of years before Columbus—whether they were Welsh, Viking, or the Lost Tribes of Israel—they would have been few, frightened, and feigning superiority.

Just like Coronado.

The reference on the state historical marker about the golden bells, and the source for similar passages found in various texts, comes from one source: a history of the expedition written decades after the fact by Pedro de Castañeda de Nájera. Born in the Basque country of Spain, Castañeda was living in what is now northwestern Mexico when he became one of Coronado's foot soldiers. The narrative was translated into English in 1896 by George Parker Winship, but the standard reference has been the translation included in *Narratives of the Coronado Expedition, Vol. II*, edited by George P. Hammond, in 1940. It is typically cited by historians as the NCE.

"The Turk claimed that in his land there was a river, flowing through plains, which was two leagues wide," according to the NCE translation, "with fish as large as horses and a great number of very large canoes with sails, carrying more than twenty oarsman on each side" [a league is about three miles]. "The nobles, he said, traveled in the stern, seated under canopies, and at the prow there was a large gold eagle. He stated further that the lord of that land took his siesta under a large tree from which hung numerous golden jingle bells, and he was pleased as they played in the wind. He added that the common table service of all was generally of wrought silver, and that the pitchers, dishes, and bowls were made of gold."

By the time the expedition reached the great bend in the Arkansas River in 1541, the *conquistadores* had already begun to suspect the Turk of fabrication and worse. Castañeda reported that, during a bitter winter spent in a pueblo in what is now northern New Mexico, following a small war with the locals, a soldier swore he had seen the Turk talking to the devil in a pitcher of water, and that he knew things—the number of Christians killed elsewhere by the native pueblo dwellers, for example— that he could not have known without supernatural help. Even his nickname, the Turk, suggested suspicion; it was given to him because to the Spanish he resembled a swarthy member of a different religion. Still, their avarice overruled their caution, and they followed the Turk's directions as he led them out of New Mexico. He was leading them in the wrong direction, deep into the Texas panhandle, before Coronado listened to another guide, had the Turk put in chains, and corrected their course to the north.

Coronado and his thirty riders picked up the Arkansas River near present-day Ford, Kansas, and Coronado christened it the "River of Peter and Paul." From there, being led by the trusted guide named Isopote, they followed the river northeast. Historians are most certain of Coronado's path along the Arkansas, because the river is such a major geographic feature, and figures so prominently in the expedition's narrative.

Coronado and his troop left the Great Plains and, generally sticking to the north bank, explored the border between the silt- and sand-filled Arkansas River lowlands and the chalky limestone beds of the Smoky Hills. They encountered villages filled with thousands of nearly naked and tattooed inhabitants who lived in beehive-shaped grass huts. They found one tattooed woman who was reportedly "as white" as a Castilian, according to Castañeda. They sent out hunting parties to feed themselves and, at one point, killed 500 bison, which they called cows. They continued until they reached the north side of the Great Bend area, where they found the village called Quivira.

It was a prosperous Wichita settlement, and the soil was rich and the game, including deer and wild turkeys, abundant, but there was no gold. Coronado had the Turk interrogated—and we can assume here that it means tortured—as to why he lied. "He replied that his country was in that region, and the people of Cicuye [the Pecos Indians in New Mexico] had asked him to take the Spaniards out there and lead them astray on the plains. Thus, through lack of provisions, their horses would die and they themselves would become so feeble that, upon their return, the people of Cicuye could kill them easily and so obtain revenge." He thought the plan would work, because the Spanish did not appear to know how to hunt or survive without corn. "As to gold, he declared that he did not know where there was any. He said this like one in despair. The men, fearing that he would give some information that would bring harm to them, garroted him." Other sources said the order for the secret execution came from Coronado himself.

Parties of soldiers were sent to the north and elsewhere, but upon their return reported finding nothing but more grass and sky. Coronado said later that he had reached the 40th parallel, the current boundary between Kansas and Nebraska, but that may be a bit of an exaggeration. He may have just rounded up, in order to count more territory for Spain. Determining one's latitude on the plains was similar to taking a north-south position at sea, that is, by taking the angle of the sun and comparing it to charts. But figuring out where one was on the east-west longitudinal scale was a different matter, and would have to wait for the invention of the chronometer a couple of centuries later. But mostly, distance traveled was estimated by dead reckoning, and a solder was assigned each day to count his steps. A typical day's march was six or seven leagues a day, some eighteen to twenty-one miles. Coronado may have simply reckoned he was near the 40th parallel by estimating he had traveled 950 leagues—about 2,000 miles—from Mexico to reach Quivira.

Based on some metal chain mail found in 1915, Coronado or some of his men may have reached a hill near Lindsborg, about seventy miles northeast of the river at Great Bend, before turning back. In 1936 the Works Progress Administration erected a stone shelter there that resembled a castle. The place is called Coronado Heights and is just one entry in a long list of place names inspired by the expedition, from Tattarax Drive in Manhattan to Quivira Road in Johnson County. Kansans have dug up all sorts of things believed to have been left behind by the Spanish. Some objects, however, are not as authentic as others. The "Coronado Sword" found in 1886 near Cimarron and displayed for decades at the Kansas State Historical Society proved to be of German manufacture, and a product of the eighteenth century, possibly for trade and lost along the Santa Fe Trail. The rusty two-inch-square piece of horse mail found near Lindsborg was lost for many years before surfacing in 1974 at an Albuquerque antique store. It has since been authenticated, is believed to be the first definitive physical proof of the Spanish in Kansas, and is currently on display at the Kansas History Center in Topeka.

"What I am sure of is that there is not any gold nor any other metal in all that country," Coronado wrote to the king of Spain, Charles I, "and the other things of which they [the Turk and others] had told me are nothing but little villages, and in many of these they do not plant anything and do not have any houses except of skins and sticks, and they wander around with the cows."

Coronado returned to New Galicia in disgrace. Not only did he fail to find riches, but he was deeply in debt for the expedition. He was also in poor health, having fallen from his horse during the return trip from Quivira, suffering a head injury from which he was not at first expected to recover. Just two years after resuming his governorship of New Galicia, he was relieved of his duties and tried by the crown on charges that ranged from malfeasance to mistreating the Indians in his mines. Found guilty, Coronado was never to have an important posting again. He was sent to Mexico City, where he served as a petty city official occupied with road repairs and other municipal quotidia. He died in 1554, after an extended illness, at the age of forty-four.

Paul A. Jones, author of *Coronado and Quivira*, said the last years of the explorer's life illustrate the danger of naming public monuments after people who continued to live after their most noted acts. "Historians looking back on Coronado from the vantage ground of four centuries must revise their estimates of his ability to command and realize that he was not a great leader nor a great character," Jones writes.

The location of Quivira was almost certainly in Rice County, home to the headwaters of the Little Arkansas River, which joins the "big" Arkansas eighty-five miles to the southeast, at Wichita. Between the rivers is an area once populated by villages made of round houses and occupied by the Wichita people, who subsisted on a combination of hunting and farming. This headwaters area had been occupied for many thousands of years before the Wichita came about 1,700 years ago, after being displaced by other tribes to the east.

In 1981, a visiting anthropologist from Luther College in Iowa was asked to take a look at a trench in a farmer's field in Rice County, and the professor, R. Clark Mallam, identified a prehistoric serpent intaglio 160 feet long. An intaglio is a man-made ditch or furrow, and the earthen depression was first noted by students on a school outing in 1917. It wasn't until Professor Mallam filled the depression with lime, and took a photo from an aircraft, that the symbol became clear to him. The serpent, which has an egg or other oval object in its open jaws, is thought to have been carved to mark a "cosmologically oriented ceremonial center made sacred by the hydrological abundance of the headwaters region," according to an article in *Kansas History*. The serpent is similar to, but a tenth the size of, Serpent Mound in Ohio, which is oriented to the summer solstice and is estimated to be about 2,300 years old. It is located in an ancient meteorite impact crater, near a tributary of the Ohio River.

The builders of Serpent Mound left no clue to their faith, other than the shaped earth that is older than the New Testament, but generally snakes are associated in Native American mythology with water, creation, and rebirth. Because the serpent is aligned with the summer solstice, it is possible that the serpent isn't eating an egg at all, but is devouring the sun, in a never-ending life cycle in which the sun is spat back out at the winter solstice. Another, less popular interpretation is that the object isn't something being eaten, but is rather the eye of the snake. Given the ubiquitous nature of serpents and eggs in world mythology, however, I'd say the smart money is on the ovoid shape being an egg.

The Rice County effigy is cruder, and possibly younger, than the one in southern Ohio. It goes down six or seven inches to a clay layer, according to Mallam's excavation in 1982. The figure is on a ridge south of three mounds containing what have been described, since the 1940s, as "council circles." As advanced by Wichita State University anthropologist Donald Blakeslee and others, the Kansas intaglio was made by the Wichita people themselves. Blakeslee has even hosted tours of the Rice County site for a few descendants of the Wichita people, who noted sage growing at the site, a plant that is sacred to them and other Native Americans.

To me, the evidence for identifying the creators of the Rice County serpent intaglio seems slight. There were some stone flakes found by Mallam in the intaglio that were from the Pecos region of Texas, which would be consistent with Quiviran or Wichitan builders, and there is an alignment with the council circle mounds, two miles to the north. But, no wooden tools or anything else subject to radiocarbon dating was discovered in the trench. As tempting as it is to link the serpent effigy with Quivira and the dawn of the Kansas historical period, the intaglio may be far older. Maybe the site was sacred to the inhabitants of Quivira, but in the same way the Old and New Testaments are to Christians. Or, I could just be wrong. After all, this is coming from a man who has never turned so much as a shovel of dirt in the disciplined pursuit of the past.

Far more convincing is that Quivira was in north-central Kansas, although competing claims have been made for locations in at least eight other states. Waldo R. Wedel, of the National Museum of Natural History, who had been a principle in the Rice County investigations of half a century earlier, wrote a retrospective in 1990 for *Great Plains Quarterly*. Wedel praised the work of Herbert E. Bolton, who in 1940 set out by auto, horse, mule, and on foot to retrace Coronado's route, and came to the conclusion that Quivira was in Rice or McPherson Counties in north-central Kansas.

"Despite some very good clues in the Coronado documents," Wedel wrote, "the identification and location of Quivira sought by the Spaniards has been a subject of lively discussion for well over a century. It has been located in many places in New Mexico, Texas, Oklahoma, Kansas, Colorado, Missouri, Nebraska, South Dakota, and even across the Missouri River in Iowa. Many of these identifications rest on an amazing disregard of the information that can be ferreted out of the Coronado documents—the distances and directions reportedly traveled, the number of days spent, the terrain traversed, and other details."

In the 1920s, our Kansas editor Jones was the subject of much newspaper-slung ridicule by rival amateur archaeologists from the Lone Star State who felt Quivira rightly belonged to them. The town of Liberal, just above the Oklahoma border in southwest Kansas, also competed for tourists in later decades, but when attendance began to fall the museum curator, Fred W. Jaedicke, resorted to arson. In 1962, he set fire to the museum, and later to another building where artifacts from the museum had been moved. After being arrested and charged, Jaedicke was committed to the Larned State Hospital, where he died in 1963.

Castañeda describes Quivira as a well-settled country similar to Spain in its variety of vegetables and fruits. There are grapes, nuts, mulberries, oats, and flax. It is a country worth returning to, he says. But, he also says that while Quivira is located on a plain, mountains can be seen in the distance. If this is true, then Rice County is out of the running, unless the *conquistadores* mistook the Smoky Hills of Kansas for mountains. That is what most historians believe, but it seems to me unlikely that men who had seen the Grand Canyon and the mountains of New Mexico would mistake a few rolling hills for mountains. Castañeda's narrative is serpentine, bouncing back and forth between locations, and was written twenty years after his visit. Perhaps his memory failed him.

Castañeda notes that a zealous Andalusian friar, Juan de Padilla, and some subordinates, including a Portuguese soldier in the service of Spain, stayed behind in Kansas. Sometime in 1542 (or perhaps 1543 or 1544), after ministering throughout the region, he angered some locals by wanting to visit a neighboring, but enemy, tribe. His hosts killed him, ostensibly while the good Franciscan was kneeling in prayer. His companions, including the Portuguese de Campo, escaped. After being captured and held as a slave for a year by the Indians, de Campo walked across much of the plains and the Southwest, and made it back some years later to Mexico, where he told the story of Padilla's death.

Today, several states claim monuments or even burial sites for Padilla. In 1936, a monument to the "first Christian martyr of Texas" was erected by the state and the Knights of Columbus at Amarillo, in the panhandle. It is one of the few monuments that depict that slaying, with Padilla on his knees between an Indian with a tomahawk and another about to let fly with an arrow.

In Kansas, there's a monument at Herington and an alleged ancient burial cairn at Council Grove. The cairn is on private land, atop a hill southwest of town overlooking the Neosho River, and its advocate was George P. Morehouse, variously a state senator, life member of the Kansas Historical Society, and president of the Kansas Authors Club. Morehouse led the effort to mark the Santa Fe Trail, which crosses the state diagonally from northeast to the southwest, and for which Council Grove was the last stop for provisions before endless days of prairie. Morehouse encountered the mysterious cairn as a boy and later convinced himself that it must be the grave of a fallen and forgotten hero—Father Padilla. Writing for the historical society, Morehouse ostensibly quotes from a Winship translation of *History of the Conquest of the Kingdom of New Galicia in North America* by Mota Padilla, an eighteenth-century Mexican historian.

"[Padilla] reached Quivira and prostrated himself at the foot of the cross, which he found in the same place where he had set it up; and all around it clean, as he had charged them to keep it, which rejoiced him, and then he began the duties of a teacher and apostle of that people; and finding them teachable and well disposed, his heart burned within him, and it seemed to him that the number of souls of that village was but a small offering to God, and he sought to enlarge the bosom of our mother, the Holy Church, that she might receive all those he was told were to be found at greater distances. He left Quivira, attended by a small company, against the will of the village Indians, who loved him as their father."

Of course, they wanted to kill him for leaving.

"At more than a day's journey the Indians met him on the warpath, and knowing the evil intent of those barbarians, he asked the Portuguese that as he was on horseback he should flee and take under his protection the oblates and the lads who could thus run away and escape. . . . And the blessed father, kneeling down, offered up his life, which he had sacrificed for the winning of souls to God, attaining the ardent longings of his soul, the felicity of being killed by the arrows of those barbarous Indians, who threw him into a pit, covering his body with innumerable stones."

At his death, according to Mota Padilla (yet another Padilla) via Winship via Morehouse, there were great signs, to wit: "The earth flooded, globes of fire, comets and obscuration of the sun." Morehouse concludes the piece by intoning, "Let us not infer that the life of Padilla and his tragic death was without its lessons."

Morehouse himself died in 1941, and is buried at Council Grove.

Whatever lessons he had for us, the strangest claim to the body of Fray Padilla goes to Isleta, New Mexico. There, in a pueblo along the Rio Grande, near the altar of an adobe mission church built in 1612, is a dugout cottonwood coffin that many thousands have believed contains his incorruptible remains. As far back as 1819, there are reports that, amid strange knocking and thumping noises, the coffin had risen like a canoe from the earth and come to rest solidly on the church floor. Upon investigation, allegedly, the corpse was found to be fresh and smelling of perfume. As late as 1936, the Associated Press reported "the martyred priest's uneasy spirit walks through the village again" and that some old men remembered the last time the coffin rose, in 1908. The AP said Padilla was "slain by rebellious Indians in 1543 at Gran Quivira, nearly 100 miles east of here." That would put the site of his martyrdom firmly in New Mexico. But, it should be noted, the AP moved the story as a Halloween feature. A fuller account of the rising coffin is given in Ray John de Aragón's 2012 book, *Hidden History of Spanish New Mexico*. He devotes ten pages to it, including a detailed description of the slaying, the sudden storm after, the friar's body being hidden in a cave by sympathetic Indians, and subsequently being taken to the mission church at Isleta Pueblo.

The Catholic Church has said, however, that the corpse is not that of Padilla, but is probably that of another brother who died about the time the church was built. No disturbances have been noted since a concrete floor was poured in the 1960s. The *Catholic Encyclopedia* records Padilla's death as November 30, 1544, but does not fix a location. Padilla heads the list of "Martyrs of the United States," candidates for sainthood given to the Vatican by an American bishop in 1941. Although Padilla is described as the "protomartyr" for being the first Catholic to die in America for his faith, his chances of canonization look increasingly slim.

The story of Fray Padilla hangs on the most slender of threads—that of a survivor recounting the tale years later, and for whom there was a powerful incentive to frame the death as heroic. Fiction or not, that Padilla's demise remains an object of roadside reverence today is indicative of the endless fascination of the devout with martyrdom. What is it about dying for one's faith that is so compelling? The root of the word *martyr* comes from the Greek *martur*, for "witness"; in Islam, the commonly used word for martyr, *shahid*, also means witness, but in Arabic. It is an affirmation of faith and a refutation of the power of the world to change one's belief. It is also subjective. A martyr is somebody who dies for *your* religion.

Five hundred and more years ago, the European superpower of Spain used religion to justify plundering the Americas under the church's "Doctrine of Discovery," which granted Christian explorers the authority to claim any lands not inhabited by those of the faith. Inhabitants who refused conversion could be killed or enslaved. After Columbus landed in the Bahamas, the doctrine was modified by treaty in 1493 that divided the New World between Spain and Portugal; other European powers, especially the upstart English, would later dispute the Iberian claims, but used the doctrine's concept of discovery when it suited. The United States has relied on the doctrine at least as far back as 1823's *Johnson v. M'Intosh*, in which the Supreme Court recognized the legality of the doctrine of conquest and legitimized the title of lands, held by the federal government, that had been obtained—or would be obtained—from Native Americans.

While the Doctrine of Discovery may seem just a historical footnote now, it shaped the future of the Americas more than any other idea; it was this doctrine, and not Columbus or Cortez or Coronado, that conquered the Americas. In 1987, John Paul II acknowledged the oppression and injustice done to native peoples when he addressed a gathering of Indians in Phoenix, Arizona. His statement was far short of an apology, however, and John Paul offered the opinion that in order to be objective, "history must record the deeply positive aspects of your people's encounter with the culture that came from Europe." He stressed the work of missionaries who strove to improve living conditions, set up schools, and introduce Indians to Christianity. "This gospel of Jesus Christ is today, and will remain forever, the greatest pride and possession of your people," he said.

In 2015, however, one of John Paul's successors *did* apologize.

"I say this to you with regret: Many grave sins were committed against the native people of America in the name of God," Pope Francis told a group of Indians and others at a hall in Vera Cruz, Bolivia, according to the *New York Times*. "I humbly ask forgiveness, not only for the offense of the church herself, but also for crimes committed against the native peoples during the so-called conquest of America."

Of the world's 1.2 billion Catholics, just over 40 percent live in Latin America. Francis, whose papacy began in 2013, is a native of Argentina. In the United States, there are 70 million Catholics, making it the largest religious body in the country; about 1 in 5 Americans are Catholic, including Kansas governor Sam Brownback. Raised a Methodist in a small town in eastern Kansas, he later spent time at an evangelical Christian Church in Topeka before converting to Roman Catholicism in 2002. He got his start in politics as the state's agriculture secretary. After terms in both the US House and Senate, and a brief run for president, Brownback was elected governor in 2010.

Which brings us back to Coronado.

Just around the corner from Brownback's office—his ceremonial office, the one he uses for public signings—on the second floor of the state capitol building in Topeka is the best-known depiction of Coronado and Father Padilla. The panel is by John Steuart Curry, a native Kansan and a lesser light of American Regionalism who, at the urging of newspaper editors, including our Paul Jones, accepted in 1937 a commission to portray the sweep of state history in a series of murals. It took some time to raise the $10,000 commission, which Kansans— including many schoolchildren—collected in dimes and dollars across the state, despite the crushing economics of the Great Depression. The governor appointed a committee of newspaper editors to oversee the project, although Curry was promised a free hand in interpreting the state's vigorous and often violent history.

Coronado and his priest are part of three panels collectively called "Tragic Prelude." Curry's most famous image—and one of the most famous pieces of public art in the world—is part of this mural: a wild-eyed John Brown with a Bible in one hand and a Beecher rifle in the other, dead soldiers in blue and gray at his feet, a twister and a prairie fire in the background. John Brown towers over the other figures in the painting, even though he is placed behind some of them, and his wild eyes and flowing hair and beard are worthy of an Old Testament prophet. It is such an iconic image that the progressive rock band Kansas used it as the cover for its self-titled debut album in 1974.

In contrast to the overpowering image of traitor-prophet-madman-martyr John Brown, stepping larger than life from the canvas of the Civil War, it might be easy to dismiss Coronado. The colors are muted, the conquistador's proud and cruel face is in three-quarter profile, and the tawny horse on which he rides seems of far more importance. Padilla walks beside him, wearing a dark skullcap and rough brown robe, clutching a golden and bejeweled crucifix to his breast with both hands. In early sketches, Padilla has a benign expression, but when Curry had committed the brother to paint, the face became skull-like, the eyes hidden in shadow, and the mouth unpleasant. The skeletal aspect is, perhaps, meant to represent his imminent death (a 1938 work, "Parade to War," gives marching American soldiers a similar, cranial visage). Three mounted soldiers are in the background, behind Padilla. The forlorn Turk walks ahead of two of the conquistadors, face downcast, dressed only in a loincloth, with something around his neck—a rope, perhaps, foreshadowing his eventual garroting.

The artist loved movies, and his depiction of Coronado was based more on Saturday afternoon matinees than any historical research. Curry ordered the conquistador's outfit from the Hollywood firm United Costumers, according to biographer M. Sue Kendall, and his horse was inspired by the Palominos popular in 1930s Westerns. The life models for Coronado were several students who successively rode a sawhorse in Curry's studio at the University of Wisconsin at Madison, where he was artist-in-residence.

In the finished statehouse panel, both Coronado and Padilla look to the left, toward a plainsman with a dead bison at his feet, and the bearded frontiersman is looking left as well, toward fanatical abolitionist John Brown.

Curry's murals were never finished.

After unveilings of "Tragic Prelude" and "Kansas Pastoral," painted in 1940 and 1941, the public backlash was swift. Many felt that Curry's portrayal of Kansas was unflattering, that he dwelled only on the negative, that a farm wife's skirt was too short and that a bull had an inauthentic stance (this last, perhaps, was because the bull's impressive testicles were fully displayed). "The murals do not portray the true Kansas," complained the Kansas Council of Women. "Rather than revealing a law-abiding progressive state, the artist has emphasized the freaks in its history— the tornadoes, and John Brown, who did not follow legal procedure." The Newspaper Enterprise Association wire service ran a nationally syndicated story in the fall of 1941 that described the dustup in Kansas in this way: "If Rudolf Hess showed up at your front door carrying Herman Goering piggyback, you would probably gasp no louder than most people do at their first glimpse of Curry's John Brown."

When Curry wanted some Italian marble removed to make room for a panel that would portray the consequences of poor soil management, the legislature balked. Some lawmakers wanted to allot money to paint over the offending images. Curry quit in 1941, left his murals unsigned, and abandoned Kansas. He died of a heart attack, at the age of forty-eight, in Wisconsin.

Long before the Curry murals, the statehouse—the interior of which was designed to look like a Renaissance palace—had inspired at least one other to depict the earliest European history of Kansas in fiction. Topeka novelist Margaret Hill McCarter—a writer of regional treacle and yet another member of the Kansas Authors Club, where she hobnobbed with club president Morehouse, of the Council Grove cairn—was inspired to write *In Old Quivira* one Christmas Eve while gazing at historical artifacts and portraits displayed beneath the capitol dome. In a dream state, the interior of the capital building becomes a sort of temple to Kansas history, with all of its rivers and valleys stretching back in time, and historical figures come to life. There's Zebulon Pike, "gracing his military dress that betokened his official rank." When the heroic Pike commands the group of Pawnees to hoist down the Spanish flag and fly the Stars and Stripes instead, it is the "voice of the indomitable Saxon spirit that speaks, and the Red Man must needs obey." The dim statehouse corridors yield to rivers of time. "A Past, the back of this Past, has its own story to tell. On these corridor walls hang sainted faces, faces of the men and women who foreran the white settler and brought the story of the blessed Gospel to the savage folk." Locked away from the rest of the artifacts there is a sword, or perhaps the Coronado Sword, found in 1886, that magically spins the story of *In Old Quivira*. There's a love story mashed up with the story of Coronado, Padilla, and the evil Turk. After being called back to minister to his "Quivira children," Padilla is stoned to death on a bluff overlooking the Neosho River—at dawn on Christmas Day.

There was no outcry over McCarter's 1908 novel. In fact, it was a best seller.

Many others have told the story of Coronado and the *Entrada* since, but the most unusual may be the work of the late Don Coldsmith, an Emporia physician who in 1980 published a novel with Doubleday called *Trail of the Spanish Bit*. Like McCarter, Coldsmith asks what story an artifact would tell if it could talk, but he doesn't resort to magic. Instead, he turns the old story on its head by centering not on Coronado or Padilla, but on a young Spanish officer who is cut off from the expedition and must depend on a plains tribe for survival. In spite of using a European character as a hook, the story is mostly about the Indians and how their lives are about to change because of the introduction of the horse. The novel became an unusually long-running series, with more than twenty books. The last book, *Moon of Madness*, was released in 2013. Because Coldsmith was my mentor, and I now the direct the writing workshop he founded with some others at Emporia State, I was asked to write the introduction to that last, posthumously published volume. It was a eulogy not just for my friend, but for an age that never was and always will be. The saga of Coronado in Kansas, equal part fever dream and prayer for absolution, had soaked the soil of the Sunflower State until we could hold no more. Future generations will offer new translations, there will be art and novels not yet imagined, and there will probably be more roadside crosses and state historical markers. But the century of McCarter and Curry and Coldsmith is done.

After the tree fell, the float trip was remarkable only in that, when the river dipped far south of the highway, it was possible to glimpse what the river may have looked like before the coming of the Europeans. One had to ignore the invasive plants, such as a variety of common reed, and had to be far enough away from the detritus of the twentieth century, such as the occasional automobile weirdly embedded in the deep cut of a bank.

But there were a few spots here, more than anywhere else I'd been on the river in Kansas, that felt like the river primeval. There were no sights nor sounds of civilization, and even the wildlife seemed remarkably unafraid of us. There were blue herons and a mallard or two and a few wild turkeys. We stopped counting the number of deer we saw, but I'm confident it topped thirty, bucks snorting in the underbrush before bounding away, and does with their babies at the water's edge, watching us with wary brown eyes. We were within a few yards of some of them before they bounded away, long white tails flagging over their backs. On the sandbars were sometimes the bones of dead critters, and Vince was looking for bison skulls, which he said sometimes appear, but we didn't find any. The only excitement was when, after dragging my kayak across the trunk and through the branches of a living tree that had fallen across the channel, I tried to get back in by sort of hopping into the seat. I knew I should have put the paddle behind me as a brace and then eased myself into the cockpit, but my lower back was howling and the proper technique would be painful.

I was impatient.

I had hung back to take some photos, and was the last one over the tree. I'd hopped casually into the kayak before, but this time the back of the seat folded beneath me, making my position precariously high, and when I lifted one of my legs from the cockpit to give me enough room to put the seat down, the kayak dumped me in the river. The water was shallow and not particularly fast, so it wasn't serious, but I felt foolish because Kevin had asked me if I needed help and I told him, "I've got it." He came back and helped me drain the water from my boat, and then I dragged the boat down to a better spot, got in, and continued. Some miles later, I lifted the Pelican case I keep my iPhone in and discovered it filled with muddy water. Somehow, it had leaked. Maybe there was some sand or grit in the seal. We stopped for a snack soon after on a sandbar, and I took the phone out of the case and found the screen was blank, and the back of the phone was hot to the touch, as if it had an infection. Without the tools necessary to remove the battery, there was little I could do to keep it from dying. It was the first time I'd killed anything electronic on the river, and my frustration and self-loathing made the twenty-first century come rushing back with a vengeance. At the take-out beneath the highway bridge south of Ellinwood, I gouged the side of my leg on a stob in the water. Later, after we had the boats and the vehicles secured, we drove back to Great Bend for a midafternoon lunch, and I didn't discover until later that as we dined blood was smearing my right leg above my tennis shoes. I hadn't shaved that morning, my hair was long and wild, and my eyes felt bloodshot from lack of sleep. I must have looked pretty rough to the other patrons.

Because it was primary day in Kansas, I was thinking about politics as we ate our ham-and-cheese omelets and baked potatoes at Perkins, where a big American flag rippled outside. In the lobby of the restaurant, a conservatively dressed middle-aged black woman was talking with a young Latina, urging her to register to vote. The young woman was in a uniform, and looked as if she might have just gotten through with one shift as a housekeeper at a local motel, and was perhaps about to start another. She looked tired. *No*, she said, *I don't vote, I am too busy. And it wouldn't make any difference.*

Vince and Kevin and I hadn't talked politics that weekend, other than noting we'd be off the river in time to vote. Kevin carried a soft-sided cooler on the river with him that was emblazoned with the McCain 2008 logo on it, but that didn't bother me. I brooked no personal quarrel with anybody who had spent time in the Hanoi Hilton. I may not agree with his politics or his choice for running mate, but I believe he is a decent man. I believe the same about George Bush 41, who had a torpedo bomber shot from beneath him during World War II, and only narrowly escaped being captured and eaten—yes, cannibalized—by Japanese officers who would later be convicted of war crimes.

But contemporary politics had consumed me for the better part of a month. Donald Trump was an enigma wrapped in a bigot. The presidential race had wrecked my sleep and haunted my days, and knowing the world was watching, had made me ashamed to be an American. When a friend of mine had asked nervously, earlier in the primary season, whether Trump stood a chance, I said no, of course not—don't worry, Trump's a joke.

Bread and Quicksilver
Elevation: 1,299' (Wichita)

The geology-water exists among stones.
The mythology-water exists in hearts.

—Albert Goldbarth

It's seven o'clock on a Monday night in July at St. Anne Catholic Church in southwest Wichita, where some three hundred people have gathered for a prayer vigil for a kayaker who disappeared in the rain-drunk Arkansas River two days earlier. The vigils, it has been reported by local media, will continue at seven every night until the kayaker has been found. Similar vigils are going on at churches in Hutchinson and Parsons, and other towns in the diocese.

This church is a rather modern one and the chapel is all air and light and wood, like a library at one of the state's better community colleges, and the crucified Jesus is suspended over an altar that proclaims, "Behold the Lamb of God." The church is named for the grandmother of Jesus, and a bilingual church flier I crib near the door portrays Anne with her hands protectively over the shoulders of Mary, who of course is wearing a blue skirt. The figures look like idealized characters from the Italian Renaissance, something from the ceiling of the Sistine Chapel. The stained-glass panels behind the altar, lit from behind by a sun that is low in the west, are a bit pop-arty. There is a representation of water in one of the panels, a blue splash of sea or river with a fish in it, and on another panel there's presumably the Garden of Eden, with a blood-red serpent. It's quiet inside the chapel—if that is what they call this modernized version of the Roman vision—and people kneel on the fold-out padded prayer benches and clasp their hands over the back of the pew in front, a rosary sometimes dangled from interlacing fingers. The only sound is the soft whirr of the HVAC, somewhere beyond the recessed lights above. Then the silence is abruptly broken by somebody's cellphone, a crazy pinball ring tone. I wonder if the call is carrying urgent news of the kayaker who has been the focus of such intense effort, both physical and spiritual, but the phone is quickly silenced.

No announcement is forthcoming.

Low-head dam beneath 21st Street Bridge.

The kayaker—a twenty-four-year-old, third-year seminary student named Brian Bergkamp—was last seen in the water beneath the 21st Street Bridge, in northwestern Wichita. The narrative relayed from authorities so far by the local newspaper, the *Eagle*, and other news outlets is cryptic, but it goes like this: Bergkamp was with four other kayakers (another seminarian and three women, all in their twenties) Saturday morning when the group ran into trouble beneath the bridge, where there's a drop of about eighteen inches. This created a boil that "snared" the kayaks, according to a Wichita fire battalion chief involved in the recovery effort, and Bergkamp left his boat to assist one of the women, who had fallen in the water. The battalion chief, Frank Buck, told the *Wichita Eagle* that Bergkamp managed to save the woman's life, but that the energy required may have depleted him too much to save himself. The other paddlers managed to reach the west bank of the river, along with three of the kayaks.

Everyone except Bergkamp was wearing a life jacket, the *Eagle* reported.

This is the fact that troubles me most about the tragedy, that a group would set out on a major river filled with rainwater and flowing at up to nine miles per hour, but wouldn't have enough PFDs for every member. Surely, there was something I didn't understand about the situation—or the narrative had been garbled in the telling and retelling.

A search involving dozens of firefighters, several boats, and even a Kansas Highway Patrol airplane, has failed to turn up any sign of Bergkamp. The two missing kayaks were located in brush about a quarter of a mile downstream, however. Crews searched over the weekend east to Amidon Street, a distance of about two river miles; by Monday, however, the water was deemed too high for firefighters to safely continue the search.

A week earlier, heavy rains had caused some streets in west Wichita to be closed, and dampened Fourth of July celebrations. Five inches of rain fell in a twenty-four-hour period. Although the city has the authority to close the river to boaters, it did not do so, either in the high-water days before Bergkamp's disappearance, or in the days to follow.

Before going to St. Anne, I had visited the spot where Bergkamp had left his kayak and, presumably, his life. Parking the Jeep at the Big Arkansas Park, just north of the bridge, I followed the concrete walkway that snaked along the west bank of the river. I walked past a pair of yellow cones meant to turn away the incautious and trotted down to where the water, frothy with what appeared to be agricultural runoff, licked at the soles of my hiking boots. Then, I took a few prudent steps back. The water had submerged parts of the concrete walkway, along with much of the grassy bank.

A quarter of a mile or so upriver cars were zipping over the I-235 bridge, and beyond that whitewater foamed from the outlet tubes at the base of the diversion dam that separates the Arkansas from the Wichita and Valley Center Floodway. Called the "Big Ditch" by locals, the floodway and associated levee was built in 1958 and protects the city from the periodic floods that used to cause millions of dollars in damage, including three floods during an eleven-day period in 1944.

The diversion dam is impassable for a boater, and a river guide posted online at the Arkansas River Coalition website notes: "rough take-out and portage to Big Arkansas River Park on river right—about .2 mile to parking lot from takeout over dike/dam, under I-235. Note: River Hazards Ahead: do not continue floating through diversion dam tubes or over low-water dam under 21st St. bridge." The ARC guide also noted that, in 2015, the city had declared the area from the bridge to Amidon off-limits to boaters.

Looking downriver, there was little sign of the dam under the 21st Street Bridge, just a difference in the color and texture of the water, and even this was largely hidden by the shadow of the bridge. Low-head dams are difficult to spot even when they are in full sunlight, and on fast water you might be on them before there was a chance to take evasive action. But, as easy as it would be to miss seeing the dam if you weren't looking closely, it would be difficult to miss the two yellow signs on the bridge:

DAM

STAY BACK 150 FEET

The sidewalk leading below the bridge to the park-like area downriver was submerged, so I climbed up the grassy slope to the deck of the bridge and waited until traffic slowed enough to allow me to cross. Then I went down to the sidewalk, which was above water downstream, where I had a good view of the water beneath the bridge. The dam, with a drop of what seemed at least two feet, ran from pillar to pillar beneath the length of the bridge. For several yards below the dam, from where the water seemed to boil, the river rolled back upstream. Once caught in those hydraulics, it would be difficult to get free, life vest or not.

It is a textbook hazard.

The force is so powerful that those who are caught in the recirculating waters below a low-head dam are often stripped not only of their life jackets, but of their clothes. Also, there's so much air being sucked down where the water meets the bottom of the dam that it reduces your ability to stay afloat, because the water is simply less dense. Even if one's personal flotation device stays in place, its effectiveness—which typically amounts to just a few pounds of lift—is compromised by what engineers call a "low buoyancy environment."

One of those engineers, Dr. Bruce Tschantz, a distinguished professor emeritus at the University of Tennessee at Knoxville, wrote in a 2014 issue of *The Journal of Dam Safety* that only three states (Illinois, Pennsylvania, and Virginia) have statutory authority for regulating public safety at low-head dams, according to a current survey. Five states have qualified authority to do so, in special circumstances, and four more provide warning sign guidance and recommendations to dam owners. Kansas and Colorado are among the majority of states that have no public safety laws for low-head dams, Tschantz reported. For most states, there isn't even an inventory of such dams.

"Kayakers, canoers, rafters, boaters, anglers and swimmers are often unaware of the dangerous forces and fast recirculating currents that these dams can produce, especially if there are no warning signs, floating barriers or portages," Tschantz wrote. "Experienced swimmers have difficulty overcoming the velocities around these structures. Stranded motor boaters, canoers, rafters, and kayak paddlers are often unable to prevent themselves from being pulled over the dam crest by the rapid drawdown current. Once they are trapped in the turbulent foam below low-head dams, life vests become less effective because of greatly reduced buoyancy. In fact, incidents have been documented where the life vests have been ripped off victims in the churning hydraulic below the dam. Overflowing water is capable of pounding trapped victims with relentless forces exceeding hundreds of pounds."

Additional dangers include debris trapped in the recirculating current, hypothermia, and disorientation. Dozens of rescuers have drowned, Tschantz noted, in attempts to free victims trapped in the countercurrent zone between the dam and downstream boil zones.

Low-head dams, Tschantz wrote, are "perfect drowning machines."

There have been more than 300 fatalities at low-head dams across the country from 1960 to 2014, according to Tschantz, with most of those deaths coming in the last few years. Of 308 recorded fatalities, more than a quarter came in the last four years. The victims also tended to be male (84 percent) and young, with a median age of twenty-seven.

Most did not have life jackets.

"Some boaters were unaware of the dam before it was too late or lost power and were pulled over by the current, while many kayakers, canoers, and rafters deliberately paddled over the dam, challenging the danger by underestimating the tremendous power of moving water while overestimating their ability to overcome these forces and currents," Tschantz noted. "Wearing a life vest while going over a dam improved the survival rate by a margin of 57 percent to 43 percent."

Every day, about ten people unintentionally drown in the United

States, according to the Centers for Disease Control, but only about one per day in a boating-relating accident.

At the Monday night prayer vigil, there has been little officially released to indicate what contributed to the accident, other than the descriptions by Buck, the battalion chief. The Wichita Police Department daily media log lists the accident as incident 16C0474451, reported at 8:42 a.m. on Saturday, July 9. "R1 [Reporting Party] reports V1 and W1-4 kayaking through the river. V1 (Victim 1) left his kayak to help W3 (Witness 3) and was lost in the current," the log states. The incident is classified as "Submersion-Public."

At St. Anne, a woman who describes herself as a friend of the Bergkamp family gives an interview to local television, and she claims that what is generally misunderstood about the tragedy is that the twenty-four-year-old seminarian had taken off his own life jacket and given it to the woman in trouble, saving her life. The message, of course, is that Bergkamp is a hero. This is the way the local media have portrayed the accident, that the Catholic community has gathered together to pray for the recovery of the body of a young man who, Christ-like, gave his life for another. A bishop would later say that Bergkamp had "lived and died in a most priestly way."

When I watch the interview with the family friend later online, I argue with the computer screen about the casual use of the word *heroic*. *Wouldn't it have been better to insist the group get some basic safety training or invest in a minimum of research on local river hazards?* It seemed to me that Bergkamp's presumed death was the opposite of heroic, because it could have been so easily avoided. It wasn't random, like cancer or being struck by lightning, but was an entirely predictable result stemming from ignorance and overconfidence. If the arrows of death at noonday fly unseen, then the Bergkamp accident was aided by a full quiver.

In the days to come, searching for Bergkamp's body will become a morbid hobby in Wichita. People with rosaries in their hands will walk the banks of the Arkansas where he disappeared, the *Eagle* reports. The paper notes that social media were reporting that a "lone candle was lit among the rocks near where Bergkamp was last seen" and that the "Miraculous Medal, a Catholic devotional, has been thrown into the river with the prayer that Bergkamp would be found soon."

Just who did the throwing and who did the praying were not specified.

Puzzling over the reference to the "Miraculous Medal," I Googled to find out more. The popular Catholic charm shows Mary standing on a globe, crushing a serpent beneath her feet, while rays shoot from her hands, symbolizing the graces she will bestow on those who ask. An inscription reads, "O Mary conceived without sin, pray for us who have recourse to thee." The popular Catholic token was the result of a series of claimed Marian apparitions by a French novice, who said she had been given a mission by the mother of God to make the medal in the image that had been revealed to her.

"The Blessed Virgin herself designed the Medal of the Immaculate Conception—popularly known as the Miraculous Medal!" declares the website of the Association of the Miraculous Medal, headquartered in Perryville, Missouri. "No wonder, then, that it wins such extraordinary graces for those who wear it and pray for Mary's intercession and help."

With the approval of the church, the first medals were struck in 1832, and the inscription about being conceived without sin—presumably, the original was in French—was the cornerstone of the campaign for the Immaculate Conception, which became doctrine in 1854. Like many non-Catholics, I often confused the Immaculate Conception with the Doctrine of Incarnation; the Immaculate Conception refers not to Jesus, but to the maternal grandmother of Jesus, St. Anne, who allegedly conceived Mary—who would become the *Theotokos*, the god-bearer—without original sin. Confusingly, this does not imply that Mary herself was of virginal birth; that would be reserved for the Incarnation. It is important to note that many Christian churches—the Anglican, the Eastern Orthodox, the Oriental Orthodox, and the Protestant—do not share the Roman Catholic view of the Immaculate Conception. I'm a Baptist, having been dunked in what I seem to recall was a kind of concrete bathtub at the age of fourteen, but I'm a bad Baptist and can't tell you what my denomination feels about the IC, except some vague recollection that it was generally confused with the virgin birth.

The Association of the Miraculous Medal brings in $9 million in donations annually. There's no mention in the association's literature of the ability of the medal to locate the missing bodies of drowning victims, but perhaps I'm just not making the connection between demonstrations of faith and evidence of favor.

But it did remind me of a couple of books by Mark Twain that I'd read in my childhood that include episodes about attempts to locate drowning victims. Twain was intimately familiar with the Mississippi, the river of all American rivers; in both *Tom Sawyer* and *Huckleberry Finn*, he describes how antebellum Missourians would attempt to locate the bodies of those lost in the river, first when Tom and his friends are mistakenly believed drowned while they're off playing pirates on Jackson Island, and again when Huck fakes his death to get away from Pap.

In both cases, the searchers fire cannons across the water in the belief that the report would bring a body to the surface (perhaps because the concussion of the report would burst organs), and float loaves of fresh-baked bread containing dollops of quicksilver. Huck catches one of these loaves from the bank where he's hiding, takes out the plug and shakes out the mercury, and reflects on his good fortune while he eats the bread.

> I got a good place amongst the leaves, and set there on a log, munching the bread and watching the ferry-boat, and very well satisfied. And then something struck me. I says, now I reckon the widow or the parson or somebody prayed that his bread would find me, and here it has gone and done it. So there ain't no doubt but there is something in that thing—that is, there's something in it when a body like the widow or the parson prays, but it don't work for me, and I reckon it don't work for only just the right kind.

I have personally witnessed two body recoveries in my life, and there was no element of superstition in either of them. Both were grim. The first was when I was a kid in Baxter Springs, and I had ridden my ten-speed down to the dam on Spring River, carefully balancing a fishing rod and some tackle, intending to catch some channel cat. What I found were the authorities dragging the body of a man out of the brown water and carrying him to a waiting ambulance/hearse. They had recovered the body just below the dam using something akin to grappling hooks. What I remember clearly was the color of his skin. The man was shirtless, and his chest and arms were a peculiar soapy blue.

I did not fish that day.

The second time was years later, as an adult, when I was on a small tourist boat on the Missouri River in Montana on a planned excursion at a writing conference. Along for the ride was my first literary agent, Barbara Puechner, her daughter, and a few writerly friends. We talked and some smoked and I watched the river, thinking mostly about the best places to fish, and wondering if I would get the chance on this trip, when we came close to the body of a swimmer that had washed down from far above. There was that same marbled, soapy blue skin. The captain of our boat asked us all to go over to the port side and look the other way while the body was captured and another boat came over to bring it in.

In my career as a reporter I've seen more corpses than I care to describe. There were the remains of murder victims, a few who lost all hope and took their own lives, the innocent and the incautious killed in traffic accidents, those trapped in fire or rent by tornadoes or smitten by hurricane winds and the floodwaters that followed. In every case I was an observer, a few times I came close to being a victim myself, and always there was a simmering outrage for the sheer meaninglessness of it all. It undermined my faith in God, corroded my belief in man, and sparked a smoldering rage. What divine purpose could there be in killing so many in automobile accidents, especially children? The only explanation was in cold physics, and not metaphysics. As to the murderers—those who killed in a lover's rage, those who murdered in the course of robberies and other crimes, the serial killers who preyed remorselessly on the defenseless or unsuspecting—well, if this was what we humans were capable of doing to one another, then what hope is there? We are all going to die one day—*die* and not *pass away*, which is a cancerous euphemism that has crept from the columns of the paid obits to infect the speech of even the most prominent of journalists—and that seems a great equalizer and wholly democratic. But the old goat song of tragedy makes one look for meaning, and where there is none, we either make one up—or become embittered. I fell squarely in the latter camp. None of the deaths I covered was romantic, even though some were dramatic, and I'm glad now that most news organizations provide training to deal with trauma and anxiety. Ten years ago and more, when I worked for daily newspapers, I pretended that witnessing so much tragedy didn't bother me. But it did.

And it does.

≈ ≈ ≈

My first float with the Arkansas River Coalition was a week after Brian Bergkamp disappeared, and it was an all-day trip, from the city canoe launch at 71st Street in south Wichita to a privately owned takeout south of Mulvane known as the Old Goat Ranch, a distance of about fourteen miles. The meet was planned for 8:30, but I arrived half an hour early, and was the first one at the launch behind Vince Marshall, the coalition's problem solver and resident river historian. He had arrived to unload some of the kayaks and PFDs the coalition loans free to those who want to paddle the river, but there weren't many beginners on this trip, because the water was still high and fast, and it was to be one of the group's longer floats. I had corresponded with Vince briefly via email, describing my project, and talked about upper stretches of the river I'd run in Colorado (we've already met Vince in an earlier chapter, but that came later chronologically than this outing). He had welcomed me to come along with the group, and asked if I had checked out the coalition's downloadable river guide of the 120 miles of navigable river from Great Bend down to the Oklahoma line. I told him I had indeed read it, been on some of the water, and suggested it would be wise for anyone thinking about paddling the Arkansas River to take a look.

Vince seldom rested that day, but was continuously in motion; when he had the loaner kayaks down from the trailer and ready to go, he began roaming the launch area, and soon he had filled a plastic trash bag. After the other paddlers arrived over the next hour, there was some complicated business of shuttling vehicles and trailers down to the Old Goat Ranch and back, and some misunderstanding on my part about who was going along and who was staying behind with the boats. Then, when it was time to launch, about a dozen paddlers of both sexes and many ages slid their boats through the mud and sand and grass to the edge of the river. The muck sucked at our heels. Wading into the water to get my kayak far enough out to float, I stepped off a concrete lip and briefly dipped in the brown water, causing some alarm for the other boaters. I said it was nothing, that I always expected to get wet, and I was getting too hot anyway. Besides, it paled in comparison to my long swim in Browns Canyon.

Soon all the boats were in the water, and we formed a pod that sometimes stretched a quarter mile along the river, the brightly colored hulls contrasting sharply with the brown and foamy water. The suds were from agricultural runoff and other waste. The river was higher than normal, and flowing at about the speed of a fast walk. It was decidedly tamer than it had been the week before. Above our heads, in the trees along the bank, and in the brush piles on the sandbars, were tattered plastic bags and other trash that were the high-water mark. Sand boils blossomed around us, and I could feel a gentle tug on the bottom of my boat when I crossed one. The only hazards were low-hanging limbs on either side of the bank and some brushy strainers like the willow trees at the heads of some of the islands and bigger sandbars. Some shallow bars lay like a crescent from one bank to nearly the other, and they whispered and shushed beneath my plastic hull until I made deeper water. Once, I misjudged and before I could make deeper water, the voice of the bar grated until it held me fast. After some frustrating attempts at rocking free, I finally stepped out, grasped the toggle at the bow, and pulled the boat into calf-deep water and flopped back inside. The water was warm, and it smelled—a creek smell, fishy and rotten—and I reminded myself to keep my mouth closed when I paddled, so I wouldn't swallow any drops that sprayed from my paddle.

I was unused to paddling with more than two or perhaps three others, and taking part in a group float was both easier, because there was plenty of help available and advice from people who had been down the river before, and a bit more frustrating, because of the logistics involved with so many paddlers. Some of them had also heard I was writing a book on the river, so I gave a few brief explanations.

Many of the kayaks in the pod were like mine, which is to say a brightly colored rotomolded plastic recreational boat for mild water; they are longer and more stable than the stubby "play" boats like the one I paddled on the sections below Granite in Colorado. My Dagger is a swirl of red and orange and yellow, but the other boats ranged from a serious banana yellow Perception sea kayak to blue and orange boats bought at big-box stores to a couple of white sit-on-tops. Some of the boats had coolers of water and food bungeed to the decks. My lunch was in a soft-sided lunch bag in the waterproof storage compartment in the stern, while my water was in Nalgene bottles carabiner-clipped inside my cockpit.

Along with these kayaks, there was also a pristine Mohawk owned by a whitewater veteran; a bright blue kayak paddled fiercely by Kevin (also from the previous chapter), the off-duty fireman, who roamed the brush along the far banks looking for the body of the seminarian; and Vince's boat, an old forest green Victory Pungo with a high prow and a ducktail stern. Vince is covered from head to toe against the sun and the spray: blaze orange top, gray nylon pants, straw hat and sunglasses, and black gloves. His paddle strokes are leisurely, the blades dipping rhythmically in the water, then lifting in low arcs that don't throw much water. I can understand his desire not to bring the river into the boat, because it looks filthy.

The river carries us on a curving, meandering course to the east and the south, and we float by a farmer who is using a machine to suck water from the river and then we pass under a railway bridge where a Burlington Northern freight thunders overhead. We stop for lunch at a sand island almost in the shadow of the Highway 53 bridge near Mulvane, beach our boats on the sand, get our lunches, and splash through a couple of rivulets in the middle of the bar to find shade beneath some trees on the other side. My hands are soaked, because I tend to paddle a bit more forcefully than I need to, the water streaming down the shaft and over the drip rings to run down my wrists and into the boat. The Band-Aid securing my wedding ring is slippery and insecure, so I pull the ring off and clip it inside the pocket of my PFD. Then I sit on the sand and clean my hands as best I can with some hand sanitizer, which is to say not very well, and then Kevin the firefighter hands me a wipe, and I finally feel clean enough to eat. I chug some cold Powerade from a Nalgene bottle and devour a couple of soggy grocery store turkey-and-swiss wraps, reflecting on how different this experience is from sitting alone on a cobble bar alongside whitewater on the upper Arkansas and having a snack to calm my nerves.

The trip concludes not long after, where the owner of the Old Goat Ranch (where there are no longer any old goats, he jokes, except the one who lives there) has put an orange cone to river left to mark the takeout. The path is mud and brush and some poison ivy, and it takes a while to carry the boats up to the meadow where the cars and trailers are parked. Vince gives me a lift back to my Jeep and trailer at the Canoe Launch in Wichita, and on the way he mentions that a few days before the seminarian was lost, he believes he saw him standing on the bank of the river, talking to some friends who were in the water with kayaks. He said he can't be sure that it was him, but it resembled the young man in the photos, including the clerical collar. The group indicated they didn't need any help.

Back at the Canoe Launch, the Jeep is intact but somebody has stolen the plastic Jerry can of water I had strapped to the cargo carrier on the tongue of the trailer. The yellow NRS strap has been cut with a sharp knife, and the two pieces left behind. Nothing else has been touched, even though the racks used to mount the kayaks on the trailer and some other things are worth far more than the old blue water jug, which I kept filled because it added weight and reduced the tendency of the trailer to "hunt" when not fully loaded. Why would anybody steal the water, I wonder? The jug wasn't easy to carry—it was bulky and weighed more than fifty pounds. I don't mention this to Vince, because it seems silly to complain about the loss of an old jug that cost less than twenty bucks new. I knew I was lucky they didn't go after, say, the battery under the hood of the Jeep. Still, that plastic Jerry can had been all over the West with me, from the furnace of the Mojave to the comb of Colorado and back, and it seemed an insult that somebody would take it. But water, as we've seen from the long-standing Supreme Court battle between Colorado and Kansas, is always worth stealing.

The prayer vigils at St. Anne lasted less than a week.

On the morning of Monday, July 18, a memorial mass was held at the Cathedral of the Immaculate Conception in Wichita, and it was reportedly attended by more than a thousand. The *Eagle* was there, and posted video online. Bergkamp's brother, Andy, a deacon at the church, gave the homily and said he was overwhelmed by the "prayers offered throughout the world." Bergkamp's fellow seminarians from Mount St. Mary's in Emmitsburg, Maryland, were also in attendance, as was Carl Kemme, bishop of the Wichita diocese.

Kemme talked about Bergkamp's faith, his work ethic, and his recent assignment at the Lord's Diner, a soup kitchen owned by the diocese, and run with volunteer help and community contributions, that serves about 2,500 free meals daily. Bergkamp and two other third-year seminarians were assigned to the soup kitchen to help them prepare for their coming ordinations and subsequent roles as parish priests. Bergkamp was not far from home, as he had grown up in Garden Plain, a town of about 800 a few miles west of Wichita. The seminarians cooked, served food, and mopped floors at the diner, which has four locations: one downtown and the other in south Wichita, and two food trucks.

At the funeral mass, according to the *Eagle* and other news outlets, the story of Bergkamp giving his life jacket to another was repeated, this time with a bit more detail—he had reached the shore with the three others and had swum back to give his own jacket to the drowning woman. "He may not have been a priest," Kemme said, "but he lived and died in the most priestly way." Kemme told the *Catholic Advance,* the house newspaper for the diocese, that "life on this side of heaven" is full of mysteries, and the mystery of the young seminarian's death "must wait until heaven to be solved."

Wichita is the largest of all the fifty-odd cities along the river in Colorado and Kansas. With a population of about 390,000, it's the largest city in the state, and 1 in 5 Kansans live in Wichita or its suburbs. As it courses through downtown Wichita, the Arkansas runs closer to my home than at any other point, a scant eighty-eight miles from my doorstep in Emporia to the river's bank.

Even casual visitors to the city are likely to know at least one of the city's landmarks, the forty-four-foot-tall steel Keeper of the Plains sculpture at the confluence of the Arkansas and Little Arkansas Rivers. The sculpture, which is a modernist representation of a warrior offering a medicine pipe blessing to the sky, was erected by the city in 1974 and is by the late Kiowa-Comanche artist Blackbear Bosin, a Marine veteran, lithographer, and artist for Boeing. A familiar ritual is the lighting of the fire pits at the base of the statue, at seven every night in summer, and dusk in winter. They burn for about fifteen minutes.

The city is named for the Native Americans who once lived here, the descendants of the tribe that Coronado met near Great Bend. The area beneath the Keeper of the Plains statue, where the rivers meet, has been the site of human habitation for centuries.

A caltrop is an ancient antipersonnel device first used against Alexander the Great's troops in Persia, and the name is derived from the Latin for "foot trap." They are nasty tetrahedral devices that create their own stable base and always have at least one spike pointing straight up. Think of a child's game of jacks, but with the jacks having dagger-sharp spikes.

Usually deployed in quantity, like sowing seeds, they were particularly effective against cavalry, capable of laming a horse. They were used in combat as recently as World War II, and modern caltrop variants are used as anti-vehicle devices, capable of puncturing self-sealing tires.

In botany, the caltrop family includes *Tribulus terrestris* (another name that derives from a word for foot trap), and this invasive plant is well-named. You've probably had the pea-sized spiny weapons of this plant stabbing you through your socks or jabbing your ankles inside your shoes, after walking through a vacant lot or down an untended alley. Its habitat is sand and gravel areas, or other places where the earth has been disturbed, especially along roadsides and railways. According to a wildflower and grasses website maintained by a Kansas State faculty member, Mike Haddock, it was introduced from southern Europe and was first recorded in the Sunflower State in the late 1800s. Most Kansans will know it as goat head or puncture vine. It can form dense mats close to the ground, with bright yellow blooms when it flowers from July to September. "The sharp, tack-like spines can puncture bicycle tires and cause injuries to the feet of animals and humans," Haddock cautions. "Puncture vine is difficult to eradicate. The seeds can remain dormant in the soil for 4–5 years."

I had first discovered the hell of puncture vine as a kid, while exploring mine dumps and rabbit hunting alongside abandoned railway tracks, but had largely forgotten this tenacious and irritating plant until I rediscovered it during a kayak trip through south Wichita. I'd had my share of insects and plants sting, stick, stab, bite, puncture, or make me break out in a rash during my time around the river, but the one insult most likely to drive me mad is goat head.

Eighteen days after Brian Bergkamp disappeared, I set my kayak once more on the Arkansas River, this time below the Lincoln Street Bridge in Wichita. I was with the Arkansas River Coalition again, for a short "Twilight Float" that had been rescheduled from the week before because of the high water. Kim was with me in her own kayak on this float, which would be tame enough for novice paddlers, and it was the first time she had been on the Arkansas with me, or on any river, for that matter. The appointed gathering time was 5:30, but we arrived early so we drove around south-central Wichita with its cheap motels and run-down businesses and desperate people shuffling along South Broadway with their faded backpacks and hollow eyes. Just a few blocks to the northwest, where the Arkansas River runs past the city's museum and gardens and joins the Little Ark beneath the Keeper of the Plains, it's a different town—clean, modern, influential, and optimistic. Stray a few blocks to the east or south, and hope seems scarce.

The city has one of the sharpest divides between rich and poor of any city in the country, according to a 2016 report from the Economic Innovation Group, a DC think tank. Using measures that included population density, median incomes, unemployment rates, and other indicators, the EIC ranked Wichita seventh for economic inequality, just behind Memphis, Tennessee.

From the river at the park-like boat launch below the Lincoln Street dam, you have a good view of the tallest buildings that rise from the heart of Wichita, on the other side of Kellogg and near the Keeper of the Plains. The urban backdrop is no less surprising because it's in Kansas. The tallest building in Wichita, and the state, is the twenty-two-story Epic Center at Third and Main, easily identifiable by its slanted, brick-red roof. Another building, 250 Douglas Place, also looms, and is the second-highest building in the state. In 1976, when the building was the Holiday Inn Plaza, an unemployed welder from Sand Springs, Oklahoma, set up a sniper nest on the roof, killing three and wounding six in eleven minutes.

The Epic Center, Douglas Place, and other buildings seem to float in the sky above the Lincoln Bridge. Scattered along the river below these municipal monuments is the city's art museum, with its John Steuart Curry "Cornfield"; Old Cowtown with its depiction of life in 1880s Wichita, and only slightly gilded by the obligatory gunfight reenactment; and Exploration Place, a science center that has an exhibit representative of 1950s Kansas, including HO scale model trains and a river that could be the Arkansas. The "Kansas in Miniature" exhibit is sponsored by Koch Industries.

Along the river on this July afternoon, there's an occasional homeless person huddled beneath a bridge. There are also white bicyclists whirring in flights along the sidewalk, black children waving from the bank, and an Asian fisherman—possibly from the Vietnamese community—setting a line in the swift water. Judging from his tackle, he's fishing for carp or catfish, both bottom-feeders. I worry about the fisherman, because the Kansas Department of Health and Environment has a standing advisory to avoid eating all bottom-feeding fish from the Lincoln Street

Dam down to the confluence of Cowskin Creek near Belle Plain, about twenty-four miles, because of PCB contamination. Polychlorinated biphenyls were widely used as a coolant and lubricant in the production of electrical transformers and capacitors from the 1930s to 1977, when they were banned in the United States because of health concerns. The federal Centers for Disease Control have classified PCBs as a "probable" carcinogen, and they are found in fatty issue and tend to move up the food chain. Eating contaminated fish is the most common way for humans to be exposed to PCBs. Because it was so widely used for so long, the toxin is relatively common in the United States, and resulted in many an aging transformer blowing on a utility pole and dripping PCB oil to the ground below. Within the Wichita city limits, there could have been multiple sources of contamination over the years, including some of the city's seventy-five identified Environmental Protection Agency Superfund sites. Some of those sites are near the Arkansas River, where it was easy to dump contaminants. Most Superfund sites in the city have been cleaned up, and as of 2016, only one remains active on the National Priorities List: a former salvage yard near 57th and Broadway in north Wichita, far from the river, where remediation efforts have failed.

I hoped the Vietnamese gentleman would eat no fish.

As our pod skims south, we near the lawns of Herman Hill Park, named for a former mayor, and a municipal landmark since 1932. The park is also the site of the Wichita Area Treatment, Education, and Remediation (WATER) Center, a local remediation project created in the 1990s, when it was feared groundwater contamination from decades of manufacturing and industry was so severe that the EPA would designate a part of downtown Wichita a Superfund site. Such a designation would wreck property values and destroy the tax base, officials feared. Wichita was the first city to tackle remediation of a pollution site it didn't create, and the impetus was clearly economic, and not public health. In addition to the concern over the tax base, parts of the contaminated site threatened the Old Town development, a plan to transform a twenty-block area that had been a hive of railway warehouses in the 1870s and that, by the 1990s, was mostly vacant. Now, it's one of the city's prize attractions, a mixed-use area filled with loft apartments, eating and drinking establishments, and light industry. But the city found itself in a protracted legal battle with the Coleman Company—famous for its white gas camping lanterns and other outdoor gear—and twenty-seven other businesses it believed should be responsible for the Gilbert-Mosley Cleanup, named for the intersection at approximately the center of the contamination. Official documents list a witch's brew of toxins, but the one that caused the most concern was trichloroethylene, a confirmed carcinogen.

TCE was first produced in quantity in the 1920s, and was used in the manufacture of some vegetable and food products and as a general anesthetic. Mostly, however, it was used as a degreaser and industrial solvent. After ten years and much legal arm-twisting, the WATER Center opened. According to information supplied by the city, the remediation project consists of thirteen extraction wells and more than five miles of conveyance piping to carry the contaminated water to the center, where it is treated by a hydraulic-venturi air stripper system. Essentially, this is a giant washing machine, in which air and water are used to eliminate the contaminants. The treated water is then released into a stream, where it flows down to the Arkansas.

The cost (as of its eleventh year of operation) has been about $81 million—about three times the initial estimate—and remediation is expected to continue until at least 2042, according to city documents. It is paid for by those firms that caused the contamination, current property owners, or lenders for properties that defaulted, according to the city. In 2004, a federal judge limited the liability against some of the existing companies, saying the city hadn't identified all of the polluters, had settled for too little with some, had asked too much of others, and had acted too slowly to prevent the spread of the contamination. A special environmental tax increment financing district was created to help pay for the cleanup. The Coleman Company was the only firm to admit to causing some of the TCE pollution, and it reached a mediated agreement with the city on its share of the project costs. The company moved its headquarters to Golden, Colorado, in 1996, then came back to Wichita, and since 2012 again has had its leadership at Golden. It is now owned by a New York firm, following a bankruptcy reorganization and sale, and most of its products are made in China.

Not far downstream from where our kayaks passed the treated water burbling from the WATER Center into the Arkansas River, we encountered an island. The island was scrubby with trees and brush, and there were a few yards of orange plastic construction netting snagged on one side. It was otherwise unremarkable except for one thing: the smell. It was a sort of sickly sweet smell, like rotting meat, but worse. The odor was stronger if you bore to the river left, as I and a few others did, including Vince and Kevin. Some of the kayakers complained about the "garbage" collecting in the river. But the odor, I knew, wasn't that of garbage. I recognized the smell as that of a decomposing body in warm weather. It was something I had first encountered in my twenties, when I was working the police beat for a small newspaper in southeast Kansas, and more recently when I was embedded with the Missouri National Guard in the days following Katrina.

I paddled up to Vince's kayak and briefly shared my thoughts. He had been thinking the same thing, as had Kevin, I learned later. There were a handful of first-time kayakers with the group that evening, including some teenagers, and it would have been inappropriate to land on the island and start searching. So we pressed on, and before long, came to Garvey Park, the take-out for our brief journey. The concrete boat launch was choked with silt and trees, so we had to haul our boats up the sandy bank, up a trail leading through some trees, and to a sidewalk that crossed a grass strip to the parking area.

I was impatient and hungry, and as Kim and I hauled our boats up to the lot where the Jeep and trailer were parked, and I stepped off the sidewalk and cut the corner and led us through the grass to the lot, I felt something pricking my ankles through my socks. I'd never been to Garvey Park before, so I didn't know the grass was covered with a thick mat of *Tribulus terrestris*. Our socks and shoes, even though we had only briefly walked on the grass, were covered with clumped dozens of burrs. It was so uncomfortable we had to change our shoes and socks before leaving the parking lot. The next day, I spent the better part of an hour using a pair of needle-nosed pliers to pluck the stickers from our socks and shoes. They were so deeply embedded in the soles of our shoes that, once gripped by the pliers, they had to be yanked or levered out with some force. I still didn't get them all, apparently, and for a month after I was picking out burrs from socks that had been washed several times.

The grass at Garvey Park wasn't the only place where the puncture vine was thick. The next day, Vince and Kevin put their kayaks in at the

Lincoln Street Dam and paddled down to the brushy island near Henry Hill. The island was thick with the stuff. Kevin, who was wearing rubber boots, got out of his boat near the head of the island and tramped over the vines, near the orange plastic construction netting. He found the body of Brian Bergkamp beneath a willow tree, caught in the branches and some driftwood and other things the river had washed up.

"Kevin called 911 and within minutes we had police and firemen swarming the banks on both sides of the river near this island," Vince later said. There was at first some discussion among the responders about whether they shouldn't just wade out from the bank at Herman Hill Park to the island, because the water was shallow, but at last a decision was made to launch a Zodiac inflatable boat to retrieve the body.

The spot is about seven miles below the low-head dam at 21st Street, and Bergkamp's body would have floated and bobbed and rolled in the water all the way through downtown Wichita, past the shining buildings and the museums and beneath the Keeper of the Plains.

The retrieval was on Thursday afternoon, and the body positively identified as Bergkamp the next day, but it wasn't until the following Monday, August 1, that the Wichita Police Department confirmed to the media that it was indeed the remains of the missing seminarian. Over the weekend, however, a fisherman told police he found half an orange life vest with part of a rosary attached to a buckle in the Arkansas River near the Keeper of the Plains. The media related the "find" and speculated on whether it was Bergkamp's. The *Eagle* ran a photo of the vest, but to me it didn't look like it had been in the water for three days, much less three weeks. Why had this story turned the *Eagle*, a fine and reliable and often hard-nosed paper, so credulous? On August 2, a spokesman for the Wichita Police said its homicide division was confident the vest and rosary were not related to Bergkamp.

Strangely, here's how the *Eagle* led the story: "The mystery of the life vest and rosary found Saturday afternoon on the banks of the Arkansas River lives on." The second graph cleared things up, but the lead indicated to me some weird sort of deference to and fascination with the entire Bergkamp affair that I didn't understand. The quality of the reporting for media across the board in Wichita concerning the drowning was appallingly soft. Why was there no mention of the hazard posed by low-head dams, or questions to authorities about whether the warning signs on the bridge were adequate, or even just a standard feature on water safety? Bergkamp's death was a tragedy, but it wasn't an act of God, and it could have easily been prevented. What was needed was less prayer and more outreach on water safety. And I wondered what the community reaction would have been if, instead of a handsome young seminarian, it had been one of the homeless people I'd seen on the streets and beneath the bridges who had fallen in and drowned? Would there have been a single prayer vigil or page 1A story?

A couple of days after the Wichita Police debunked the rosary and vest story, the Catholic News Service—which is the primary source for national and world news for the church's many publications in the United States—moved a story that is notable because it didn't allow the truth to interfere with a narrative that was more compelling: "The seminarian had been missing since he saved the life of a woman who fell into the Arkansas River on 9 July. . . . The Wichita *Eagle* Daily newspaper reported that a fisherman had spotted a piece of life vest floating in the water with a rosary attached to it. That discovery led to finding the body of the missing seminarian."

And yet, despite—or because of—the shoddy reporting and hokum at the edges, it was clear the community was moved by the tragedy. There was an outpouring of grief, recognition of a promising life cut short, concern for the family, and probably some emotions that were difficult to express. Perhaps I was being too hard on the *Eagle*. Journalists do a great job of handling facts—the Gilbert-Mosley Cleanup has cost $81 million, for example—but we're not so good at conveying the authentic emotional impact of an event. Part of it is that we don't know what's really going on in the hearts and minds of our subjects, only what they say and do. I may be able to come close to portraying someone else's inner state by reporting that is grounded in careful observation, telling details, and the use of accurate and relevant quotes, but I can never peer inside them. There is only one person whose thoughts and feelings I can confidently report, and that person is me.

When I was watching from the back at that prayer vigil at St. Anne church, I don't know what those gathered there were thinking or feeling. But I can say that I was struck by their faces. When the prayers and the chanting started, the tension of the quotidian seemed to fall away; there was no trace of self-consciousness tugging at the corners of their lips, no furrowed brows, no furtive glances at watches or smart phones. At least for most, this was true. They projected what I can only and imperfectly describe as a social, if not spiritual, communion. These were honest faces begging for their Michelangelo. It was easy for me to believe that in this group of people—these young and old, businesspeople and working poor, some with shoulder-slung oxygen and others shining with health, many serious of purpose and a few looking relieved just to find a place to rest, and one who gave me a scalding glance, perhaps because I wasn't on my knees and praying—there was a collective desire to do good, to lend comfort and help to others, to sit in silent fellowship with others, to silently reflect on the immutable nature of life and death. At least, that's what I choose to believe. Amen. Don't listen to the old goat song of death.

A few days after the seminarian's body was recovered, I contacted a former student of mine, Kelsey Ryan, who is now a reporter at the *Eagle*. There was a public safety story about low-head dams that needed to be written, I texted her, and for an expert source I suggested she contact Tschantz, the professor who placed the excellent piece on the perfect drowning machines in *The Journal of Dam Safety*. Go save some lives, I told her.

Trespasses
Elevation: 850' (Shoal Creek)

Nick stood up on the log, holding his rod, the landing net hanging heavy, then stepped into the water and splashed ashore. He climbed the bank and cut up into the woods, toward the high ground. He was going back to camp. He looked back. The river just showed through the trees. There were plenty of days coming when he could fish the swamp.

—Ernest Hemingway, "Big Two-Hearted River"

As I've discovered—and as Nick presumably would as well—there are never enough days to fish the swamp.

My father grew up during the Depression and his definition of success was if you and your kids had enough to eat. His given name was Carl, but his family called him Junior, and he was little more than a kid when he joined the navy to avoid the draft. Because he could type, he got a job as a yeoman on the battleship *Pennsylvania* during World War II, and typing and filing paperwork suited him fine because he figured the government would want to take care of a ship that big, and at least he wouldn't have to personally shoot anybody. After the war, he got a job as a salesman at Sears and Roebuck in Joplin, Missouri, and he was a good one because he was charming and would talk to anybody. He quit Sears for a while and tried his hand at owning a service station, after taking some mail-order course on running your own business, but he couldn't make a go of it and eventually went back to Sears. I don't remember much about the service station, except that it was on a curve on Route 66 at the south end of Baxter Springs, and across the street was a liquor store that also sold fishing tackle. I must have been, what—five or six years old? Oh, I also remember that one day I was running around like a little fool and cracked my head on the brick wall between the office and the service bay, and that I still have the dent in my skull to prove it.

My father understood the necessity of making a living, but he lived to fish. He used everything from cane poles to Ted Williams spincast reels to his personal favorite, a Pflueger Supreme baitcaster that was prone to making a bird's nest of the braided line. He cussed that reel, but stayed with it because it was somewhat expensive and, therefore, good. He made

My parents in 1945.

me fish from the time I was small, but I didn't really begin to enjoy it until after I was grown. He dragged me on fishing trips that ranged from Lesser Slave Lake in Alberta, Canada, to Toledo Bend in Texas. Every March 1, we'd be standing at dawn on the cold and graveled bank of Roaring River State Park at Cassville, Missouri, waiting for the whistle that signaled the opening of trout season. He was always restless, putting miles between himself and hope, sure that the fishing must be better someplace else. He even tried saltwater fishing a time or two. But I never saw him happier than when we would float Shoal Creek, a few miles from home. Shoal Creek is a shady Ozark stream, a tributary of Spring River. It flows west out of Missouri. We'd put in our little flat-bottomed aluminum boat near Lowell, Kansas, skirt the edge of the Empire District Electric Company reservoir, and then float for an hour or two just above where it joins Spring River. Dad would wear a beat-up old straw hat, and we'd drink ice water from an old red-and-white insulated jug. We'd usually fish topwater, lazily tossing the lures up beneath the tree branches close to the bank. If we made the lure dance just right, the water would explode as a big bass went after it.

Those float trips on Shoal Creek were forty and more years ago, but I am shocked by the power of the memory. Those trips are distant now not only in time, but in law. When we would go on those floats, we didn't have to ask anybody for permission to do it; the assumption was that streams navigable by boat belonged to everyone.

The Kansas Water Appropriation Act of 1945 says: "All water within the state of Kansas is hereby dedicated to the use of the people of the state, subject to the control and regulation of the state in the manner herein proscribed." The act was adopted when the state went to the "first use" prior appropriation doctrine. When seniority of a water right couldn't settle a dispute, it prioritized water use in the following order of importance: domestic, municipal, irrigation, industrial, and recreational. Even though the act declares that water belongs to everyone, it essentially strips the rights of just about everyone except those who have a vested interest or a prior appropriation, those who are making money in some fashion from the water, or public drinking supplies.

But federal law takes precedence over state law, and federal law says navigable streams are public. You could boat down a river or stream as long as you didn't trespass on private property. If you were the landowner, even if you owned both sides of the stream, you couldn't stretch a fence across to prevent boaters from passing.

But that's just what a Cherokee County farmer named Jasper Hayes did in 1988. Hayes was incensed over the carefree canoeists who floated over from Missouri and, while crossing his property on their way to the takeout at Lowell, behaved in ways that Hayes did not approve of. They were, he alleged, littering, sunbathing in the nude, and having sex. So, he stretched some bailing wire over the creek. When somebody cut that, he put some steel fence up. When that was removed, he finally put up an electric fence.

A float guide for Holly Haven Outfitters filed a complaint.

Chris Meek, the Cherokee County attorney, did what most prosecutors would have at the time: he sided with the canoeists, believing that paddlers had a right to public waters. He filed a declaratory judgment for Holly Haven and ordered the electric fence taken down. But Cherokee County District Judge David Brewster ruled in favor of Hayes because Shoal Creek did not meet the federal definition of navigable, because it was unlikely to be used as a highway for commerce for local products.

Meek appealed, and the case eventually worked its way up to the Kansas Supreme Court. On the side of Meek and the paddlers were the Kansas Canoe Association and the Kansas Wildlife Federation. On the other side was the powerful Kansas Farm Bureau lobby, which had fought the establishment of the Tallgrass Prairie National Preserve, at Strong City in the Flint Hills.

Because state law didn't define navigability for a stream, the case hinged on the federal definition. But that further complicated the matter, because federal law required that the *title* to a navigable streambed had passed to the state at the time of its entry to the union. In 1990, the Kansas Supreme Court ruled. Shoal Creek was commercially navigable, because outfitters had used it for float trips, but its *title* hadn't passed to the state when Kansas became a state on January 29, 1861.

The ruling criminalized paddling in Kansas.

There are only three rivers that are considered legally navigable in the state: the Arkansas, the Kansas, and the Missouri (but even on the Arkansas, I've had farmers on the bank shake their fist at me when I paddle by). For all other waterways—unless they are wholly public, such as in the case of a municipal lake or federal reservoir—you need the permission of the private landowners to boat them. Some still dare to paddle without asking permission, but they are trespassing.

An excellent account of *Meek v. Hayes* can be found in George Frazier's recent book, *The Last Wild Places of Kansas*. Frazier, a Lawrence software developer and writer, set out to legally paddle a section of the Marais des Cygnes that he had floated years before. He would have to get the permission from all of the thirteen landowners in Osage and Franklin Counties. He got permission from twelve, but not the thirteenth, so he never made the trip.

Frazier calls the Marais des Cygnes and Shoal Creek and others the "renegade streams" of eastern Kansas. "They are highways of history, highways of wildlife, highways of adventure, highways of the imagination, highways to the last wild places of Kansas," Frazier writes. "They are also, like it or not, highways clearly marked 'no trespassing.'"

Private land is a religion in Kansas, and any attempt to increase the available amount of public land is regarded as blasphemy. Kansas ranks dead last in public land ownership, with just under 1 percent of the state's 82 million square miles owned by the state or federal government.

Colorado, which has large national forests and tracts owned by the Bureau of Land Management, is ranked ninth. Alaska is first.

The Arkansas River represents a public corridor that stretches 411 miles, from the border with Colorado in the west to Oklahoma in the south. Even though it is designated as a navigable river, for much of the western third of the state the only way you'd get a boat down it would be to trailer it behind a four-wheel drive. In the parts of the state where it does carry water, access is a problem, and if you want to boat it you'd better be prepared to carry your boat up and down sometimes precarious embankments below highway bridges. There are some exceptions—such as the public access areas provided by the City of Wichita—but for the most part, reaching what is legally acknowledged as a public resource is challenging. In 2016, the river from Great Bend to the Oklahoma state line was federally designated as a National Water Trail, to be managed by the Kansas Department of Parks, Wildlife, and Tourism. Not much changed, however, following the designation. Along the 192 miles of river below Great Bend, there are only twenty-two designated public access points. Groups like the Arkansas River Coalition are working to make more, but they need help.

Access to the wild is essential.

It has struck me that truth hides in lonely places. When you leave home and go, say, to the desert or the side of a mountain—or stand in the middle of a fast-moving river—you're leaving your usual defenses behind. Just as your every step takes on more significance with the more extreme the territory, so too does your thinking. One deliberate step, one deliberate thought, one thoughtful paddle stroke after another. Once the social constructs and the polite lies and legal fictions that make civil society possible slough away, you're left with the essential self. You may not like what you find, but you won't know how you really feel about things until you confront yourself.

My mother seldom went on any of my father's fishing trips, and especially not on any of the trips to Texas or Canada. Once, she did go to the Lake of the Woods in Minnesota, but all I remember about that trip is that the fishing was lousy and my parents argued a lot. They had married young, before he shipped out on the *Pennsylvania*. Her name was Mary, and she had little education but loved books. She learned to drink while she was living in navy quarters in California, waiting for him to return from the Pacific. They had two children—my brother, Jim, and me. They eventually separated but never divorced, and by the time my mother died of cancer, at age fifty-nine, they were strangers.

I don't know all of the reasons for their unhappy marriage, but I am sorry they suffered so. Much of it was likely caused by depression and alcohol, emotional and physical distance, and the other commonplace things that people do to hurt each other. In spite of having been presented with a model to avoid, I have made many of the mistakes I swore I never would—especially the commonplace ones—and have hurt myself and others. I won't blame the depression, because ultimately you are responsible for making the best of the hand you're dealt. As I grew older, and after I had a wedding ring flung at me from across a courtroom, I got better at managing things. Or at least I got better at preventing catastrophic hurt. One of the things I used was mileage. I found it easier to disengage than risk emotional hurt—even after I married Kim. There's always an excuse: a magazine article, a book to research, a crazy project to follow the Arkansas River down from its headwaters.

Back when my parents were fighting, and my father was doing a lot of fishing, and my mother was doing a lot of drinking, I spent a considerable amount of time one summer in an old waxy canvas tent that I had pitched in the backyard. I must have been twelve or thirteen. I spent a lot of time reading in that tent, and the stuff I read was a crazy mix of things: Hal Lindsey's *The Late Great Planet Earth*, Frank Yerby's *The Foxes of Harrow*, and a lot of Hemingway. I knew there was meaning in "Big Two-Hearted River" that was important, but it took me years to understand it. The story is about Nick Adams, a young man on a lone fishing and camping trip in the Northwoods, who is uneasy about going into a swampy area of the forest after big trout.

> Nick did not want to go in there now. He felt a reaction against deep wading with the water deepening up under his armpits, to hook big trout in places impossible to land them. In the swamp the banks were bare, the big cedars came together overhead, the sun did not come through, except in patches; in the fast deep water, in the half light, the fishing would be tragic. In the swamp fishing was a tragic adventure.

Nick did not want it. He didn't want to go up the stream any further today.

That was published in 1925, but it might as well have been describing much of my father's life, or mine. The sharp attention to detail to drive out unpleasant thoughts, the unease with shadowy places where the water is fast and deep, the fear of hooking fish in places where it was impossible to land them. Even when I was a teenager, I knew it was about something more than fishing.

My father gave me only one piece of advice about women, about the time I was reading Hemingway in that tent in the backyard. "There's nothing pretty about the open end of a gut," he said, referring to the female anatomy in a way that horrified me at the time. It still bothers me, and I'm ashamed at having written those lines, because I don't want readers to hate him. If he had reasons for feeling that way, he never elaborated, and I never asked. But I am glad that I never came to share his sentiment. The statement may not seem as shocking now as it did then, back in 1972 or so, but in the first draft of this manuscript I was uncomfortable enough to leave it out.

Twelve years after I finally left that tent in the backyard, my mother called me back to that house to show me that she had breast cancer. We had grown apart, and she often called only when she was drunk, so when she summoned me one Thanksgiving week, I was patronizing. She was drinking a can of Coors at the kitchen table, the one I was so used to as a boy, where I had put up my typewriter and written so many nights away. Instead of telling me what was wrong, she pulled back her robe and showed me the ruin of her right breast and the blackened hole that led into her ribcage. I took her to the hospital, but she was dead by Christmas.

To live is to risk tragic adventure. But without risk, there is no chance for growth, no hope for connecting in any meaningful way with another. While I have had the common share of misadventure and sometimes tragedy, I have also been lucky enough at times to find meaning—and have occasionally been smart enough to recognize it. A few years ago, before we were married, Kim and I met for a weekend trip to Bennett Spring, a state park near Lebanon, Missouri. It was November, but it was unseasonably warm, and we did a lot of walking and exploring in the woods, which were brilliant with fall color. Much of the park was built by the Civilian Conservation Corps, and those rustic Depression-era bridges and buildings lend a nostalgic character. The spring is stocked with trout, and it was catch-and-release season, so I bought a daily trout tag and spent a little while casting a rooster tail into the water with the ultralight rig I carry in the Jeep. I caught a fish, a fine two-pounder that fought well, his rainbow sides flashing in the water, and after landing him I was careful to release him unharmed. Late that afternoon, we put steaks and ears of corn on a grill at a campsite overlooking the park, and drank ice-cold Coronas as the food cooked. Kim's red hair shone like the leaves of the trees in the late afternoon sun, and I wanted her in the way that a circle seeks completion. I didn't have to tell her what I was reading; she knew what I was reading, and likely had read it too and could tell me what I didn't understand about it. I clumsily recited from memory some lines from John Donne's "The Bait," written about 1601. It begins with a line borrowed from an earlier poem by Christopher Marlowe, and then answers that poem; while Marlowe idealizes romantic love, Donne makes love a choice that both pleasures and ensnares.

> Come live with me and be my love
> And we will some new pleasures prove,
> Of golden sands and crystal brooks,
> With silken lines and silver hooks.

"There will the river whispering run," I said to Kim, still quoting. "Warmed by thy eyes more than the sun." And I knew that this would be, at the end of my life, the one perfect day I would remember.

Swells from Ancient Oceans
Elevation: 869' (Pawnee, Oklahoma)

Before I could turn and seek the door, there came a really terrific shock; the ground seemed to roll under me in waves, interrupted by a violent joggling up and down, and there was a heavy grinding noise as of brick houses rubbing together.

—Mark Twain, *describing the 1865 San Francisco earthquake in* Roughing It

At 7:02 this morning, Saturday, September 3, I was shaken awake by a rumbling in our second-floor bedroom. To say I was soundly asleep would be an understatement; I had written late in the night and into the morning, and had finally gotten to bed around 3 a.m. It was the kind of sleep I jokingly called the *primordial snooze*. But the shaking of the house brought me wide awake. At first, I thought it was the continuation of a mild nightmare (a frequent one, about being on the river and threatened by some vague but immediate peril). Then, I thought perhaps Kim was shaking me to get up and deal with some emergency. But in a few seconds, I snapped awake and knew the trouble was something else. The shaking grew stronger, the bed moved beneath me, stacks of books and the bookcases swayed back and forth, and even the walls seemed to be moving. The 120-year-old Victorian wood-frame house with the weak foundation I'd never gotten around to repairing creaked and growled like a wooden ship being tossed in a storm. This was the strongest motion I'd felt during any of the handful of earthquakes that I'd felt in the last five years, and like the others, I knew this one probably originated in Oklahoma, just south of the Kansas line. Instinctively, I also felt this was the biggest yet. As it continued I glanced at my watch, noted the time, and ran to the top of the stairs. While the house still trembled, I called down the narrow stairs, and from her office Kim answered that she was all right. By the time I reached the bottom, the growling had stopped. Kim's eyes were large and threatening tears. She was frightened, and said she never wanted to feel that again, because an earthquake was much worse than a twister. Why, I asked? *Because you expect tornadoes in Kansas, not earthquakes. There's no place to run to.*

In my office, I found a few things were knocked off the shelf behind my desk, including a Zippo lighter (I don't smoke, but it was a gift from

Earthquake-damaged Arkansas Valley National Bank Building, Pawnee, Oklahoma.

Butch) and a five-inch figure of Edgar Allan Poe. There were also some new cracks in the plaster high on the wall, near the ceiling. I sat at my laptop and waited for the automated email from the US Geological Survey to tell me how big the quake was. After the largest earthquake in Oklahoma history had struck in 2011, I had signed up to be notified of all quakes within a few-hundred-mile radius with a magnitude of 2 or greater. Since then, I have received nearly 6,000 alerts, indicative of the earthquake swarms in Kansas and Oklahoma. Most of the quakes were small, but a few exceeded magnitude 4 (more on magnitudes later). In Emporia, I had felt some of those stronger ones, including a time when I was lecturing and felt the classroom floor shimmy. When the USGS did send me an email, twenty-eight minutes after the shaking, it gave the quake a magnitude of 5.6—tying the one in 2011 for the record— and placed the epicenter eight miles northwest of Pawnee. *Note:* The Wednesday following, the USGS announced it had reexamined its data and upgraded the September 3 quake to 5.8, making it the largest in Oklahoma history; the 2011 quake was also upgraded, to 5.7.

Pawnee is a small town eight miles from the Arkansas River in north-central Oklahoma. It is also 207 highway miles south of Emporia, and by the time we arrived that afternoon, the sidewalks had been swept of loose bricks and other debris. The center of town is the intersection of Sixth and Harrison, and about half of the businesses in the block to the west were behind caution tape or otherwise barricaded. Pawnee's population is just 2,190, and the cordoned area represented a considerable fraction of the downtown business district. No buildings collapsed, but many had cracks or other apparently minor damage, with the historic Arkansas Valley National Bank building on the northwest corner of the intersection getting the worst of it. A couple of square yards of sandstone facing was shaken loose from near the top of the building, on the second story. In relief on the east side of the building is PAWNEE CO BANK, but the name was changed before the bank opened in 1918. Behind the orange tape with the repeating DANGER warnings was a folding sign for the Cheatham real estate agency that said the building was for sale at a "New Price." Maybe somebody in Pawnee had a sense of humor. As we walked downtown, Kim noticed small details that had escaped me: a broken flowerpot here, goods jumbled in a shop window, a globe from a streetlamp on the ground.

Few townspeople were about, but there were plenty of reporters, some of them doing standups in front of the Arkansas Valley National Bank building. I counted nine news vehicles when we arrived, and a few more came after. One of the television journalists, a young man in a crisp blue shirt, said he had found the only casualty of the quake, a man just outside town with a bandaged head who said a brick had fallen from his chimney. Around town, there were crews checking for natural gas leaks, some state cars outside the courthouse, and a convenience store that was open but not pumping gas. Oklahoma governor Mary Fallon had earlier declared a thirty-day state of emergency for Pawnee County, and the state's corporation commission had ordered 37 disposal wells shut down closest to the epicenter. The 37 are among about 3,200 active wastewater wells in the state, which are suspected to have contributed to the earthquake swarms which have increased every year since 2009. Just three months ago, in June 2016, the USGS released, for the first time ever, a one-year seismic forecast for the central and eastern United States that included the risk from *induced* earthquakes. The area at highest risk for induced earthquakes, according to the survey, was along the Kansas-Oklahoma border; when weighted for population density, the biggest risk was for those in Oklahoma City, with a population of more than 600,000.

Despite the amount of attention paid to the earthquake swarms by the press, the public, and lawmakers, the science of induced earthquakes is generally misunderstood, according to the USGS. Although hydraulic fracturing—fracking—is responsible for some of the felt earthquakes, most are caused by the injection of wastewater through disposal wells. The majority of this wastewater is not the spent slippery solution used in fracking, but is instead something called "fossil water" from the distant past. It is also called produced water.

"Produced water is the salty brine from ancient oceans that was entrapped in the rocks when the sediments were deposited," writes a pair of experts in a 2015 issue of the journal *Seismological Research Letters*. "This water is trapped in the same pore space as oil and gas, and as oil and gas is extracted, the produced water is extracted with it. Produced water often must be disposed in injection wells because it is frequently laden with dissolved salts, minerals, and occasionally other materials that make it unsuitable for other uses."

The experts, Justin L. Rubinstein and Alireza Babaie Mahani, said that only 10 percent of wastewater injection is fracking solution; the rest is this prehistoric saltwater that is difficult to clean and unsuitable for drinking. I was glad for the handy graphic that Rubinstein and Mahani included in their piece, which allowed me to understand an industry I had observed all my life, but not given much thought to until I was literally shaken awake.

The area around Pawnee, like nearly all of Oklahoma and much of southern Kansas, is dotted with oil and gas wells, which are easily identified by their bobbing horseheads, walking beams, and twirling counterweights. Both oil and gas can be produced from the same well, and some wells have been in continuous production for decades, and there are some wells that have been constantly producing for a century. The Ora Graham Farmwell #6, behind the Pizza Hut in El Dorado, Kansas, for example, has produced more than a quarter of a million barrels since its discovery in 1919. New wells are uncommon, however, since the revenue from oil and natural gas (as of September 2016) has fallen below the cost it takes to prospect and drill. What has increased profitability for established fields, however, is fracking.

Hydraulic fracturing is a decades-old technology that, in a sense, causes small earthquakes to create new paths for the flow of oil and gas—and that ancient saltwater.

The first commercially successful oil well in Kansas was drilled in 1891 at Neodesha, and by 1925 the state ranked fifth in oil-producing states. Oil production peaked in the 1950s, with 122 million barrels per year. There are still working oil and gas wells scattered in clusters across southern Kansas, although the state has dropped out of the top ten in oil production. But in the last decade or so, new technologies have brought production back to oil-bearing Mississippian rocks in areas that were once thought tapped out. This porous limestone layer, which is about 360 million years old, was formed when the area that is now Kansas was below the equator, covered by shallow tropical seas. This was before Pangea broke up and the continents drifted to their current locations. The Mississippian shale layer is typically only fifty feet thick, and lies about a mile beneath the surface, according to a Kansas Geological Survey publication. The new technologies that permit oil recovery from it are horizontal drilling and hydraulic fracturing. Both techniques are expensive, and only commercially viable when crude oil prices are high. As I write this, oil is at $46 a barrel; the historic low in the past two decades was $17 in 1998, and the high, $155, in 2008.

Oil is still a major industry in Cowley and Sumner Counties, both the production of it and its transport. The Kansas section of the Keystone XL pipeline runs across prairie and farmland and dips beneath the Arkansas River near the Chaplin Nature Center, above Arkansas City. Capable of delivering more than half a million barrels of oil a day through its thirty-inch diameter pipe, the section was completed in 2011. It is part of Phase II, the Keystone-Cushing extension, which runs from Steele City, Nebraska, to the oil distribution hub of Cushing, Oklahoma. The $8 billion pipeline is designed to more efficiently link the shale oil fields of Alberta, Canada, with American refineries in the Midwest and the Gulf Coast. In November 2015, President Obama rejected TransCanada's permit for the final phase of the project, through South Dakota and Montana, citing environmental concerns. Approving the pipeline, he said, would have undercut the status of the United States as a world leader against climate change.

Also shaken awake by the earthquake on September 3 was Rex Buchanan, director of the Kansas Geological Survey, at his home in

Lawrence, about 290 miles away. He said he knew immediately it was an earthquake, and uttered a silent prayer: *Please, let it be in Oklahoma.*

Buchanan is the genial man who, as depicted previously, challenged me about what to do about depletion of groundwater in western Kansas. In the same interview, he described how earthquakes came to dominate his working life after 2014. Buchanan recalled he was "getting bashed on all sides." The oil and gas industry was unhappy that he was pinning the quakes on it, he was getting pressure from lawmakers, and the environmentalists were unhappy that he wasn't using the word "fracking."

The biggest recorded quake in Kansas history, at magnitude 4.9, came on November 30, 2014, and struck forty miles south of Wichita. It was felt as far away as Memphis, Tennessee, and near the epicenter, in the tiny community of Milan, it broke windows and dumped shelves. Scientists with the US Geological Survey concluded the quake was likely the result of wastewater injection.

Buchanan said he worked with the Kansas Corporation Commission, which in 2015 imposed restrictions that limited the amount of wastewater injection in five seismically active areas by 60 percent. That undoubtedly helped to reduce earthquakes, he said, but the drop in crude oil prices probably contributed as well. When the price of oil goes back up, even with the present wastewater limits, earthquakes may again increase in frequency and intensity.

When I asked him how large an earthquake we might ever expect in Kansas from wastewater injection, assuming that limits or other measures failed, he thought for a moment. Then, he answered: 6. That's somewhat above the magnitude of the quake that struck Pawnee.

A magnitude 6 earthquake, according to the USGS, would be considered "very strong" and result in the following: "Damage negligible in buildings of good design and construction; slight to moderate in well-built ordinary structures, considerable damage in poorly build or badly designed structures; some chimneys broken."

The measuring of earthquakes is a complicated business; magnitude measures amplitude waves on a seismogram, while intensity measures effect. Effect includes experiences, such as being awakened, and damage, such as bricks being dislodged. Ordinarily, magnitude is used to describe quakes, because it is not as subjective as scales of intensity. The amount of energy released increases dramatically from one magnitude to the next. The difference between a magnitude 5.8 quake, similar to the one at Pawnee, and an 8.7 quake, for example, is this: the 8.7 is about 23,000 times stronger, according to the USGS. For comparison, one of the strongest quakes ever recorded on seismograph, the 2004 Indian Ocean earthquake, which created a tsunami that killed 280,000 people, was between 9.1 and 9.3.

The quake Twain described was a magnitude 6.3.

Coyote's Song
Elevation: 1,188' (Oxford)

Here we are, slipping away in the early morning of another Election Day. A couple of us did vote this morning but we are not, really, good citizens. Voting for the lesser evil on the grounds that otherwise we'd be stuck with the greater evil. . . . We will not see other humans or learn of the election results for ten days to come. And so we prefer it. We like it that way. What could be older than the news? We shall treasure the bliss of our ignorance for as long as we can.

—Edward Abbey, *Down the River*

Cave Park, on the west bank of the Arkansas River in the tiny community of Oxford, Kansas, is clean and well-maintained and is the best public place below Wichita from which to launch a kayak. There's a broad concrete boat ramp and steps that lead down to the river, plenty of space to park, and picnic tables and other amenities. The park is located at one end of the Black Dog Trail, and the other end is in my hometown in Baxter Springs; the Osage built and used this wide path, named for one of the tribe's three chiefs, for hunting and trading in the early to mid-nineteenth century. I was disappointed to find that there is no cave at Cave Park, but that it is instead named for a local physician and mayor.

Dr. C. F. Cave was superintendent of the State Home for the Feebleminded in Winfield, on the Walnut River ten miles to the east, and he regularly gave lectures on eugenics and invited schoolchildren to tour the home, telling them in 1913 that "seventy to eighty percent of the cases of imbecility were due to inheritance." He was an advocate for sterilization and often brought along some of the 500 inmates of the home when he gave lectures, at local high schools and libraries, and he attributed all of their physical ills and perceived moral shortcomings to incestuous parents or marriages between mental defectives. He assured his audiences that the unfortunates couldn't have lost their minds, because they "never had minds to begin with," that sawdust and fruit tasted the same to them, and that they didn't feel pain. All told, they amounted to about 5 percent of the population of the state, institutions across Kansas were filled with them, and their care cost $162 per year. Cave was in favor of eventually eliminating this drag on Kansas society by stricter laws.

Before launching on a chilly November dawn.

"State laws should prevent their marriage and sterilization should make their increase impossible," the *Winfield Daily Free Press* reported on one of Cave's lectures in 1913. Cave got many of his ideas from eugenicist Henry Goddard, who a year earlier had published *The Kallikak Family: A Study in the Heredity of Feeble-Mindedness*. This was a case study of a pseudonymous family (*Kallikak* hammered together the Greek words for *beautiful* and *bad*), twin branches of which had issued from a Revolutionary War hero who married and had children with a Quaker woman, and earlier had a child with a "feeble-minded" tavern girl. The legitimate side of the family bred upstanding citizens, Goddard claimed, while the illegitimate descendants were criminals or imbeciles. Goddard's work has been discredited, because other factors were likely responsible for the unhappy Kallikaks, including poverty, malnourishment, alcoholism and fetal alcohol syndrome. Worse, the entire Kallikak saga was invented by Goddard; both sides of the family were legitimate, and the union with the tavern girl was fiction.

The pseudo-science of eugenics was popular in the late nineteenth and early twentieth centuries, and its ideas about racial hygiene appealed to those of white European stock who feared blacks, immigrants, and the poor. Goddard used the Binet intelligence test as a hammer, and every disadvantaged group was a nail. In 1913, he instituted intelligence testing at Ellis Island, and declared 80 percent of immigrants traveling steerage were feeble-minded. He introduced the word *moron* to popular culture (under Goddard's system, a moron has an IQ of 51–70, an imbecile 26–50, and an idiot 0–25). At one point in his career, after testing racial groups in the US Army, Goddard claimed Americans as a whole were unfit for democracy.

In 1913, Kansas passed the state's first sterilization law, aimed at "habitual criminals, idiots, epileptics, imbeciles, and the insane." It was up to a judge to enforce. In 1917, the law was modified to allow sterilizations to proceed without the court. About 3,000 individuals were sterilized between 1913 and 1961, the last year of sterilizations. The peak for sterilizations was in the mid-1930s. About 2 in 3 of these individuals were male, and the majority were sterilized because of mental illness, not mental incapacity. Most of the procedures were done at the state hospital at Winfield.

Kansas ranked sixth in the nation for sterilizations.

The state also promoted eugenics through its "Fitter Families" contest at the Kansas State Fair, with "fitter" referring not to physical fitness, but so-called Darwinian fitness. The competition encouraged the breeding of superior children, just as one would breed superior livestock. "The object of these contests," said the *Topeka Daily Capitol* in 1922, "is to demonstrate to the people that the well known principles of heredity and scientific care which have revolutionized agriculture and stock breeding apply to the next higher order of creation, the human family." Since 1903, Kansas had a marriage restriction law on the books, which forbade all men, and women under the age of forty-five, from marrying alcoholics and the "feeble-minded" under the penalty of a $1,000 fine or three years in jail.

In 1998, the Winfield state hospital was closed. It came after more than a hundred years of scandal, the first of which was in 1894, when it was discovered the superintendent was castrating patients to prevent masturbation. By the 1930s, the hospital's original charter of education was largely abandoned for one that can only be described as incarceration. The hospital and other state institutions were reformed in the 1940s following a series of newspaper articles by the *Topeka Capital-Journal* and the *Kansas City Star*, and patterned after the progressive ideas of Topeka psychiatrist Karl Menninger. The hospital continued to have its ups and downs in the decades that followed, including overcrowding and budget crunches and scandals about the discovery of whips, chains, and thumbscrews. The final blow, however, was the growing recognition that the developmentally disabled possessed the same civil rights as other Americans, and that they deserved behavioral treatment—not segregation.

The Winfield hospital is now a prison, administered by the State Department of Corrections. Its inmate population, which hovers around 500, is about the same as the patient count was during C. F. Cave's tenure.

Eugenics and its wrong-headed ideas about mental incapacity and state control of reproduction were swept away by the Nazi horrors during World War II, including the forced sterilization and euthanasia of the mentally ill. From an evolutionary standpoint, there are advantages to maintaining a large and sometimes messy gene pool.

Dr. Cave is all but forgotten today, except for the municipal park that bears his name. In spite of his interest in now-disfavored eugenics, Cave seems to have been a disciplined and hard-working physician, according to the local newspapers of the time, and was a capable amateur radio operator and a medical corps volunteer during the Great War. He seems to have been a man of his time and place, well-intentioned but given to common prejudices, and preaching rationalization as fact. When I mentioned eugenics to Kim, she immediately responded with what the character Tom Buchanan says in *The Great Gatsby*, in gushing about a fearmongering book about growing minority populations worldwide. "It's all scientific stuff; it's been proved," the wealthy and arrogant Buchanan says.

One afternoon in summer, while Kim and I were scouting locations along the river just above the Oklahoma state line, we followed a dirt road into the Kaw Wildlife Area below Arkansas City. I knew there was a boat ramp on the east side of the river, at Grouse Creek, but I wanted to see what was on the other, west bank. We drove down the rutted road and found ourselves in a dead-end turnout where a motorcycle and a handful of pickups were parked. There were some people milling about the vehicles, and they watched as we parked the Jeep.

"They seem sketchy," Kim said.

They're just fishing, I assured her.

"I think we've walked into a drug deal."

No, I said. They probably think we're the game warden or something.

"Okay," Kim conceded.

There were a couple of rugged types with tall fishing poles, standing on the high bank and looking out over the water. The men near the pickups were leaning against the tailgates and had cans of beer in their hands. Their clothes looked like they had been worn for days, and their hair was matted beneath their worn baseball caps.

We got out of the Jeep and I retrieved the camera from the back and as we passed the men, I gave a casual *How's it going?* but got no reply. They wouldn't even make eye contact.

The trail led down to a high bank that had a good view of the river. The water was wide and brown, and flowing moderately, and we could see the sandbars stretching along the bend of the river on the other side. We couldn't have been more than a half mile or so from Oklahoma. Consulting my GPS, and taking into account the distances already traveled, I now knew exactly how long of a journey I'd undertaken: 747 miles. The area was heavily wooded and branches hung over the bank like a curtain. There was no possibility of any access here, because the bank was thirty feet above the water, and too steep and muddy to climb. Just to the north of us was a stump that had been marked with some orange paint from an aerosol can, meaning *Keep Out.*

While I was examining the bank, Kim climbed up into the fork of a big oak tree. She stood there for a moment, looking upriver, her arm out as if she was giving a benediction. Amused, I raised the camera to my eye and made a few photos. Far in the background were the pickups and the men clustered around them.

That's when I saw the gun.

It was a large-framed semiautomatic handgun with a stainless slide, and a young man in his twenties was holding it low in front of him, with his finger curled inside the trigger guard. An older man with dark hair and the most ragged baseball cap of all had a long gun, and he was working the action, as if to seat a round. Neither of the guns was the kind you'd expect hunters to carry.

"Let's go," I said.

Still in the tree, Kim asked me what was wrong.

I told her, and said we were going to walk as confidently back to the Jeep as we could, and then she was going to get in first. There wasn't much room at the turnout, and if one of the drivers of the pickups backed out just a few feet, we'd be trapped. As we approached, the younger man put the pistol in his waistband and let his shirt hang over it. The older man with the rifle put it in the bed of his pickup.

As we passed them, I slowed, allowing Kim to get a few steps ahead.

I looked the young man in the eye.

"See you later," I said.

"Yeah," he said.

Then I walked to the Jeep, where Kim was waiting. I started the engine, then backed slowly out, cut the wheels, and pulled forward out of the turnout. For a good long while I looked in my rearview mirror. I don't know what the intentions of the men back at the river were, but their affect was disturbing. They carried their guns in a way that said they were ready to use them.

At Cave Park, on a Saturday morning on the first weekend of November, I met Vince and Kevin and about forty-six other individuals for what turned out to be one of the Arkansas River Coalition's biggest floats of the year. The concrete boat ramp was packed with kayaks (and one canoe), and after our launch shortly after 9 a.m., our pod of colorful kayaks stretched for half a mile down the river.

The Arkansas here is broad and shallow, and curves in ever-widening sweeps to the east and then the west, with shifting sandbars in the middle of the river and on the inside of the curves. Picking the right line down the river meant either smooth paddling or hearing the scrub of sand and gravel beneath the plastic hull, and sometimes having to get out of the boat and pull it across a high spot. My lava-colored Dagger was riding lower in the water than usual, because it was loaded with an extra thirty pounds of camping gear, stowed in the bow and the stern and lashed to the rear deck; I was among the eight individuals who planned to continue paddling after the others took out at midafternoon, and to camp on a sandbar about ten miles downriver that night.

Having watched Vince and Kevin for many miles of river paddling, I had adopted some of their gear, including neoprene gloves to protect my hands, and rubber boots that came up over my calves. I had originally thought the boots a bit silly when I first started paddling with them, and wore either my wetsuit booties or low-topped paddling shoes, but had discovered the rubber boots were not only practical in the mud and muck when putting in and taking out, but also offered protection from the many goat head stickers and stobs along the bank.

As we were putting in at Cave Park, a boat that had been turned into a floating duck blind putted down the river, and we later could hear the popping of their shotguns. We caught up with them a couple of miles down the river, tucked up against a notch in the bank, their spread of decoys bobbing on the water. They may not have been too happy to see our parade of kayaks, but they waved pleasantly enough as we paddled by. It didn't feel much like duck weather to me, even though the calendar said the season was in full swing. It had been a little chilly when we started out, but the day grew increasingly warm, and it was in the 70s, with clear skies and little wind, by midmorning.

Our group stopped for lunch on a sandbar, and while we were relaxing in the sunshine, a yellow and white Piper Cub (or a very similar type of plane) came upriver, flying low. The occupants waved as the plane sailed over us, and the moment seemed like a postcard: the brightly colored plane against the expanse of autumn sky, the rainbow of kayaks pulled up on the sandbar, the river and the trees that were just now beginning to turn on either bank. One of the newer paddlers, a young man, had upset his boat in the middle of the river, and a fire was started to dry him out.

Paddling with us was a stream biologist, with the entirely appropriate name of Ryan Waters, from the Kansas department that oversees wildlife and parks at Pratt. Waters said he had spent a lot of time on the river seeking peppered chub, a small fish that is found almost exclusively in the shallow, sand-bottomed waters of the Arkansas River basin. It is endangered in Kansas, having lost 90 percent of its habitat to pollution, dams, and cycles of drought. The decline of the peppered chub in Kansas began about thirty years ago, but has accelerated in the past ten years to the point they may no longer be a viable population.

The most invasive fish species in Kansas, as in other states, are Asian carp. Originally brought into the American South from China in the 1970s by fish farmers to help clean up commercial ponds, the carp have spread to many lakes and rivers, where they displace native species. The silver carp, which can grow as large as 100 pounds, is especially troublesome because of its reflex to jump several feet out of the water when frightened. When disturbed by an approaching motorboat, the carp can fly out of the water and land in uncovered boats, injuring passengers. While silver carp have been found in many rivers in the state, including the Kansas and Missouri, they have not yet been spotted in the Arkansas.

Shortly after the plane went by, there was the sound of another motor approaching from the south, and at first I thought it was another airplane. What appeared surprised me, because I'd never seen one before on a Kansas waterway. It was an airboat, with a screaming V8 motor driving a huge caged aircraft propeller in the back, and the driver and his passengers riding in high seats up front. The sound of the boat shattered the peace in a way the aircraft hadn't. The roar from airboats is from the prop wash, which averages about 150 mph, and not from the engine exhaust. The operator throttled back as he came abreast of us, then surged forward again after passing us, and the boat slalomed away like a downhill skier. As we made our way south, we encountered several more airboats, and each time I regarded them as mechanized nuisances. This wasn't the Everglades. They were too much boat, too much horsepower, too much noise. Perhaps my impression would have been different had I not been in a kayak, which glides nearly silently at water level; on the river with the airboats, it felt a little bit like peddling a bicycle in the same lane as an 18-wheeler.

Beneath the bridge at Rainbow Bend, some eight or nine miles downriver, I beached my kayak high on the sand and helped some of the day floaters clamber up the steep bank with their boats to the waiting cars. Earlier in the morning, we had shuttled the cars down to the turnout on the east side of the bridge. For those of us who were overnighting, we had to shuttle our cars again to the intended takeout. When we returned from that trip, I found Vince surveying a brushy area just beyond the turnout.

He said that some time before at the spot, he had taken his dowsing rods and found a grave a few yards in the brush. He said it was the grave of a woman, probably from the late nineteenth century, when there would certainly have been a farm here near the river. Another paddler asked him how he knew it was a woman, and Vince said the rods will point in one direction for a man and another for a woman. Because Christian burials are generally done with the body facing east (that is, with their feet to the east), he can then determine the gender. All human beings emit energy he said, even after death, and the dowsing rods are just tools that help us focus the lingering energy that our bodies detect. His technique is a bit different than Tom Monaco's, the cemetery dowser in Colorado, but otherwise their approach is similar. Because Vince believed so strongly in dowsing, and I didn't want to hurt his feelings, I kept my skepticism to myself.

We took to the river again, and floated past the old Rainbow Bend oil field, which had its peak production in the 1920s. On the weekend we were on the river near Rainbow Bend, the Dakota Access Pipeline was the target of a massive protest, involving thousands of people, near the Standing Rock Sioux reservation. The tribe said the pipeline, which would run from North Dakota to Illinois, would threaten its way of life and sacred sites, and environmentalists were concerned about water contamination in the event of a leak, because the pipeline would run beneath the Missouri River.

After paddling a few miles beyond Rainbow Bend, and following two great gentle curves in the river, our overnight group approached a large sandbar on the east bank that Vince said had made a good camping spot on past trips. There was an airboat parked at the head of the sandbar, and the operator was lounging with a beer in his hand while his ferocious-looking dog ran madly about. From our spot a few yards out in the water, we asked if the airboater was intending to stay. He gave a noncommittal answer, and said there was another sandbar just around the bend. Vince said that this sandbar was better for camping, and that we were considering landing a bit farther down, but on the same bar. We paddled on, and by the time we got the boats hauled up on the bar, a few hundred yards down, the airboater had fired up his motor and roared off.

The sandbar was large and flat, with some trees clustered on the higher points, and plenty of driftwood. It was really more of an island than a sandbar, because there was a spring-fed stream on the east side, with a high bank beyond. The stream was not broad, but it seemed deep enough to paddle, and it was obviously running because it glittered in the sunlight.

It was about four o'clock when we began to set up camp, and we chose locations that were twenty or thirty yards apart from one another, and I made my camp even farther apart from the rest, because I didn't want to bother anybody in case I snored.

Within thirty minutes, I had my camp established, with the same REI tent that I'd used the previous Christmas in the mountains, and elsewhere. Inside, there was my down sleeping bag, a small inflatable pad, and a stuff sack of clothes that I'd use for a pillow. I placed a blue tarp on the ground, weighted it with rocks against a wind that had just kicked up, and set up a small cooking area, with my MSR stove and my alpine pack containing my food and other essentials. Although some of the campers intended on boiling river water for cooking and drinking, I had brought my water in three quart Nalgene bottles. The water here was definitely clearer than the stretch from Wichita to Mulvane, but I was still worried about fertilizer, pesticides, and other contaminants. With the help of another paddler, I carried my kayak up and placed it on the blue tarp. It was handy to be able to stow things in the boat, and to have the rear deck to use as a seat and the hatch cover as a flat area on which to eat meals.

By five o'clock I had brewed a cup of coffee and eaten a bit of chocolate. I must have been hungrier than I thought, because the snack picked me up considerably. Vince and some of the others came by, carrying their boats, and asked if I wanted to go with them in exploring the stream that cut along the east side of the bar. I declined, because I wanted to catch up on my note-taking. I asked them what spring it was, and Vince said he didn't know that it had a name, it was just one of the many in the area around Geuda Springs, which had once been famous for its mineral spas.

In 1902, a staff member of the University Geological Survey (now the Kansas Geological Survey) compiled an exhaustive survey of the state's springs in *Special Report on Mineral Waters*. E. H. S. Bailey included history, photographs, and chemical analyses of the waters, which were believed by many to have therapeutic properties.

"In the south-central part of the state, on the line between Cowley and Sumner counties, is situated a remarkable group of springs that has been known since the earliest settlement of the state," Bailey writes. "These springs may be easily reached from Arkansas City, seven miles, by a branch of the St. Louis & San Francisco railroad. The town is only eight miles from the undulating plains of Indian Territory. It is about a mile from the Arkansas River. . . . In the vicinity, especially to the north, there are numerous salt springs, so that many of the streams are quite saline in character."

The spas were located at the north end of town, just beyond the west bank of the Arkansas River. In addition to the spas, Bailey noted, there was also an operation to bottle the spring water. The name of the town, which is pronounced "Good-ah," may have a Native American origin. Bailey says it may have come from an Indian word meaning "healing springs," and that the area was thought to have been a favorite Native American camping area.

Vince and the others returned from their exploration of the spring-fed stream after only fifteen minutes or so, saying that the water had soon become too shallow to continue. Looking over at the stream channel, I saw that it had dropped several inches since our arrival, revealing broad patches of sand, and was now flowing sluggishly, if at all.

Later, I joined the others around a campfire where good-sized deadwood logs had been positioned to provide seating. In addition to Vince and Kevin, there was a couple that had paddled the group's lone canoe, a scoutmaster who ran a plumbing business in a small town about 100 miles north of Wichita, a young couple who were new to paddling, and the Arkansas River Coalition's float coordinator, Wally Seibel.

Seibel, who is in his seventies, started out as a wilderness backpacker, but as age began to catch up with him he became a kayak camper. He considers himself more of a camper than a paddler, because he doesn't run whitewater, and he's adapted the skills he learned backpacking to river camping. He's a small man, but with big hands that wield a paddle well, and he's surprisingly flexible, able to bend low over the rear deck of his kayak to slip beneath downed trees. Because he dislikes the heat and the bugs that come with summer, the fall is his favorite time to camp. As he sat off to one side of the group, heating his dinner on a camp stove, and checking his work with the light from a red LED headband lamp that thankfully saved our night vision, he seemed content. I asked him what his favorite section of the river was, and he said the areas far above Wichita, particularly between Alden and Sterling.

There was the usual campfire talk, and we took turns talking about our best and worst experiences on the water. I briefly mentioned my swim at Zoom Flume, and the scoutmaster had several stories that generally involved getting some kid out of trouble, and Vince talked about the time during a summer float when an older man who was a first-time kayaker had suffered heatstroke and had to be towed to the takeout. Then Kevin told the story of the dead tree that had fallen near us at Great Bend, and Vince and I agreed it had been strange. Kevin disappeared to roam in the darkness along the edge of the river, and we could see glimpses of him every now and then, a bearlike shadow moving against the water, and he eventually came back later with some type of heavy animal bone, perhaps from a cow, that looked as if it had been on the bar for decades. It occurred to me that on the four occasions I'd been on the river with him, he had always been searching the banks for something. Earlier, I had found a deer coccyx in the sand, not far from where I pitched my tent, but I left it where it was, because it creeped me out.

At around 8:30, I bid the other campers goodnight. I had gotten up that morning at 5:30—hours before my usual daily routine—to drive from my home in Emporia to Cave Park in time for the launch, and I was beat. But I needed a bit of time to unwind before turning in. At my camp, I fired up the stove and heated water for hot chocolate, watching the intense blue flame. Then I sat on the rear deck of my kayak and held the warm cup in my hands, looking at the few stars that peeked through the mostly cloudy sky. I was glad for the fleece pullover and the stocking cap, because the air from the river was chilly. Vince had picked a good spot to camp, because there were no lights from houses or farms to spoil the view. If you looked very closely to the south, you could see the winking red light from a broadcast antenna or perhaps a wind turbine, but that was all.

Inside the tent, I stripped down to my underwear, but kept the stocking cap, and burrowed into the sleeping bag. The tent was on a nice flat spot, so I wasn't leaning in any direction, and the sand made an excellent foundation for the inflatable pad. I thought about how comfortable I was, and how different it had been, in the same tent and the same bag, along the river at Christmas at Hecla Junction, some 723 miles upstream. I had to agree with Wally: fall camping was the best. I hadn't even seen a mosquito or other bug that evening on the sandbar. About ten o'clock, a lonesome coyote began to yap and howl somewhere in the night, and gradually other coyote voices began to join in. In twenty minutes, their song was so great it sounded like the night world now belonged to the coyotes. That was okay with me, because I've always had a special place in my heart for coyotes.

I hate that people hunt them, especially those that shoot them from helicopters (yes, this is legal). They are a nongame species in Kansas, and a predator of livestock, so the season on them is year-round, and there is no bag limit. And even though they are not officially designated a furbearing animal by the state, the value of their pelt harvests ranks second in the state, according to the Kansas Department of Wildlife and Parks. The most efficient way the pelts are harvested is by foothold trapping of the animals.

The trickster is an archetype found in preindustrial societies around the globe and, among the plains Indians of North America, he is typically represented as the coyote. "The ambiguous, curiously fascinating figure of the trickster appears to have been the chief mythological character of the paleolithic world of story," Joseph Campbell writes in *The Masks of God: Primitive Mythology*. "A fool, and a cruel, lecherous cheat, an epitome of the principle of disorder, he is nevertheless the culture-bringer also."

In the Pacific Northwest, the trickster is the raven; in the woodland Northeast, the Great Hare; in the forests of Europe, Reynard the Fox. While Christian mythology has confused him with Satan, the original trickster is a rich and contradictory figure, a shape-shifter whose business is adaptive transgression.

"One reason native observers may have chosen coyote the animal for Coyote the Trickster is that the former in fact does exhibit a great plasticity of behavior and is, therefore, a consummate survivor in a shifting world," writes Lewis Hyde in *Trickster Makes This World*. Once, coyotes hunted in packs, Hyde says, as wolves do. But now coyotes are solitary hunters. "Watching coyotes hunt in packs, the eighteenth-century wolf might well have said to them, 'This is my way, not your way.' But two hundred years later the wolf is trapped in his 'way,' is endangered, while coyotes are eating purebred poodles in Beverly Hills."

By eleven, the coyote cacophony had stopped, leaving the river valley once again in silence, except for the occasional owl deep in the woods. It felt good lying in the tent, stretched out in my warm bag, not having looked at a screen—not on a television, not on my laptop, not on my smart phone—in nearly twenty-four hours. I hadn't even brought my iPhone on this trip, because after I bricked my old iPhone in the river below Great Bend, the new phone I got was taller and wouldn't fit in my old case. It was just as well, because I wanted a break from constantly checking the news.

Lying in the bag staring into the darkness, I thought about the previous Christmas Eve, and then thought about Kim, and did not presume to imagine what she was doing. Instinctively, I touched my wedding ring with the tip of my thumb, to make sure it was still there. I'd been obsessed with not losing the ring during my journey, but now I knew that even if it had bounced across the deck of the kayak and disappeared into some deep and rapid hole, I would have lost nothing. The ring could have slipped away, returned to the earth beneath the water and joined bits of alluvial gold in a bedrock fissure at the bottom of the snowmelt river, and it wouldn't have changed anything. It was my anxiety and resorting to emotional and physical distance that had been the real problem. The ring isn't the thing it stands for.

I had undertaken the journey down the river seeking the baptism of wilderness, a confirmation of self-authenticity, some great revealed truth about our place in nature. What I discovered was not a single revelation, but a series of small ones, an incremental range of mental and emotional steps. I found the limits of my ability and endurance—and yes, ambition. I have failed to do what I had intended; I've paddled most of the river, hundreds of miles, but not all of it. The difference between our intentions and what is possible may be a measure of our hubris—or at least our hypocrisy. We are all of us the Orth Steins and the Baby Does, the miserably lost Zebulon Pike, the powers that clashed at Ludlow and the fearful nation that imprisoned Japanese Americans at Camp Amache. We may claim moral superiority when we think of the peak disfigured by the Climax mine, but as long as we drive automobiles in which some parts—the axle shaft in my Jeep, for example—are hardened by molybdenum, we are deceiving ourselves. As long as we continue to belly up to the casino buffet and eat cheap steaks without thinking of who is butchering the beef or caring how much water from western Kansas was used to grow the corn that fed the cow, then we are not reckoning the real cost.

What is needed now—and what was needed, always—is an unflinching appraisal of our values and an authentic relationship to others and to the earth. Real commitment requires sacrifice. And the consequences of our actions transcend our lifetimes.

≈ ≈ ≈

In my stuff sack was *Down the River*, and I returned to its printed pages
with Luddite glee. I had read it once, and was reading it again, pausing
on passages I had highlighted here and there. On an early page, the one I
had started when locked out of the motel room in Salida: "Here we are,
slipping away in the early morning of another Election Day. . . ." But then
I skipped a few pages, and found a passage I had not highlighted. It was
Abbey talking about immigration, and he suggests closing the border and
giving every illegal immigrant "a good rifle and a case of ammunition"
and sending them back to take care of things themselves. "If this seems
a cruel and sneering suggestion," Abbey writes, "consider the current
working alternative: leaving our borders open to unlimited immigration
until—and it won't take long—the social, political, economic life of the
United States is reduced to the level of life in Juarez. Guadalajara. Mexico
City. San Salvador. Haiti. India. To a common peneplain of overcrowding,
squalor, misery, oppression, torture, and hate."

Abbey wrote that back in 1980. He would die nine years later, at the
age of sixty-two, and the controversy created by his anti-immigration
rants would follow him to the grave. He denied accusations of racism,
and said his position was based in a desire to protect the wilderness from
an onslaught of humanity. Yet there, in *Down the River*, he's not talking
about what immigration does to the wilderness. He's talking about
his fear of what illegal immigration does to us, not to the land, and he
uses alarmist language that would likely find an audience in the 2016
presidential campaign. Never mind that the number of illegal immigrants
in the United States peaked at 4 percent of the population in 2007, and
then declined during the Great Recession. It's currently stabilized at 3.5
percent, or about 11 million, according to a report from the Pew Research
Center.

As much as Abbey was a hero of my youth—I always wanted a Jeep
because Hayduke drove one in *The Monkey Wrench Gang*—I have to
now admit that he was, judging by his own words, a self-satisfied bigot.
It wasn't just his rants on immigration, but his contempt for the political
process, which in 1980 seemed charmingly anarchistic. Today, however,
the global movement to just burn it all down is not informed by deep
reading or thinking, but by a poorly articulated desire to commit political

arson. Abbey got many things right, including his observation that institutions were crushing the life out of the average American, but he went too far in suggesting that we shirk the obligations of citizenship. We no longer have the luxury of indulging the smug paper anarchists who feel themselves above the fray.

I sat up in the bag, found a notebook, and began scribbling.

It's now Sunday morning, and the polls will open in little more than 48 hours. I'm relieved that it will all soon be over, and perhaps we can get on with things. The polls are still predicting a Hillary Clinton win, despite the FBI director's attempted palace coup. I favored Bernie Sanders in the primary, but supported Hillary after because I believe—without hyperbole—that Donald Trump is a fascist who represents an existential threat to American democracy. Fascism is not just a mixture of authoritarianism and militant nationalism, but the convergence of state and corporate power. It's the Colorado militia mobilizing to protect the interests of the Rockefellers from striking miners and their families in the tent colonies, and the lies with which Ivy Lee libeled the dead. It's the depletion of water in western Kansas so that farmers can break even growing corn to feed to cattle that become $14.99 steak dinners. And it's the refutation of science, to the benefit of the petro-chemical industry, by a presidential candidate who has said he believes global warming is a hoax created by the Chinese.

But my vote won't matter much in red-locked Kansas, because the state hasn't gone for a Democrat in the White House since Lyndon Johnson in 1964. The state's winner-take-all six electoral votes will almost surely be awarded to the improbable Republican nominee.

Donald Trump.

How could this have happened?

We normalized Trump's candidacy and let him off the hook for a range of behavior that would have disqualified any other candidate, from his refusal to follow decades of tradition in releasing his tax returns to his mocking personal attacks on journalists to his hateful speech, bigoted policies, and outrageous hypocrisy. Mass deportation, building a 2,000-mile wall, and Muslim watch lists. We must take him at his word. A racist wrapped in a fragile ego, Trump encourages hate 140 characters at a time. The exclamation marks alone should be enough to disqualify him. To listen to him speak is embarrassing and terrifying at the same time. I don't want the launch codes anywhere near his raging id. How can anybody believe this man is mentally stable, much less

think he is qualified to be president? Nearly every poll says he'll lose, but I'm
still anxious. The country is roiled by some strange and unthinking anger.

The greatest threat to Abbey's wilderness, nearly four decades on, is not
illegal immigrants, but the white voters who—largely or partly because of their
own bigotry, which of course they, like Abbey, will deny—who would choose
a candidate who sees the wild as just another commodity to be exploited. My
unhappy realization is that, if Abbey were alive today, he would likely say
to hell with the whole mess and spend Election Day on the river. Burn, baby,
burn.

The sound of low voices and the rustling of cooking, sudden laughter,
the popping of the campfire. Christ, it was still dark. Just half past six by
my watch. The time had changed overnight, but I hadn't reset my watch,
and in my groggy state couldn't immediately remember whether it was
supposed to be an hour later or an hour earlier. But no matter how I spun
the dials, it would not delay the dawn.

I pulled on a down vest over my long underwear, crawled out of my
tent and lit the stove to boil water. Hunched over the blue flame, I stared
unseen at the group of campers around the campfire, an animal lurking in
the darkness. I could not be fit company until I'd had at least one cup of
coffee from my insulated mug. I breathed deep the crisp, wood smoke–
tinged air and took stock of my surroundings. Dew coated every exposed
surface, dripping from the rain fly of the tent and beading on the deck
of the kayak. The air was still chilly, but not cold. Just above 50. The sky
had cleared and the Milky Way and several thousand other stars glittered
overhead; the moon, approaching the first quarter, was high above.

After the requisite coffee, I joined the group around the fire and
warmed my hands while we made small talk. The young couple, Dean and
Triscilla, shared without complaining that they'd been cold in their tent,
and she clutched a blanket around her narrow shoulders. Kevin allowed
that he liked his new tent, which his wife had bought for him online,
for only $39, because it was big enough for him to stretch out. Vince
was eating something he'd whipped up for breakfast—I never did figure
out exactly what it was—and he was keeping an eye to the west, where
weather was expected.

Gradually, clouds crept in from the west, blocking out the moon and stars, and the wind picked up as it got closer to dawn. By the time the sun had cleared the horizon, we had broken camp and stowed our gear in the boats. The sunlight shot over our dark sandbar and lit up the trees on the opposite bank, a brilliant streak of gold between a silver sky and a river of lead. I took a few photos, which delayed me for a few minutes while most of the others launched. Then I pulled on the rubber boots, walked the kayak out into a half a foot or so of water, and braced the boat by putting my paddle across the rear of the cockpit while I climbed in. I shook as much water as I could from my boots, adjusted my neoprene gloves, and flipped the paddle over so the blades were going in the right direction. I paddled out a few yards into the water, then spun the boat around to watch as Vince and a few others got ready to launch. That's when I noted the high-water mark on the sand.

There was a dark, wet band eight or nine inches on the bank above the water, measuring how much the river had dropped during the night. I thought of Hunter Thompson writing that in 1968, with the right kind of eyes, you could see where the wave of the American Dream had reached the high-water mark and begun to roll back. Now, after a forty-eight-year roller-coaster ride of high hopes and bad dreams, had things finally bottomed out? Could you see the low-water mark with the right kind of eyes?

The morning was as chilly and inhospitable as you would expect in November, even though the day before had been unseasonably warm. The coffee had made me civil, but it had not relieved my tiredness. I had slept plenty, eaten well, and had stayed dry during the trip. There was no excuse for my fatigue except, perhaps, existential fatigue. The remaining six miles before the takeout would be full of low places we'd have to drag our boats over. We'd be paddling against the wind. There shouldn't be any significant hazards, but the river changes so quickly that every section is new, each time you put your boat to water. I shoved away from the bank, turned my bow into the wind, and looked for the right line to cross the tail of the gravel bar to the safer channel.

Acknowledgments
Elevation: 1,197' (home)

It is well before dawn on a winter's day, and outside it is chill and wet—but warming after several days of snow. It seems the stuff will never stop melting. From my warm and book-strewn study, I can hear the water dripping from the gutters that I haven't touched once in the eight years I've owned this 120-year-old house on Constitution Street. My plan was always to fix the rusted and leaky gutters, which are as old as the house, but there have always been more interesting, more important things to do, including the project that has resulted in the book you now hold. While the rainwater has slowly eaten away at the foundation of this old house, I've roamed to the far blue mountains of Colorado and back, read hundreds of books, interviewed scores of people, and written the nights away. My goal was to produce a deep and intimate portrait of the Arkansas River. If I have succeeded, it is only because I had many fine people and a few good institutions lending support to the project.

I will cite the individual to whom I am most indebted first, and that is my wife, Kimberly Horner McCoy. Although she has been a co-conspirator in many shared adventures along the river, she spent patient confinement in this house with the leaky gutters during those times when it was impractical or impossible for her to follow, especially when I was *on* the river in snow or white water. She has sacrificed much for me, including leaving her native state of Missouri and often setting aside her own work to assist in mine. The only consolation I can offer her is my love and the prospect—or threat, perhaps—of future adventure.

Kim Hogeland, my editor at the University Press of Kansas, deserves special thanks for seeking me out, after having read one of my magazine pieces, to ask whether I had any ideas for a book that might be appropriate for her catalog. She has championed the river project ever since, and I am thankful for her expert editorial hand. I am also grateful to my agent, Doug Grad, whose literary agency in Brooklyn is always a happy landmark when visiting a shore that is strange to me.

My colleagues at Emporia State University offered unfailing support, encouragement, and friendship. The university was instrumental by granting me a one-semester sabbatical to begin the project. My journalism students should be commended for their patience, because I know they've heard me talk about the writing of this book far too often, to the point at which just hearing the phrase "immersive research" could provoke violence.

To the many individuals who generously shared their time and expertise with me: thank you. Some, such as Brandon Slate, gave far more than could be expected. He also showed me how to be safe on the river, or at least he tried. And finally, to my friend Karl Gregory, who operated a one-man river shuttle service for much of the journey, and who volunteered for the longest and coldest night I've ever passed in the wild, I can only say: *Thanks, brother.*

A word on my approach may be in order here as well. In this post-fact world, a little clarity could be refreshing. Or, it could just be a sign that I am a relic from a past age that clings to the principles of verifiable fact and reliable sources. *So be it.*

Because this is an account of an annotated journey down the Arkansas River, much research went into providing the cultural and historical context for each chapter, and I have liberally cited the source material. I am grateful to the many authors and experts, living and dead, who have shared their wisdom. Any errors or misinterpretation of fact, however, are mine alone. The opinions I've expressed should be attributed only to me as well, and they reflect an evolving philosophy as I journeyed down the river. Time will tell whether they were informed by wisdom or by folly.

Some day, when the snow has melted and the sun returns, and the gutters finally stop dripping on the foundation, I may get the big aluminum ladder from the garage and begin repairs. The house certainly needs it. After the gutters, I should think about slapping on a coat of paint as well, because it has peeled so badly in some places that it's beginning to look like a refugee from a ghost town. But then, I would have to move the kayaks stowed in the garage to get to the ladder. Even with no book to finish, it might seem a shame to waste a beautiful spring day standing on a ladder when one could be on the river.

Some foundations require water.